Walt Whitman's Reconstruction

The Iowa Whitman Series

ED FOLSOM, *series editor*

Walt Whitman's Reconstruction

POETRY AND PUBLISHING BETWEEN MEMORY AND HISTORY

Martin T. Buinicki

UNIVERSITY OF IOWA PRESS IOWA CITY

811 WHITMAN

University of Iowa Press, Iowa City 52242

Copyright © 2011 by the University of Iowa Press

www.uiowapress.org

Printed in the United States of America

Design by Richard Hendel

The University of Iowa Press is a member of Green Press Initiative
and is committed to preserving natural resources.

Printed on acid-free paper

Library of Congress Cataloging-in-Publication Data
Buinicki, Martin T., 1972–
Walt Whitman's Reconstruction: poetry and publishing between
memory and history / Martin T. Buinicki.
     p.   cm. — (The Iowa Whitman series, ISSN 1556-5610)
Includes bibliographical references and index.
ISBN-13: 978-1-60938-069-4; ISBN-10: 1-60938-069-x (pbk.)
ISBN-13: 978-1-60938-070-0; ISBN-10: 1-60938-070-3 (e-book)
1. Whitman, Walt, 1819–1892 — Political and social views.
2. Reconstruction (U.S. history, 1865–1877) in literature.   3. United
States — History — Civil War, 1861–1865 — Literature and the war.
4. Authors and publishers — United States — History — 19th century.
I. Title.
PS3242.S58.B85 2011
811′.3 — dc22   2011015085

For my family

Contents

Acknowledgments / ix

Abbreviations / xi

1 **Walt Whitman's Reconstruction** / 1

2 **Periodicals, Politics, and the New Paper World** / 15

3 **Whitman and the Elusive Site of Memory** / 49

4 **"By the Roadside" and Whitman's Narrative of**

Poetic (Re)Awakening / 77

5 **Whitman's General** / 109

6 **Reconstructing His Story** / 134

Notes / 151

Bibliography / 169

Index / 177

Acknowledgments

This book would not have been possible without the generosity and support of a number of people who may not fully realize the debt of gratitude that I owe them, and I am happy to have a moment here to offer some slight recompense. First, I am grateful to my colleagues at Valparaiso University, who encouraged me throughout my work, reading drafts of materials and always lending a kind word when the going got rough. Stephanie Frederick and the rest of the Christopher Center Library staff have shown great patience with me as I tasked the interlibrary loan system to the limit, and I truly appreciate their help. I was also fortunate to be the recipient of a Valparaiso University Research Professorship early in the writing process, which allowed me to make much swifter headway than I would have otherwise. I am delighted to be a part of an institution that cares so much about teaching and scholarship.

While working on the manuscript, I also had the great privilege to take part in Wayne Franklin's History of the Book seminar at the American Antiquarian Society in Worcester, MA. Much of the material that we read and discussed inspired my thinking on this project, and I was able to spend valuable time doing research in the incomparable archive. The staff at the AAS are truly wonderful professionals, and I value every opportunity that I find to work with them. Likewise, I was able to spend several productive days at the Library of Congress in Washington, D.C., and I appreciate the efforts made on my behalf by the staff to help me make use of the valuable materials held there.

While I was in D.C., Martin Murray gave me a walking tour of the city, highlighting places where Whitman lived and worked, and he listened patiently as I discussed my project, then still in the very early stages. I am deeply grateful for the gift of his time and expertise. Likewise, my book has benefited from the wisdom of several Whitman scholars who have read some of this material in draft form, including M. Wynn Thomas, who gave valuable feedback on an early version of the "By the Roadside" chapter, and the anonymous reviewer of the completed manuscript. I also delivered early material from this work in a Midwest Modern Language conference panel chaired by the always generous and gracious Kathleen Diffley, who has gone out of her way to encourage me throughout my career. One of the true joys of my profession is being able to work with and learn from such a wonderful group of scholars. I am also very thankful to have had the opportunity to work with Holly Carver, Charlotte Wright, and the rest of the staff at the University of Iowa Press. They have helped tremendously through each step of the publication process. Jennifer Bennett's careful eye for detail has made this a much stronger book, and I am grateful to her as well.

Much of what I know about Walt Whitman, and about being an academic, I learned from Ed Folsom. My participation in his Whitman seminar at the University of Iowa started a long-term fascination with the poet, and I knew that Whitman would be the subject of my second book long before the first was even completed. I am continually inspired by Ed's passion, energy, and commitment, and I am deeply honored to have him as a mentor and a friend.

Like the subject of this book, I oftentimes find myself straining against the limitations of the text, trying to make it do more than the marks on the page allow. Where Whitman often succeeds, however, I never feel my lack of the poet's gift so acutely as when I turn to write of my family. My wife Andrea makes everything possible, and I sometimes think that I would keep writing books just to have the opportunity to keep thanking her, always knowing that it is never enough. My sons Will and Jack make every day an adventure, and they constantly remind me of the joys of reading, writing, and telling stories. I hope they will seek out their names here with eager fingertips, read them aloud, and feel some inkling of the pride that I feel in them.

An earlier version of chapter 5 was published as "'Average-Representing Grant': Whitman's General" in *Walt Whitman Quarterly Review* 26.2 (2008).

Abbreviations

AAS   American Antiquarian Society. Worcester, MA.

Corr.   *The Correspondence*. 6 vols. Ed. Edwin Haviland Miller. New York: New York University Press, 1961–1977, vol. 7, ed. Ted Genoways, Iowa City, IA: University of Iowa Press, 2004.

LG   *Leaves of Grass*, Comprehensive Reader's Edition, edited by Harold W. Blodgett and Sculley Bradley. New York: New York University Press, 1965.

Leaves 1855   *Leaves of Grass*, 1855 ed. *The Walt Whitman Archive*. Ed. by Ed Folsom and Ken Price. ⟨whitmanarchive.org/published/LG/1855/whole.html⟩.

MDW   *Memoranda During the War*. Ed. Peter Coviello. New York: Oxford University Press, 2004.

PW   *Prose Works 1892*. 2 vols. Ed. Floyd Stovall. New York: New York University Press, 1963–1964.

WMB   Ed Folsom. *Whitman Making Books / Books Making Whitman: A Catalog and Commentary*. Iowa City: Obermann Center for Advanced Studies, 2005.

WPP   Betsy Erkkila. *Whitman the Political Poet*. New York and Oxford: Oxford University Press, 1989.

WWC   Horace Traubel. *With Walt Whitman in Camden*. 9 vols. Vol. 1: Boston: Small, Maynard, 1906. Vol. 2: New York: D. Appleton, 1908. Vol. 3: New York: Mitchell Kennerley, 1914. (Vols. 1–3: Rpt. New York: Rowman and Littlefield, 1961.) Vol. 4, ed. Sculley Bradley, Philadelphia: University of Pennsylvania Press, 1953. (Rpt. Carbondale: Southern Illinois University Press, 1959.) Vol. 5, ed. Gertrude Traubel, Carbondale: Southern Illinois University Press, 1964. Vol. 6, ed. Gertrude Traubel and William White, Carbondale: Southern Illinois University Press, 1982. Vol. 7, ed. Jeanne Chapman and Robert MacIsaac, Carbondale: Southern Illinois University Press. Vols. 8–9, ed. Jeanne Chapman and Robert MacIsaac, Oregon House, CA: W. L. Bentley, 1996.

Walt Whitman's Reconstruction

1. Walt Whitman's Reconstruction

I cannot let my momentous, stormy, peculiar Era of peace and war, these States, these years, slip away without arresting some of its specimen events—even its vital breaths—to be portray'd and inscribed from out of the midst of it, from its own days and nights— not so much in themselves (statistically and descriptively our times are copiously noted and memorandized with an industrial zeal)— but to give from them here their flame-like results in imaginative and spiritual suggestiveness.... In another sense (the warp crossing the woof, and knitted in,) the book is probably a sort of autobiography; an element I have not attempted to specially restrain or erase.—Walt Whitman, from "Note at End of Complete Poems and Prose," 1888*

On May 23rd, 1865, the combined might of nearly the entire Union army gathered for one last march. Two hundred thousand strong they came, wending their way through the streets of Washington, D.C., for a magnificent Grand Review in the nation's capital. It would take two full days for this mass of men and machinery to complete its final task before disbanding. Many soldiers would return home, while some would go on to take up their duties in the southern states. Out of sight of the cheering crowds, still others lay dying in Army hospitals. For now, however, the occasion was a celebration, to be sure, and a momentary homecoming—schoolchildren waved signs, including one that read "The Public Schools of Washington Welcome the Heroes of the Republic."[1] The review was also a show of strength for a country that had only a month before been shocked to its core by the assassination of Abraham Lincoln. In a demonstration of governmental continuity, the newly installed president, Andrew Johnson, attended the review flanked by his generals and cabinet.[2] It is hard to imagine that this new president could serve as anything but a reminder that, while the war was finally over, the hard work of bringing the nation back together after four bloody years had only just begun, and the outcome was anything but a sure thing.

The poet Walt Whitman was among the throng that watched the spectacle unfold over the course of those two warm summer days and, as he had done throughout the war, he reported on the event in detail in a letter to his mother, Louisa Van Velsor Whitman:

> Well, the Review is over, & it was very grand—it was too much & too impressive, to be described—but you will see a good deal about it in the papers. If you can imagine a great wide avenue like Flatbush avenue, quite flat, & stretching as far as you can see, with a great white building half as big as fort Greene on a hill at the commencement of the avenue, & then through this avenue marching solid ranks of soldiers, 20 or 25 abreast, just marching steady all day long for two days, without intermission, one regiment after another, real war-worn *soldiers*, that have been marching & fighting for years—sometimes for an hour nothing but cavalry, just solid ranks, on good horses, with sabres glistening, & carbines hanging by their saddles, & their clothes showing hard service, but they [are] mostly all good-looking hardy young men—then great masses of guns, batteries of cannon, four or six abreast, each drawn by six horses, with the gunners seated on the ammunition wagons—& these perhaps a long while in passing, nothing but batteries—(it seemed as if all the cannon in the world were here)—then great battalions of blacks, with axes & shovels & pick axes, (real southern darkies, black as tar)—then again hour after hour the old infantry regiments, the men all sunburnt—nearly every one with some old tatter all in shreds, (that *had been* a costly & beautiful *flag*)—the great drum corps of sixty or eighty drummers massed at the heads of the brigades, playing away—now and then a fine brass band—but oftener nothing but the drums & whistling fifes—but they sounded very lively—(perhaps a band of sixty drums & fifteen or twenty fifes playing "Lannigan's ball")—the different corps banners, the generals with their staffs &c—the Western Army, led by Gen. Sherman, (old Bill, the soldiers all call him). (*Corr*, 1:260–61)

Although the poet claims the review is "too impressive" to describe, his letter suggests both the scale of the march itself and the traces of the conflict that the soldiers carried with them. Whitman later drew upon his description of this day for other purposes, including similar phrases in his collection of war writing *Memoranda During the War* (1875–1876) and then again in his 1882 autobiography *Specimen Days*. For now, however, the poet's time and attention were consumed both by the spectacle of the mass of soldiers marching—"good looking hardy young men" filling the streets—and, as his journals attest, the many wounded still lying in a far worse state in Washington's hospitals. Like President Johnson, these soldiers were a reminder of the war and its costs, while the presence of the freed slaves marching through the capital suggested the many and varied tasks still facing the country, foremost among them stitching the Union back together and integrating the freed African Americans into the postwar nation.

This work would extend from schoolhouses and statehouses in the South to the halls of Congress in Washington and, in a kind of historical shorthand, came to be known as "Reconstruction." In the federal government, it would include amending the United States Constitution, guaranteeing all citizens equal rights before the law and ensuring the voting rights of African American men. For federal troops, it meant taking up positions in the South to support the newly established state governments and to protect the freed slaves from reprisal and exploitation. Over the course of the next twelve years, the Reconstruction era would see the impeachment and acquittal of Andrew Johnson, the election and reelection of General Ulysses S. Grant to the American presidency (in spite of numerous scandals), the rise of the Ku Klux Klan and the growing oppression of African Americans in the South, and a disputed national election in 1876, the resolution of which would see the final collapse of Republican governments in the South and the end of federal troop intervention there.[3] While the controversial agreement that enabled Rutherford B. Hayes to become president in 1877 marked the end of official Reconstruction,[4] the work of binding the nation's wounds following the cataclysm of the Civil War, and of securing equal rights for all of its citizens, are challenges the United States has continued to face down to the present day.[5]

For Walt Whitman, living and working in Washington, D.C., in the years immediately following the war's end, Reconstruction meant not only navigating these tumultuous years with his fellow citizens, but also coming to terms with his own memories of the war, marked by the sight of innumerable casualties and the stories of remarkable courage told to him by the soldiers he treated in the hospitals. Preserving what he felt to be the essence of these experiences became a central concern for the rest of his life. A critical time for the nation, the postwar years were also a time when the poet dealt with significant personal losses and physical illness even as he expanded and cemented his place in the American literary landscape. Just as national Reconstruction would continue long past its ostensible end in 1877, Whitman's own reconstruction would continue until his death in 1892.

The poet's work following the war was profoundly influenced by the remarkable changes taking place in the publishing industry in the postwar years. The exponential growth of periodical publications fed by new technologies and new markets was transforming the publishing world and the profession of authorship that the poet had pursued for well over two decades. Whitman's increasingly numerous appearances in periodicals as both author and subject demonstrate how he adjusted to these changing realities in an effort to reach out to the wider audience now available to him. The years after the war would see Whitman transformed from newspaper editor and staff journalist to celebrity contributor and nationally recognized public lecturer, a transformation driven as much by material developments in the nation as by his own professional and poetic ambitions.

While all of these developments are vital to any understanding of Walt Whitman's personal reconstruction, they are inadequate if not examined in the context of the considerable poetic and personal reimagining that is the hallmark of these years. Numerous critics have discussed the editions of *Leaves of Grass* that Whitman produced after the war in terms of this process, most significantly the 1881 edition, and biographers have carefully documented the personal setbacks, including a stroke and his mother's death. Surprisingly, however, to date there has only been one book-length study that examines the poet strictly in terms of Reconstruction, Luke Mancuso's important *"The Strange Sad War Revolving": Walt Whitman, Reconstruction, and the Emergence of Black Citizenship, 1865–1876*.[6] Mancuso discusses each of the poet's major postwar publications specifically in terms of Reconstruction legislation, focusing primarily on the congressional debates regarding amending the Constitution to preserve the rights of the newly liberated slaves. Given the importance of the issue of African American citizenship, Mancuso's choice makes a great deal of sense. At the same time, however, his work's scope does not account for the interplay between the politics that marked the present moment and the poet's evolving response to his memories of the cataclysm from which the nation had just emerged.

Similarly, M. Wynn Thomas devotes two chapters of his important work *The Lunar Light of Whitman's Poetry* to the poet's response to the war and to his efforts to come to terms with his experiences in the hospitals. In studying the poet's writing, particularly the "Drum-Taps" poems and Whitman's response to Abraham Lincoln's assassination, Thomas offers a subtle reading of the poet's psyche, suggesting that some of the poet's memories "threatened his mental equilibrium."[7] At the same time, he highlights how Whitman worked to preserve his painful personal experiences as part of a national history and memory, becoming, in Thomas's evocative phrase, "the prophet of the past" (*Lunar Light*, 278), seeking to preserve the memory of the war to inform the future. Thomas offers a compelling and significant close reading of much of Whitman's major Civil War writing, both in terms of how it reflects the poet's personal struggles with his memories and how they came to inform his larger poetic project.

Whitman's response to his memories was unquestionably affected by the material changes taking place around the poet as he pursued his profession. The reconstruction of "one of the roughs,"[8] as he described himself in the 1855 *Leaves of Grass*, into a widely recognized public figure was facilitated by the nature of the press during the years after the war. In very concrete ways, the ability of writers to reach a mass readership and influence the reception of their work changed dramatically following the conflict. The struggle had produced a transportation and media infrastructure that could at last accommodate the kind of national audience that Whitman had long imagined in his writings. The number of rail lines had greatly increased to transport troops and supplies, and these improvements allowed for far easier transport of goods, including books and periodicals. In 1865, approximately seven hundred magazine titles were in publication, a number that almost doubled by 1870.[9] The increase in subscribers as well as in advertising revenue also made magazines much more stable venues than they had been in the earlier part of the century, even with the increased competition. Whitman quickly seized this increasing opportunity to reach his readers. He was no stranger to the periodical press, of course, having begun his career as a journalist and editor, but, following the war, magazines served as an important vehicle for pursuing his aims. As Amanda Gailey has recently observed, "In the 10 years between the 1871–72 and 1881–82 editions, Whitman dramatically increased his rate of publishing poems in periodicals. . . . By this point in his career, Whitman was deftly and frequently using periodicals as a way to give his poetry and himself an ongoing public relevance beyond the pages of *Leaves of Grass*."[10]

Much of that relevance in the postwar period was a result of the poet's well-known service in the Union hospitals, and Whitman approached the war in his writing as a crucial moment both in the nation's history and in his own, part of a shared narrative that his writing both reflected and shaped. For Whitman, Reconstruction was not simply an act of moving forward from the wreckage left behind by the war or of reconciling two opposing sides. For the poet who is often thought of as looking toward the future—who "laid in [his] stores in advance"[11]—his postwar writings are frequently preoccupied with "backward glances," attempts to make sense of his memories and to integrate them into his work and the arc of his life and career as well as into the triumphant story of the nation. The poet's concern for what he derisively called the "cold and bloodless electrotype plates of History" (quoted in Thomas, *Lunar Light*, 234) forces us to consider how Whitman regarded the war in the far less concrete form of memory, the inexpressible impression of events that eludes the historian's pen. If, as he famously lamented, the "real war will never get in the books,"[12] he still never accepted that the real significance of the conflict would consequently be lost; indeed, his own writing dwells on precisely those kinds of episodes that he repeatedly asserts can never adequately be described. Even when he claims his words fail him, then, he nevertheless insists on documenting the gaps, as when he notes "[The war's] interior history will not only never be written, its practicality, minutia of deeds and passions, will never be even suggested" (*MDW*, 7). Never suggested, save by Whitman himself, who, as Thomas notes, strove to see "the present and future put in touch (that sense so vital to Whitman) with the real 'interior history' of the past" (*Lunar Light*, 234).

The tension between attempting to retain some sense of these lost moments by creating what Pierre Nora terms *lieux de mémoire* (sites of memory), while simultaneously documenting in specific terms the heroism of the soldiers and the events in the hospital, is evident in the changes between the 1875–1876 text *Memoranda of the War* and his 1882 autobiography *Specimen Days*. The poet who witnessed and did his best to record the unspeakable suffering in the hospitals and listened to the harrowing tales of the battlefields stands between the representational work of history as he rendered it in his personal archive—the names, dates, and events in his notebooks—and the finally unrepresentable agony of those years signified in the mute bloodstains that he claimed spot those same notebooks. Along with his memoranda, Whitman came to see the traces of the war in his own stroke-ravaged body, his weakened physical condition providing a form of silent testimony, a sign forever indicating the war's cost.[13]

But this physical memory contrasts sharply with the historical record of the conflict that became a prominent public preoccupation during the 1870s, a fascination with events that Whitman tapped into with his writing and with his lectures on Abraham Lincoln. The poet's early interest during the late 1860s in recasting the Civil War in terms of the Crusades demonstrates that, at least in the beginning, the poet was searching for a way to view the conflict in a historical framework.[14] As he researched the project, Whitman hand-copied a passage from a May 1844 article on the Crusades from the *North British Review* and noted in the margin, "The analogy between all this & the exciting scenes at the breaking out of our own war."[15] He would repeatedly link the Crusades to the United States in his notes, as he did when he jotted the line, "The Crusades of the 12th & 13th centuries are tallied by the American war of the 19th."[16] As he initially considered how he would construct the history of the war, then, the poet went quite far afield in looking for a suitable framework.

Despite his initial enthusiasm, however, Whitman's contemplated work never took shape. His abandonment of the project indicates that, despite his claims of finding an analogy for the Civil War in the Crusades, either the war itself or the histories he was reading during his research offered no adequate precedent for him to follow. Rather than a reworked historical narrative, mediated through the accounts of another struggle, what he would offer instead was a war read through his own life and memories. Consequently, understanding the various "backward glances" the poet casts in representing the war and his experience requires a close attention both to his feelings about the conflict and to the nation's burgeoning interest in the record of that conflict.

To describe Walt Whitman's reconstruction, then, requires shifting attention away from the Civil War itself to concentrate instead on the poet's postwar views on and recollections of the struggle. This is not an easy endeavor, for the war looms large in any account of the poet and his work. Indeed, it would be hard to top Walt Whitman's own estimation of the impact that the Civil War had on his life and poetry. As he famously notes in "A Backward Glance O'er Travel'd Roads," "Without those three or four years and the experiences they gave, 'Leaves of Grass' would not now be existing" (*LG*, 570). Given the importance of the war, critics have followed Whitman's own lead in carefully studying the poet's experiences during the conflict by way of his poetry and prose. Moving reconstruction to the fore means focusing less on his experiences during the war itself and more on his process of reconsidering it and, even more significantly, the ways that he reconstructs his experiences as they slip inexorably into the past. To examine Whitman's reconstruction requires an almost constant stepping back to examine how he frames his memories, rather than concentrating on the events they recall, a difficult process of which the poet himself became progressively more conscious. This is evident in his increasing reification of the "blood-stain'd" immediacy of his wartime notebooks and in his apparent desire to reach the substance of his memories without getting caught up in the deliberate process of remembrance, his preference for "the Untold and Unwritten History of the War—infinitely greater (like Life's) than the few scraps and distortions that are ever told or written" (*MDW*, 7–8), even as he continued to tell and write his own history of the war.

In spite of the challenges, however, much can be gained from undertaking a new examination of Whitman during the postwar period. It was during the years that followed Lee's surrender that Whitman revised his poetic project to account for the shocks and disasters that had befallen the Union, and it was during that same period that "Walt Whitman," the public figure that came to hold a prominent place in American letters, took shape. The confluence of these events is hardly coincidental. If the war had shaken the poet's belief in a national democratic vision that could embrace contradictions and the conflicting views of both North and South—"slavery and the tremulous spreading of hands to protect it, and the stern opposition to it" (*PW*, 2:743)—its aftermath brought a resurgent desire for the kind of Union that Whitman had long described. In short, by the 1870s his poetic vision was of a piece with a larger political and literary movement seeking reconciliation and a resurgent nationalism. *Leaves of Grass* has never been associated with the "romances of reunion" of the time, but Whitman's call for a bard who would "not be for the Eastern states more than the Western, or the Northern states more than the Southern" (*PW*, 2:446) was much easier to imagine in a nation tired of sectional conflict, and it was echoed by writers in the popular press after the war.

While unity, adhesion, and the bonds that link Americans were themes of Whitman's poetry before and after the war, they took on a new and pressing relevance following the war's conclusion; however, the poet was hardly silent regarding the political upheavals that marked the years of Reconstruction, nor was he blind to the significant challenges the nation faced. As Mancuso and others have discussed, these years saw the release of some of Whitman's most overtly political writings, including the three essays that were eventually collected and published as *Democratic Vistas*. What remains open for debate, however, is the degree to which the poet's writings actually engage the particular political crises of the moment, such as the extension of the right to vote to African Americans. Thomas F. Haddox, for example, argues of *Democratic Vistas* and the revised version of "Poem of Many in One" (1856) entitled "As I Sat by Blue Ontario's Shore" that "Whitman does little more than allude to these issues before he moves past them, gesturing toward a future in which these conflicts have been resolved even as he continues to invoke the same model of national unity that he had championed in 'Poem of Many in One.'"[17] Mancuso reaches a starkly different conclusion, arguing that Whitman's "rhetorical images" in *Democratic Vistas* "placed [it] squarely in the public debate over the franchise" (52). Mancuso even suggests that the work reinscribes the gap between the new constitutional language and its effect, writing, "The 'spirit' of reconciliation between the races remained at arm's length, despite the 'appearance' of the fifteenth amendment and *Democratic Vistas*, though such texts constructed an America as the 'mother of the true revolutions' of social solidarity between strangers" (70). He concentrates primarily on the text's relationship to legislative discourse of the time: both exhibit the distance between their apparent aspirations and performances. As a result, the work is more than simply an extension of the earlier poetry; beyond what may or may not be explicitly addressed in the text, Mancuso sees *Democratic Vistas* itself as quite literally a work of Reconstruction. In his study of Whitman and the constitutional debates, he extends this line of argument to many of the poet's postwar works in his systematic analysis of the major publications.

If one goes beyond the particular question of enfranchisement and examines Whitman's writings in terms of the changing nature of the partisan press and the political campaigns of the postwar years, one gets a better sense of the poet's engagement with a range of contemporary issues. Haddox is correct in stating that the poet, particularly in his verse, often gestures toward the future and speaks in apparently broad terms. But a closer attention to the venues for Whitman's work and the changing nature of his popular reputation can tell us more about how the poet navigated this tumultuous period. If his published statements on race seem oblique or fleeting during this period, for example, his interest in issues of class and labor movements, issues closely linked to race in party politics of the time, provides greater insight into the poet's engagement with the challenges facing national reconciliation. The changing nature of his feelings toward Grant, for example, demonstrates how he balanced his career as a public servant, his doubts about issues such as the tariff and the franchise, and his desires for a unifying national figure who could take up the mantle of his beloved Lincoln. The general-turned-president looms large in any discussion of Reconstruction, although the poet's response to him has gone largely unexamined by critics. Understanding how the poet's views on the war, politics, and on his own art shifted over time requires beginning with his response to Grant's appointment as commander of the Union forces and examining the poet's writings on Grant up until the general's death in 1886. Such an analysis represents one instance where the analysis of Whitman's reconstruction must begin with the war itself, as Whitman's response to the general as he took command provides the baseline for his evolving views on the man as he became president, international celebrity, and, like Whitman himself, autobiographer.

Whitman's reconstruction was political, poetic, and public, and his prose writings, like his poetry, form a major part of the postwar figure that he presented to the nation. If his message of unity was getting a new hearing from an audience hungry for reconciliation, it was only one of many that readers had to choose from. The tendency to view Whitman's later work through the prism of the war has hampered efforts to read his work in the context of the Reconstruction literature that was growing in popularity as Whitman's postbellum work appeared. If, in the political realm, there was a tendency to wave the bloody shirt, in the pages of books, newspapers, and magazines, there was a growing call for the "hatchet to be buried." This literature would later be supplemented and ultimately supplanted by a drive to document the events of the war, as partisan debates over the justice of the cause gave way to arguments over tactics and strategic errors. Such a shift did not occur overnight, of course, but grew as the 1860s came to an end and as Reconstruction as a legislative enterprise was abandoned in the 1870s. Looking at Whitman's engagement with the political issues of the day with an eye toward his awareness of his public self and the larger literary scene can provide new insight into his views and how his writing changed following the war.

A reconsideration of the enigmatic and vexing "By the Roadside" cluster first included in the 1881 edition of *Leaves of Grass* demonstrates this forcefully. The cluster has received comparatively little critical attention, and when it is discussed, it is often seen simply as a random assortment of unrelated shorter poems. Although it includes one of Whitman's most reproduced works ("When I Heard the Learn'd Astronomer"), it is largely overshadowed by the "Drum-Taps" cluster that immediately follows it, yet another instance of readers' attention shifting from Whitman's postwar reconstructions to his war experiences and writings. If we examine the cluster in light of how division and conflict shape the persona's views in these poems, however, we see the poet creating a narrative of fractured and failing poetic vision, a vision that can only be restored through the cleansing violence of war. In this cluster, Whitman inverts Washington Irving's story of Rip Van Winkle: where Irving's hero sleeps through the Revolutionary War to awaken to a world dramatically changed by events, Whitman's speaker determines to sleep *until* the coming of war. Only war, the speaker suggests, will allow him to regain his vision and allow the nation to emerge whole once more: "Then I will sleep awhile yet, for I see that these States sleep, for reasons; / (With gathering murk, with muttering thunder and lambent shoots we all duly awake, / South, North, East, West, inland and seaboard, we will surely awake.)" (*LG*, 279). The "electric shock" and the "drum-taps" that fill the first poem of the next cluster will serve as the speaker's wake-up call: "By the Roadside" can be read, then, as a purposeful poetic prelude to the "Drum-Taps" cluster; with these two working together, Whitman constructs a poetic narrative of martial reawakening. The war is reimagined after the fact as a necessary shock to restore both the poet and the United States. The two clusters form the speaker's own "romance of reunion," dramatizing how the war leads to a transformed poetic vision and renewed purpose. "By the Roadside" positions "Drum-Taps" and by extension the Civil War itself as a necessary cataclysm in the development of Whitman's persona. The poet uses the cluster to reconstruct his poetic story, transforming the national crisis of the war into a poetic one as well.

While Whitman's writing took on the additional work of reunion following the war, the poet was also concerned that such reunification not come at the cost of forgetting those lost in the conflict that put the nation at risk. This concern would become increasingly obvious as the years passed, but it is clear that even in the 1870s the poet was preoccupied with how he, the war, and its combatants would be remembered. For Whitman, these were all inextricably linked. In the beginning of his autobiography *Specimen Days* (1882), he emphasizes the fact that much of the book's significant matter comes from his war writings and, at first blush, it appears he has merely lifted his earlier *Memoranda* into the second work, once again holding up those pages "blotch'd here and there with more than one blood-stain" (*PW*, 1:2) for public scrutiny. As such remarks indicate, from the outset Whitman saw the book as offering yet another iteration of his memories of the Civil War, and critics have rightly looked to its pages for insights into Whitman's views on the conflict. Long after Reconstruction had officially ended, the poet's work of reconstruction continued.

Despite this shared material in the two postwar volumes, there is a striking feature in the opening pages of *Specimen Days* that sets it apart, and that is the mingling of genealogy with the descriptions of illegible family gravestones with which the poet begins his autobiography. Where in earlier writings Whitman seems to find significance in the graves marked "UNKNOWN," his early depiction of his own family life suggests unease with historical gaps. While in an earlier poem, "As the Time Draws Nigh" (1860, 1871), the speaker is able to reassure himself, "O soul, we have positively appear'd—that is enough" (*LG*, 488), by the time Whitman turned to reflect upon his own life and on the war in *Specimen Days*, he sought a more permanent record. Such a record would serve to preserve the "truth" of himself and his family, the fallen soldiers North and South, and the president that he loved so dearly, and it would outlast the illegible grave markers on the family plot. He found such an enduring memorial, of course, in his own writing, as in the 1881 poem "As at Thy Portals Also Death," a tribute to his mother: "To her, the ideal woman, practical, spiritual, of all of earth, life, love, to me the best, / I grave a monumental line, before I go, amid these songs, / And set a tombstone here" (*LG*, 497). Here the language of dissolution that marks earlier poems such as "This Compost" (1856, 1881) is replaced with an air of monumental permanence.

Immediately following this memorial to his mother in the "Songs of Parting" cluster, Whitman writes in "My Legacy" (1872, 1881),

> But I, my life surveying, closing,
> With nothing to show to devise from its idle years,
> Nor houses nor lands, nor tokens of gems or gold for my
>   friends,
> Yet certain remembrances of the war for you, and after you,
> And little souvenirs of camps and soldiers, with my love,
> I bind together and bequeath in this bundle of songs.
>
> (*LG*, 497–98)

Whitman's postwar writing tells us a great deal about the life of the poet and the changing circumstances in which he found himself. Ultimately, however, Walt Whitman's reconstruction is devoted to the construction of both a lasting memorial and an abiding historical record, a project extending well past 1877. In his writings after the war, the poet strives to inscribe both the events and the import of the Civil War and of its aftermath, as well as his own struggles and triumphs, in letters that will not be obscured by time or the elements, just as innumerable years must pass before his tomb, that improbable temple of granite of Whitman's own design, at last sinks into the earth.

2. Periodicals, Politics, and
the New Paper World

Editions! Editions! Editions! like the last extra of a newspaper:
an extra after an extra: one issue after another: fifty-five, fifty-six,
sixty-one, sixty-seven—oh! edition after edition.
—*Walt Whitman to Horace Traubel, 1889*

Walt Whitman's Civil War writings, while voluminous and complex, were only one small eddy in a river of texts that emerged from the confluence of the wrenching national conflict and the dramatic transformation of the publishing industry. While the outbreak of the war momentarily shocked Northern publishers—Thayer and Eldridge, publishers of the third edition of *Leaves of Grass*, went bankrupt (Loving, 239)—it also produced a boom in war-related publications in the North.[1] Even before its conclusion, the war gave rise to a then-unprecedented number of poems, stories, and novels, and indeed, it has been a central preoccupation of writers ever since. Poetry meant to inspire and console family members frequently appeared alongside news from the front, and at the war's end, the retelling and reimagining of the war was a task taken up by writers both famous and obscure and, increasingly, the participants themselves, as editors and publishers solicited former officers to share their perspectives. This proliferation of texts owed a great deal to the massive changes taking place in publishing in the 1860s. As with so many other writers, then, Whitman's written attempts to come to terms with the war he experienced coincided with this fundamental transformation in both his nation and his profession.

Nowhere are these changes more apparent than in the rapid developments that swept periodical publication. In many ways, Whitman was better positioned than most writers to navigate the new landscape that took shape after the war. Throughout his long career, including the height of his fame as a poet, Whitman never left behind the periodical culture in which he had gotten his start. Even after he began publishing his multiple editions of *Leaves of Grass*, the poet continued publishing both poetry and prose in newspapers and magazines much as he always had. As Amanda Gailey points out, however, as time went on, he came to see periodical publication as not only a way to increase his reputation but also to promote the latest edition of his book. Gailey suggests that while these publications offered him both publicity and another source of income, they also squared with his poetic philosophy: "Periodicals gave *Leaves of Grass* legs. They moved the poet into the busy streets of democracy he sought to articulate and celebrate" (417). Whitman's practice, therefore, dovetailed with industry advances in productive and revealing ways and enabled him to reach his readers at a key historical moment.

Despite these significant professional and poetic resonances, Whitman's periodical publication after the Civil War has only recently begun to garner sustained attention. While his early writing has long been examined for the insights it might offer into the foundations of *Leaves*, his later publications have been discussed much less frequently, in part because, for a long period of time, these works remained uncollected.[2] As work like Gailey's indicates, there is a great deal to be learned from examining the changes that the poet made between periodical and book publication, and the periodicals themselves can serve as an important indicator of the poet's evolving literary influence. Of course, Whitman's engagement with the magazines and newspapers of the time also forces us to reassess the break critics have sometimes assumed took place in 1855 between the "dandy" editor of the 1840s and the "rough" of *Leaves*. The revolution in his poetry did not necessarily coincide with a complete revolution in the approach to his profession that he had cultivated in the early part of his career; however, the context in which Whitman pursued publication in periodicals changed dramatically, particularly after the Civil War. A greater understanding of the material developments in production and the changing political landscape of periodicals provides insight into Whitman's appearance in the press in the years of Reconstruction. Periodicals shifted to accommodate changing readerships and changing partisan divisions, and close attention to the poet's publishing venues reveals how the poet's national reputation developed, how he shepherded that reputation, and how his postwar publications contributed to the historical narrative of the war that was being created. These works also shed additional light on Whitman's positions on some of the most pressing political issues of this tumultuous time in American politics.

THE UNFOLDING PAPER WORLD

While Whitman pursued a publishing strategy reminiscent of his early days as an editor, the market in which he operated was undergoing a significant transformation. The Civil War was a moment of both crisis and opportunity for American publishing, and the years that followed witnessed a flowering in periodicals that had not been seen since the early heyday of magazines in the 1820s. There are a number of reasons for this. First, the necessities of war yielded an infrastructure that allowed for both the shipment of raw materials of publication and the national mailing of periodicals themselves. On a purely technical level, the national readership that Whitman long craved only truly became feasible following the end of the war. Second, the war helped foster and promote a culture of readers for periodicals. As Charles G. Steffen points out, newspapers had long attempted to make themselves a fixture in American life, promoting free circulation and the establishment of reading rooms in publishers' offices, effectively clearinghouses where both editors and the public could find a copy of any number of publications.[3]

More than any other event, however, the Civil War made newspapers essential to their readers. As Alice Fahs remarks,

> Reading habits changed dramatically with the onset of war, a
> fact that numerous observers noted both north and south. News-
> papers suddenly became an urgent necessity of life, with readers
> eagerly gathering at bulletin boards outside newspaper offices
> in order to read the news as soon as it was printed. In Boston,
> Oliver Wendell Holmes reported that one person he knew always
> went through the "side streets on his way for the noon *extra*, —he
> is so afraid somebody will meet him and *tell* the news he wishes
> to *read*, first on the bulletin-board, and then in the great capitals
> and leaded type of the newspaper." The newspaper was "imperi-
> ous," according to Holmes. "It will be had, and it will be read. To

this all else must give place. If we must go out at unusual hours to get it, we shall go, in spite of after-dinner nap or evening somnolence." (19)

The hunger for news of the war that drove the newspaper business also extended to magazines, at least in the North, which was unhampered by the material and production limitations that rapidly plagued the southern states. Magazines like *Harper's Weekly* that provided numerous illustrations of war events trumpeted their images and saw increased demand (Fahs, 49). Even literary journals like the *Atlantic Monthly* saw their circulation grow as their content shifted to war subjects; Fahs notes a particularly striking example: "James T. Fields . . . advertised the June 1861 number of the *Monthly* as 'An Army Number,' with the claim, 'The especial adaptation of the contents of this number to the wants of the reading public at the present time has induced a number of patriotic gentlemen of Boston to subscribe for 10,000 copies as a gratuitious [*sic*] donation to the officers and privates of the Army of the United States'" (53). This last remark suggests another way in which the war contributed to a culture of periodical reading that had not existed prior to the war. The large number of men in camp created a ready-made readership for magazines and newspapers, particularly in the North, with some papers, like the *Army & Navy Official Gazette* (1863–1865, American Antiquarian Society), springing into existence solely to serve this particular reading constituency. Whitman saved several 1864 issues of the *Armory Square Hospital Gazette*,[4] the small paper of one of the hospitals in which he spent the most time ministering to wounded soldiers, and in *Specimen Days* he asserted that he published in its pages (*PW*, 1:288).

Like many, Whitman was an avid reader of the papers during the war, and they served as more than sources of information. He frequently clipped and preserved articles detailing events during the conflict.[5] As Ted Genoways has demonstrated, the poet did not simply draw inspiration from newspaper reports but even the language for some of his poems written during the war, noting that at least two works—"Cavalry Crossing a Ford" and "An Army Corps on the March"—share diction with stories in the *New York Times*.[6] While Genoways makes clear that the poems, and more significantly their placement in *Drum-Taps*, resist the kind of strictly chronological and historically located narratives of their journalistic sources, the influence of the reports on the poetry suggests one of the ways that attention to the periodical press can reveal more than simply bibliographic information regarding venue. Periodicals continued to inform his writing in the postwar years. In his later prose accounts of the conflict, Whitman quotes frequently from newspapers, as he does in *Memoranda During the War* when describing Andersonville ten years after the war (*PW*, 1:323). The proliferation of newspapers and magazines offered not just places to publish, but material as well, raw paper goods to be refashioned into the story of the nation.

It was not just the significant developments in infrastructure and readership that transformed the periodical culture in which Whitman cut his teeth during the 1840s and 1850s, however. The "stuff" of paper itself was changing: one of the more striking advances that took place during this period was in the making of paper. Prior to the war, nearly all paper was made of "rag-stuff," fibers taken from the pulp of rags. During the conflict, the demand for paper and the scarcity of rags led to soaring prices for the simple material; one firm's records indicate that prices more than doubled from roughly six cents a pound in 1862 to nearly fifteen cents a pound in 1866.[7] The demand for rags for newspapers over the years led to some macabre anecdotes regarding their sources. One persistent myth holds that a Maine papermaker named Augustus Stanwood became so desperate for rags during the 1850s and 60s that he imported the bandages from Egyptian mummies for use as paper.[8] And, in an anecdote that seems to literalize Whitman's "blood-drips" and the physical connection between his work and the body, in 1892 businessman Horace Hosmer of Concord, Massachusetts, offered this remembrance of the nearby Maynard paper mill of the 1850s:

> There was a Paper Mill up stream which I used to visit occasionally. After the Crimean War 5 tons of soldiers white shirts came to this mill at one time just as they were taken off the dead bodies, matted with blood, and were made into writing paper. I weighed

one of my shirts and it weighed ¾ of a pound, so there must have been the blood of 1000 men coloring the waters of our beautiful river.[9]

This recycling of bloody material is clearly suggestive for thinking about the ways Whitman sought to transcend the boundary between bodies of people and bodies of work, and, with Whitman's preoccupation with the bloodstains on his Civil War notebooks, it also points to the way that the suffering of war was permeating his pages even in the early editions of *Leaves of Grass*. Paper could literally re-present the material effects of war in its pages, its very substance emerging from the wreckage as producers sought to feed the escalating demand. The anecdote graphically illustrates the desperation of papermakers seeking to meet an exceptional appetite for their commodity.

This desperation led to experimentation with new fibers and eventually the breakthrough of using wood fibers to create paper, an innovation that allowed for cheaper manufacturing.[10] Mills began changing over in the 1860s and increasingly used wood during the 1870s; by the 1880s nearly all of the newspapers were using wood-pulp paper. Historian David C. Smith writes, "Newspapers chose the new paper most widely. A major result was the cheapening of the papers in price and an extension of coverage of items with the result that by the turn of the century the newspaper had gone down in price from ten to perhaps one cent, and the size of the paper had risen from four pages to often ten or more" (138). Prices for paper dropped so dramatically in the decades following the war that Smith argues "a paper world seemed to unfold in the 1880's and 1890's" (139) as all manner of products took advantage of the wood-pulp paper.

In addition to paper manufacturing, printing technology also continued to improve. Whitman would have witnessed firsthand the introduction of electrotyping, a process by which copper plates of typeset pages were produced through electricity-conducting molds. These plates were much more durable than regular stereotype plates, and they became the standard for large print-run texts such as newspapers and magazines during the 1840s.[11] In 1855, Jacob Abbot wrote that the Harper brothers published nearly everything using electrotype plates,[12] necessitating large underground vaults beneath the publisher's building: "The accumulation of electrotype plates in a large establishment that has been long in operation is very great. In the Harper Establishment [*sic*], the stores now on hand are enormous. Those of the Magazine alone are rapidly approaching ten thousand. The plates are stored in subterranean vaults built under the streets that surround the building."[13] Whitman boasted of the 1856 *Leaves* in a letter to Emerson that "these thirty-two Poems I stereotype, to print several thousand copies of" (*LG*, 730), and Whitman's friend John Burroughs later wrote that "a batch of a thousand copies" was produced.[14] Publishers generally only used plates for large runs, so his decision to stereotype is a sign of his optimism.

Plates would only truly become an issue for the poet and for *Leaves of Grass* in 1860: the subsequent auctioning of the durable electrotype plates for the edition by Thayer and Eldridge and their eventual purchase by Richard Worthington, who began publishing unauthorized copies using the plates in 1879, became a notorious episode in the poet's career. The creation of the plates in the first place, however, suggests the aspirations of the poet and his publishers for a larger audience. As one commentator for the *Westminster Review* acidly remarked of the Thayer and Eldridge edition,

> When a volume containing more obscenity and profanity than is perhaps elsewhere to be found within the same compass, presents itself in all the glories of hot-pressed paper, costly binding, and stereotype printing, and we believe as a fourth edition, it is manifest that it not only addresses, but has found a public of a much wider class, and it becomes a question how such a book can have acquired a vogue and popularity that could induce an American publisher to spend so much upon its outward setting-forth.[15]

Regardless of Whitman's own eventual misfortune with the plates, the increasing use of the electrotype was crucial, for the boom in periodical publishing following the war could only be sustained by the more durable plates that rose to prominence in the 1850s and allowed print runs of several thousand copies. Similarly, during the 1860s, the cylinder presses first used in the 1840s became more and more common as their design improved in 1858 and then 1865: "These machines did not incorporate radically new features but, by combining minor improvements with new standards of mechanical accuracy, they first challenged and then overcame the lead enjoyed in the mid nineteenth century by the platen machines."[16] Although the flat-plate machines continued to be used for certain texts because of their greater accuracy and generally higher quality, they were neither as fast nor as large as the cylinder presses.[17]

The results of all of these changes in readership and the innovations in production are easily seen in the jump in the number of publications and periodical subscriptions following the war. While noting that the data do not readily distinguish between newspaper and magazine titles, Frank Luther Mott states that in 1865 there were seven hundred titles, nearly doubling by 1870, and doubling again by 1880 (3:5). Mott estimates that by 1885, there were 3,300 periodical titles (3:5). The number of readers grew dramatically as well. While he notes that exact circulation figures were often closely held secrets or liable to public exaggeration, it is clear that the numbers significantly increased:

> By 1874 the *New York Weekly*, a cheap story-paper, was advertising 350,000—which it thought "the largest circulation in the world." But it went down a bit by the eighties, as its prototype the *New York Ledger* had; and the *Youth's Companion* went up, achieving by 1885 the largest circulation of the period outside of the group of mail-order papers—385,000. The House of Harper had two periodicals with lists running over 100,000—the *Monthly* and the *Weekly. Scribner's Monthly* was also in that class; by 1885, (as the *Century Magazine*) it had reached 200,000. *Godey's* had over 100,000 in 1865. . . . Altogether there were more than thirty periodicals which were quoted at 100,000 circulation or over between 1865 and 1885. (3:6–7)

These numbers provide a stark contrast with a magazine like the old warhorse *North American Review*, which had a peak prewar subscription list of 3,200 in 1830 (Mott, 2:231–32). It was a new age for American magazines.

While Whitman had published in periodicals for many years before producing *Leaves of Grass*, he had never reached an audience like the one he had access to following the war. In the absence of the advances described above, Whitman's prewar publishing venues were of necessity more provincial. The first edition of *Leaves of Grass* itself enjoyed a limited print run of 795 copies and limited distribution (*WMB*, 12). The same obstacles of technology and infrastructure that limited the scope of periodicals were at work in book publishing, as well, although, as Ronald J. Zboray notes, significant advances were already being made by 1855,[18] particularly thanks to the railroad, an innovation that military necessity would vastly expand during the war years. Whitman, who self-published his first edition with the help of a printer of legal forms (*WMB*, 8), would finally come much closer to the national readership he described in the preface to the 1855 edition in the pages of postwar magazines such as the *Galaxy* and even ostensibly local papers such as the *New York Daily Graphic*. New York was firmly established as the publishing center of the nation after the war, and many of its productions were widely distributed throughout the country.

Whitman's newspaper publications allowed for much more inexpensive distribution of his ideas. Newspapers enjoyed a significant advantage when it came to the postal system, for example: while sending a letter five hundred miles cost three cents in 1863, and a magazine two, a newspaper could be sent for 0.38 of a cent.[19] Congress eventually acted in 1879 to make the situation more equitable by dropping the price of mailing magazines: "The postal act of March 3, 1879, which gave second-class mailing privileges to magazines . . . was recognition of the stature which magazines were achieving in the years of accelerated industrial and economic growth in America that began with the Civil War and continued through the remainder of the nineteenth century."[20] This increase in Whitman's ability to reach a broader audience was equally true for his newspaper and magazine publications. While the culture of reprinting had long meant that newspapers were never strictly regional, since their stories and articles were frequently appropriated and republished, the extensive reach of publications only increased following the war.

WHITMAN IN THE MAINSTREAM

The poet published in many newspapers and periodicals in the years following the war, and these contributions, combined with the growing number of profiles, interviews, and other mentions of the author, helped shape his increasingly recognizable public persona. In its catalog of periodical publications, the online Walt Whitman Archive currently lists thirty-two poetry publications prior to the Civil War, dating as far back as 1839. Following the war, Whitman published a staggering 128 poems in periodicals ranging from local newspapers to national magazines, including the *Atlantic Monthly* and *Harper's*. When one considers the number of readers that these periodicals were reaching after the war, it is easy to see that the poet was becoming a significant public figure.

In some ways, Whitman was poised for such a rise even before the war. Gailey points out how Whitman's 1860 publication "Bardic Symbols" in the *Atlantic* both improved his reputation and helped to prepare the ground for the appearance of the 1860 edition of *Leaves* a few months later (416–17). It is perhaps indicative of the poet's desire for mainstream acceptance that he acceded to James Russell Lowell's demand to delete two lines from the work, the kind of acquiescence he almost never displayed when it came to his poetry (Mott, 2: 501–2). Susan Belasco notes how striking Whitman's agreement is, pointing out that Fannie Fern had cited his refusal to agree to editorial changes as one of the strengths of his verse.[21] While the appearance of his poem in 1860 suggested his acceptance by the Boston Brahmin set, his 1869 publication of "Proud Music of the Storm" in the *Atlantic* was even more significant.[22] The poem was published anonymously, but Whitman himself drew attention to his authorship of the work in the *Washington Star* just prior to the poem's appearance (Gailey, 423). If "Bardic Symbols" represented Whitman's entrée to the confirmed literary establishment, then "Proud Music of the Storm" was the poet's postwar return to a literary culture that was in the process of reconstituting itself in the wake of the conflict.

The poem itself gestures to the war in the opening stanza: "You sounds from distant guns with galloping cavalry, / Echoes of camps with all the different bugle-calls, / Trooping tumultuous, filling the midnight late, bending me powerless, / Entering my lonesome slumber-chamber, why have you seiz'd me?" (*LG*, 403). As the poem progresses, however, these sounds that suggest a specific recollection of previous strife are first replaced with the sounds of victory and the suffering of the wounded and grieving, only to be subsumed into a far more universal song: "All songs of current lands come sounding round me" (*LG*, 406), emphasizing the present harmony over the past conflict and suggesting a universal music ranging from East to West, from "the Egyptian harp of many strings" to "Luther's strong hymn" (*LG*, 408). By the poem's conclusion, the significance of the songs that the speaker is hearing contracts to serve a specific poetic function:

Haply what thou hast heard O soul was not the sound of winds,
Nor dream of raging storm, nor sea-hawk's flapping wings nor
    harsh scream,
Nor vocalism of sun-bright Italy,
Nor German organ majestic, nor vast concourse of voices, nor
    layers of harmonies,
Nor strophes of husbands and wives, nor sound of marching
    soldiers,
Nor flutes, nor harps, nor the bugle-calls of camps,
But to a new rhythmus fitted for thee,
Poems bridging the way from Life to Death, vaguely wafted in
    night air, uncaught, unwritten,
Which let us go forth in the bold day and write.

                             (*LG*, 410)

While the dream that the speaker experiences incorporates the recent struggle into a universal context of music, part of the "storm" that encompasses the globe, when the speaker awakens the storm is rendered into a kind of poetic license. It is an aesthetic gesture, well suited for the explicitly literary magazine in which it was published, and seemingly well suited for the magazine's increased subscription list. From 1863 to 1870, the subscription list increased from thirty-two thousand to fifty thousand (Mott, 2:505). While the magazine enjoyed a reputation as perhaps the premier literary magazine in the United States, prior to the war it was also accused of being overly provincial, with editors and contributors rooted in New England. This had changed by the 1870s; William Dean Howells remarks of the postwar period, "The fact is we were growing, whether we liked it or not, more and more American. Without ceasing to be New England, without ceasing to be Bostonian, at heart, we had become southern, midwestern, and far-western in our sympathies" (quoted in Mott, 2:506). Whitman's 1869 publication offered him a far more national literary imprimatur, and his tone matched that wider audience.

If publishing in the *Atlantic* helped to solidify the poet's literary reputation, his publication in magazines such as the *Galaxy* and, in 1874, *Harper's Monthly Magazine*, contributed still further to his national exposure and reputation. *Harper's* had ruled the magazine world in terms of its number of readers almost from its inception, and it emerged from the war years even stronger than before. After beginning in 1850 with 7,500 subscribers, by the Civil War it had a circulation of two hundred thousand, a figure that dipped during the war years before the magazine surged again in 1864 (391–93). Publication in its pages signified a mainstream respectability that the poet had never previously possessed, as the editors firmly held to the notion that theirs was a family publication. The public controversy regarding *Leaves of Grass* that had led to Whitman's dismissal from the Department of the Interior only a few years before seemed long forgotten when, in February 1874, *Harper's* published "Song of the Redwood-Tree," with its invocation of a nation on the rise, looking toward the future:

> But more in you than these, lands of the Western shore,
> (These but the means, the implements, the standing-ground,)
> I see in you, certain to come, the promise of thousands of
>   years, till now deferr'd,
> Promis'd to be fulfill'd, our common kind, the race.
> [. . .]
> Fresh come, to a new world indeed, yet long prepared,
> I see the genius of the modern, child of the real and ideal,
> Clearing the ground for broad humanity, the true America,
>   heir of the past so grand,
> To build a grander future.
>
> (*LG*, 210)

This encomium was followed only a month later in the magazine's pages by "Prayer of Columbus," a poem that numerous critics have seen as offering as much of a portrait of the poet's own melancholy regarding his physical condition and aging as of the historic figure that it claims to represent.[23] At the same time, an invocation of the discoverer of the New World represents the sort of safe topic that would serve Whitman and the mainstream sensibilities of the magazine. While Whitman admitted the biographical element in private correspondence, publicly the poet sought to ensure that his work received a more historical reading by including a long introductory paragraph on its subject:

> It was near the close of his indomitable and pious life—on his last voyage, when nearly 70 years of age—that Columbus, to save his two remaining ships from foundering in the Caribbean Sea in a terrible storm, had to run them ashore on the Island of Jamaica—where, laid up for a long and miserable year—1503—he was taken very sick, had several relapses, his men revolted, and death seemed daily imminent; though he was eventually rescued, and sent home to Spain to die, unrecognized, neglected and in want. . . . It is only asked, in preparation and atmosphere for the following lines, that the bare authentic facts be recalled and realized, and nothing contributed by the fancy. See, the Antilliean Island, with its florid skies and rich foliage and scenery, the waves beating the solitary sands, and the hulls of the ships in the distance. See, the figure of the great Admiral, walking the beach, as a stage, in this sublimest tragedy—for what tragedy, what poem, so piteous and majestic as the real scene?—and hear him uttering— as his mystical and religious soul surely uttered, the ideas following—perhaps, in their equivalents, the very words.[24]

Perhaps wary of biographical readings, Whitman insists that his readers consider only his pronounced subject: "It is only asked, in preparation and atmosphere for the following lines, that the bare authentic facts be recalled and realized, and nothing contributed by the fancy." For the poet who previously argued in *Democratic Vistas* that the reader "must himself or herself construct indeed the poem" (*PW*, 2:425), this direction is strikingly restrictive. He provides graphic stage management—"See, the Antilliean Island, with its florid skies and rich foliage and scenery, the waves beating the solitary sands, and the hulls of the ships in the distance. See, the figure of the great Admiral, walking the beach, as a stage, in this sublimest tragedy"—

focusing the reader's attention on his historical subject; and, further removing both himself and the reader from the drama, the poet suggests that his language may even be analogous to the explorer's actual language: "Hear him uttering—as his mystical and religious soul surely uttered, the ideas following—perhaps, in their equivalents, the very words." The effect of this introduction is to distance Whitman as much as possible from the poem itself, a striking move for a poet who frequently sought to collapse the distinction between himself and his work. Such distancing would have served to make the poem more palatable to editors who may have been squeamish about including the still-controversial poet in their magazine, and, in an era of uneasy national reconciliation, its subject is one that could appeal to readers regardless of sectional rivalries.

The perspective taken in the introductory note is all the more remarkable when we consider Whitman's correspondence regarding the poem. He wrote to Ellen O'Connor, the wife of his once-good friend William O'Connor, "As I see it now I shouldn't wonder if I have unconsciously put a sort of autobiographical dash in it" (*Corr*, 2:272). A little more than two weeks later, he wrote to his friend Peter Doyle, "I have a poem in the March *Harper* as I believe I mentioned in my last. (I am told that I have colored it with thoughts of myself—very likely)" (2:278). There is no determining from whom he might have heard this, but it is clear that it was his own impression if not his overt objective, and the repetition of this comment indicates that autobiographical intent was likely at work. This suggests that his introductory note to the poem is rather disingenuous, or at least an attempt to shield himself from perceived criticism for daring to compare himself to such a historic figure. At the same time, however, there is no denying that both the note and the subject matter of the poem itself are far removed from the candor and controversy that had previously defined the poet's public persona, and, like "Song of the Redwood Tree," this work represents a move toward more recognizable (and acceptable) national themes. Whitman himself wrote of these poems to his friend Rudolf Schmidt, "I suppose it is hardly necessary to tell you that I have *pitched* and *keyed* my pieces more with reference to fifty years hence, & how they will stand mellowed and toned *then*—than to pleasing & tickling the immediate impressions of the present hour" (*Corr*,

2:310). This may have been the case, but, in publishing his poem in such a prominent periodical, addressing an apparently noncontroversial theme, Whitman was also firmly situating himself within the cultural landscape of his time.

POLITICS AND PUBLISHING
THE CASE OF DAVID G. CROLY AND
THE *NEW YORK DAILY GRAPHIC*

While magazines like *Harper's* were essential in securing Whitman's public reputation, his newspaper publications were becoming increasingly visible and further contributing to his fame as an author. At the same time, they offered him a reliable venue during a time of personal misfortune and poor health. Most critical in this latter regard was his association with the *New York Daily Graphic*. Whitman published in its pages almost from its very beginning in 1873, and the timing was fortuitous for the poet. As Belasco remarks,

> At the beginning of 1873, Whitman suffered a debilitating stroke and just as he was beginning to recover, his mother, Louisa Whitman, died. In many ways, 1873 was the most difficult year of Whitman's life, as he struggled with his health and grief and also with his persistent feeling that he was failing to become a major American poet. But Whitman rallied and continued writing, publishing his poems and prose articles in periodicals, and trying new venues such as the *New York Daily Graphic*, which was among the first tabloid-format newspapers. ("Walt Whitman's Poetry," whitmanarchive.org)

An examination of Whitman's correspondence during this time demonstrates just how crucial the *Graphic* was for the ailing poet. As he wrote to his mother in 1873, "I am getting along well, but it is very, very slow—I cannot begin to apply my brain to regular work yet—though, for all that, I have written two or three little poems for the *Graphic*, a N.Y. daily evening paper just commenced—(one of them was in the number for last Wednesday)—they pay me moderately" (*Corr*, 2:204). In November of that year, the paper published letters from the poet describing Washington and even, as he put it to Doyle, "a portrait of my beautiful phiz." (2:259). The paper also published a biographical account of the poet in January 1874 entitled "A Biographical Sketch—An American Poet Graduating from a Printer's 'Case'" (2:283n). Even as his physical condition imposed a degree of physical isolation, the *Graphic* quite literally put Whitman and his life before the public eye. The emphasis on his background in printing and the appellation "American Poet" dovetailed nicely with Whitman's preferred narrative of his identity.

As these contributions and articles suggest, the *Graphic* aided in Whitman's continued emergence as a public figure who transcended the confines of purely literary circles at a time when he was personally more homebound than ever. Despite his physical limitations, his newspaper publications marked a return to Whitman's editorial roots, only this time with a much larger platform and reputation. The paper published selections of his *Memoranda* prior to its appearance as a discrete volume, and, as part of a prolonged study and critique of the popular spiritualist movement, it published the following letter from Whitman on December 19, 1874: "Your notes inviting me to write about Spiritualism reached me during a late severe spell of illness, which will account for their not being answered at the time. I thank you for your courtesy, but I am neither disposed nor able to write anything about this so-called Spiritualism. (It seems to me nearly altogether a poor, cheap, crude humbug)" (2:318). This brief notice indicates Whitman's role as a public intellectual, at least within the pages of the *Graphic*, which sought his views on cultural issues as one of several regular commentators. This was a role that Whitman would play increasingly during the 1870s as journalists sought him out for interviews on any number of subjects, from religion to politics.[25]

Perhaps the clearest evidence of the poet's growing prominence and evolving public identity can be found in the poet's inclusion in the newspaper's first special Christmas issue, the *Christmas Graphic*, "for sale at news-stands throughout the United States."[26] He wrote to his friend William Burroughs, "I am writing very little—have a piece, a *melange*, prose and verse, in the '*Christmas Graphic*'—(comes out in a week or so,) in which I say a brief word about Emerson" (2:318). The glowing announcement of the Christmas issue suggests the kind of production of which Whitman was now a part:

The Graphic Company will bring out during the month of December AN EXTRA CHRISTMAS NUMBER of THE DAILY GRAPHIC, and intend that it shall be the most perfect and beautiful specimen of printing ever issued from a great newspaper establishment. It will be entirely separate and distinct from the regular issue of THE DAILY GRAPHIC, and will comprise twenty pages, including a four-page cover, illuminated from elegant designs in red, blue, black, and gold, and chromo-lithographed to make it a model of artistic engraving and presswork.[27]

In addition to this detailed description of the material object itself, the editors proudly announced the contributors to the volume, offering "original papers expressly for the Christmas Graphic." These included Richard Henry Stoddard, who received top billing, and "KATE FIELD, the popular authoress, lecturer, and comedienne," "'Peleg Arkwright,' whose poems illustrative of low life in New York have attracted such marked attention," "'Jennie June,' the well-known essayist," and others, some with and others without follow-up descriptions. The fact that the sixth entry in the list is simply "A Christmas Garland in Prose and Verse by WALT WHITMAN" is indicative of the poet's prominence in 1874. While he clearly did not need introduction or description, he also did not receive top billing, and his entry received none of the accolades granted the others, whose inclusions were referred to as "charming," "sprightly," or "wise and witty." Nevertheless, his inclusion in such a mainstream holiday publication aimed at a wide audience, much like his publication in *Harper's* a few years later, suggests how his reputation had developed and mellowed since he first emerged on the public scene.

As the *Graphic*'s announcements of the eventual (and repeatedly delayed) appearance of the annual continued, the descriptions fell away and Whitman received billing over Stoddard (although he still had to give pride of place to Kate Field and "Anon."). On the day of its release, the publishers trumpeted that it was "FOR SALE BY NEWS AGENTS EVERYWHERE" and that it was "far superior in its art matter to any art journal ever published, and in its literary matter to anything that has ever appeared in a newspaper, and when we assert this we include the choicest publications of the London *Graphic* and the art periodicals of other countries."[28] The *Christmas Graphic* indicates the growing technological sophistication and ambition of newspapers following the war. While there is clearly no small degree of hype in the *Graphic*'s pronouncements regarding the quality and availability of its product, the reviews that followed the annual's release do support some of its claims, at least so far as publishers throughout New England and New York are concerned. At least eleven newspapers made reference to the annual, and the *Graphic* proudly cited the glowing reactions to the work.[29]

While the *Graphic*'s efforts to cater to a large and mainstream audience in the 1870s can partially explain its courting of Whitman, it is important to remember that its editor, David G. Croly, had also been a longtime supporter of the poet. Whitman remarked to Traubel in 1889, "I wrote things for The Graphic back there, you know. Croly was really good to me."[30] Until Jerome Loving's recent biography of the poet, little had been said regarding the connection between Croly and Whitman, which is surprising given Croly's dubious distinction in American history. As Edwin Haviland Miller remarks, in 1864 Croly coauthored a work entitled *Miscegenation*, "which proposed the blending of the two races for the survival of civilization."[31] Although Miller does not mention it, Croly and his coauthor George Wakeman are commonly credited for coining the title term, and Miller also fails to point out that the work was published as a hoax, intended to discredit the Republican Party by suggesting that the party supported the then-radical views that the pamphlet espoused.[32] Loving echoes Miller's description of Croly, which itself draws from the *Dictionary of American Biography*, as an "iconoclast and a reformer" and states that the work "may have been a spoof intended to smear the Republican, or Union, party."[33] While certain aspects of the work itself might strike modern readers as open and forward-thinking, and while Croly's widow would later refer to the "half joking, half earnest spirit in which [it] was written,"[34] its primary goal was precisely to stoke racist fears.[35] In one representative passage, the authors argue,

It is idle to maintain that this present war is not a war for the negro. It is a war for the negro. Not simply for his personal rights or his physical freedom—it is a war, if you please, of amalgamation, so called—a war looking, as its final fruit, to the blending of the white and black. . . . Let it go on until church, and state, and society recognize not only the propriety but the necessity of the fusion of the white and black—in short, until the great truth shall be declared in our public documents and announced in the messages of our Presidents, that it is desirable the white man should marry the black woman and the white woman the black man. . . . The next step will be the opening of California to the teeming millions of eastern Asia. The patience, the industry, the ingenuity, the organizing power, the skills in the mechanic arts, which characterize the Japanese and Chinese, must be transplanted to our soil, not merely by the emigration of the inhabitants of those nations, but by their incorporation with the composite race which will hereafter rule this continent.[36]

The entire pamphlet is written in a similar vein, offering a view of the conflict and of the future that is designed to play upon the racist fears and prejudices of readers. In advocating for the necessity of "miscegenation," the authors comment on the current political landscape, asserting that the Democratic Party "attempts to divert discussion to senseless side issues, such as peace, free speech, and personal and constitutional rights" (49), while the Republican party is "in effect, the party of miscegenation" (50). While the pamphlet was not universally received as its authors intended, it is clear, as Katherine Nicholson Ings notes, that the authors "did not condone a word they wrote [and] hoped to repel their readers with their ironic endorsement of interracial romance."[37]

Given Croly's participation in such partisan dirty tricks, it is not surprising, then, that a few years later he also published a biography in support of the 1868 Democratic candidates for president and vice president entitled *Seymour and Blair: Their Lives and Services.* This significant element of Croly's career has gone largely unnoticed, but, as historian David W. Blight notes, "White supremacy was the cornerstone of the Democrats' strategy in 1868, and with vice-presidential candidate Blair leading the offensive, they conducted one of the most explicitly racist presidential campaigns in American history."[38] One slogan stamped on campaign buttons read, "This Is a White Man's

Government."[39] Croly's association with this campaign raises questions regarding his affinity for Walt Whitman. Of course, Whitman had been a supporter of the Democratic Party before the war, and even in 1859 he expressed a preference for Douglas over Lincoln: "Disunion is impossible; Defeat is unbearable; *ergo*, Douglas is inevitable."[40] As this remark suggests, by the 1850s Whitman's association with the Democratic Party was primarily driven by his desire for Union and his concern that the Republicans would bring about Civil War (373–74). David S. Reynolds notes that in later years the poet would tell others that he voted for Lincoln in 1860 (136), and his general favor for Lincoln and other Republican presidents is well known; however, his warm association with a figure like Croly during the 1860s and 1870s suggests the two men may nevertheless have shared ideas and beliefs that strengthened their friendship at a time when the poet's views on race caused a bitter quarrel with one of his closest allies, William O'Connor, a staunch abolitionist and supporter of equal rights (Loving, 346–47).

While not commenting upon Whitman's relations with the man who helped to coin the term "miscegenation," critics have long recognized the poet's ongoing concern regarding race and sexuality, with most agreeing that Whitman's personal views on the subject, both before and after the war, often appear to belie the more liberal and accepting expressions of his poetry. Most notably, in the early temperance novel *Franklin Evans*, the poet presents an ill-fated interracial marriage as one of the lamentable consequences of drunkenness.[41] Indeed, the results of the union seem almost the mirror opposite of the positive claims made in the *Miscegenation* pamphlet. As Debra Rosenthal remarks, the novel links intemperance and interracial romance as forms of degradation: "Whitman conflates temperance and racial discourse to show that miscegenation, like alcohol, is a dark blot on the U.S. character and a threat to a healthy U.S. C/constitution."[42] Thus, while the seemingly progressive arguments made in Croly's pamphlet fly in the face of the poet's own representations of interracial union, recognition of *Miscegenation*'s political double-cross allows for the intended oppositional reading that reveals the same fear of interracial mixing that Whitman expressed in his novel. The poet stated similar concerns even after the war. In Whitman's 1875–1876 publication of

Memoranda During the War, for example, there is a passage entitled, "Results South—Now and Hence," in which he states,

> The present condition of things (1875) in South Carolina, Mississippi, Louisiana, and other parts of the former slave states—the utter change and overthrow of their whole social [*sic*], and the greatest coloring feature of their political institutions—a horror and dismay, as of limitless sea and fire, sweeping over them, and substituting the confusion, chaos, and measureless degradation and insult of the present—the black domination, but little above the beasts—viewed as a temporary, deserv'd punishment for their Slavery and Secession sins, may perhaps be admissible; but as a permanency of course is not to be consider'd for a moment. (Did the vast mass of the blacks, in Slavery in the United States, present a terrible and deeply complicated problem through the just ending century? But how if the mass of the blacks in freedom in the U.S. all through the ensuing century, should present a yet more terrible and more deeply complicated problem?). (*PW*, 1:326)

While not addressing "miscegenation," the references to the "measureless degradation and insult of the present" and "the black domination" indicate Whitman's discomfort with race relations in the postwar era, the same kinds of fears upon which Croly's pamphlet was intended to play.

Whitman later disavowed *Franklin Evans*, and he removed the above passage when he incorporated his *Memoranda* into his sprawling autobiographical collection *Specimen Days and Collect* of 1882. Noting changes like this one, Ed Folsom has argued that the poet seems to have been careful in editing out the majority of his most vitriolic statements regarding race from reprintings and subsequent editions of his work: "He kept such statements out of his enduring books, almost as if he recognized his own retrogressive position on race."[43] This certainly may be true of the poetry, but the poet's relationship with Croly and his writings about the war during the 1870s demonstrate how attention to Whitman's publishing practices, in this case his association with the *Daily Graphic*, can enhance our understanding of the poet's political positions on issues of race and party after the war.

Given the rapidly changing publishing business and the tumultuous political scene, it is not surprising that Croly's Democratic activism during the 1860s has been obscured. Despite his efforts during the 1860s, once he left the *World* and became editor of the *Graphic*, Croly repositioned himself in a postwar nation where many publications were working to reach a wider audience, even as racial and political tensions were continuing to rise, particularly in the South. Indeed, in 1872, the editor left behind the question of race entirely to author the book *The Truth about Love: A Proposed Sexual Morality Based upon the Doctrine of Evolution, and Recent Discoveries in Medical Science*, which one biographer describes as "a remarkably frank exploration of sexuality and 'the passion of Love,'"[44] a text that, with its dismissal of the moral value of virginity and call for legal prostitution, may have been strong stuff even for Whitman.[45] At approximately the same time, Croly also launched an ill-fated periodical entitled *Modern Thinker* "which ran only two bizarre issues, one in 1871 and the second in 1873."[46]

Croly was clearly pursuing other interests, and the desire to move beyond the sectional struggles of the 1860s coincided with the expanding market for periodicals and the growing role that advertising revenue played in changing the nature of periodicals. As Gerald J. Baldasty notes, "Attention both to the general concerns of advertisers and the complex newspaper business also demanded that readers be attracted to the newspaper in large numbers. To answer this need, publishers and editors attempted to produce a paper vivid in its graphics and interesting in its content that would please any potential reader. The key to the emerging newspaper was diversity."[47] Not surprisingly, this meant that the traditionally outspoken party politics of papers like the *New York World*, where Croly got his start, were growing increasingly untenable. At the same time, the specter of scandals in the Grant administration contributed to a growing distrust of government:[48] "The result was a certain distancing from politicians, the growth of the press more or less as an autonomous institution rather than an adjunct to political parties. . . . By the end of the century, it became standard editorial policy for the press to present news based on facts, rather than producing the political essays that characterized so much of the antebellum press" ("Nineteenth-Century Origins," 416; 417). Newspapers still covered politics after the war, of course, but without the same partisan edge that had marked them in the 1840s, when Whitman himself was an editor. Evidence also suggests that, in addition to a movement away from overt party affiliation, newspapers generally reduced their coverage of politics substantially in the postwar era, while at the same time dramatically increasing stories on crime, "society and women[,] [and] leisure activities" (*Commercialization of News*, 122–25). While the *Daily Graphic* might be tagged as one of the earliest tabloid newspapers in New York, it would not be long before its content would be pretty much indistinguishable from that of other major newspapers.

If Croly was seeking to distance himself, at least publicly, from the partisan battles of the 1860s as he pursued new projects and audiences with the *New York Daily Graphic*, then he and Whitman were well suited to one another.[49] In 1874, the paper published Whitman's poem for the graduation at Tufts, "The Song of the Universal." The occasion for the poem's composition, its place of publication, and its subject all point to the poet's apparent disengagement from current crises. David S. Reynolds notes of the poem, "The generalities had crucial importance, for [Whitman] was now seeking to soar above the pros and cons of American life and view them abstractly, from a height. . . . America's current problems? No need to worry about them, the poem assures us: they will go away in time, since the good will win in the end" (514). The poem's very title suggests the distance the poet was traveling from the increasingly divisive politics of Reconstruction.

Such a move away from the pressing political and racial conflicts extended not only to the poetry Whitman was writing during this period, but to his revisions of earlier work as well. This is indicated by his treatment of race in his poems. Folsom and Price examine this extensively in Whitman's revisions of his poem "The Sleepers," particularly the "Lucifer" section, which features the voice of a slave cursing his master. They note,

> The Lucifer passage lingers in *Leaves* through the first two post–Civil War editions as a kind of vestige of Whitman's antebellum

desire to voice the subjectivity of the slave, to give the slave power and agency to imagine that that poetic act might be enough to change the slavemaster's perception of slaves, to coerce the slave-masters into recognizing the humanity in those they treated as objects and possessions, as less than human. In the late 1870s, however, as Whitman revised his book for a new edition that would be published in 1881, he made a stunning decision. He deleted the "Lucifer" section of "The Sleepers," crossing it out on his working copy of his 1871–1872 edition and marking two "d's" (one in pencil and one emphatically in dark ink) to indicate to the printer to omit the section.[50]

Such a change is of a piece with other actions Whitman took during this period. In 1870 the poet published his prose work *Democratic Vistas*, a work that featured the revision and synthesis of two articles that had been published in the *Galaxy* in 1867 and 1868, along with a third essay that had never been published. While claiming to be a response to Thomas Carlyle's attack on black suffrage in "Shooting Niagara: And After," the work really offered little in way of rebuttal:

> [Whitman] begins *Democratic Vistas* saying he will not "gloss over" the issue of universal suffrage, but that is exactly what he does: he discusses equality between the sexes, but after obliquely raising the issues of race in the opening pages, the essay veers away, never to return, except in some small-print notes at the end, notes that he did not republish with *Democratic Vistas* after the initial reprinting. (*Re-Scripting Whitman*, whitmanarchive.org)

While this is clearly an example of the poet's ambivalence regarding issues of racial equality during this period, it also suggests the poet's search for a "vista" above the fierce partisan politics of the time. Despite the conflicts surrounding him, Whitman appears to have preferred to see this as a period of personal and national healing, telling one correspondent, "All continues to go well with my health &c. The Union now promises to reconstruct—(after a violent and somewhat doubtful struggle.) My leg is not much different, & I still have an occasional spell with the head—but I am *much better*" (*Corr* 2:237). The conflation of his personal condition with his assessment of the political climate is unmistakable, and it is possible the poet did not wish to continue probing the nation's wounds.

His periodical publishing in the 1870s reinforces this sense of a press and a poet that are both postpartisan. Just as Croly's mainstream *Graphic* represented a move away from the political divisions of the 1860s, Whitman's appearance in Horace Greeley's *New York Daily Tribune*, a paper that had been a prominent advocate for abolition before the war,[51] also suggests the changing nature of newspapers, since both provided venues for the poet despite the widely disparate views of their editors. Greeley's own political career presents a picture of the changing party dynamics as the country sought to rebuild itself: "The liberals sought reform and conciliation in dealing with the South and turned to Greeley as their candidate. The Democratic Party, with which he had fought all his life, also nominated Greeley for the presidency, and he accepted."[52] As Greeley noted when stepping down from the editor's position upon his nomination, "The *Tribune* has ceased to be a party organ, but the unexpected nomination of its Editor at Cincinnati seems to involve it in a new embarrassment."[53] While his claim that his nomination was "unexpected" may be accurate given what at first seemed long odds, the position was hardly unsought by the ambitious editor. Still, the statement indicates the new necessity for at least the appearance of impartiality on the part of the press.

Although Greeley was defeated in a landslide, his political career indicates how the old divisions were shifting in the postwar years. What had previously been separations along lines of racial attitudes were shifting more explicitly to divisions along issues of class. As Heather Cox Richardson argues in her study of race and labor in Reconstruction, conservative and moderate Republicans, concerned that the former slaves were abandoning ideas of individual enterprise and advancement for class struggle, increasingly found common cause with Democrats. In the months leading up to the 1872 election, she writes,

> Greeley continued to develop the theme of the disaffected black worker in his newspaper, attributing to African Americans the same negative qualities pinned on white organized labor by its enemies. . . . Picking up the popular image of "communists" who argued about political theory while their wives struggled to feed

the children, Greeley contrasted the lazy black men with their wives, whose "industry" was "noticeable."[54]

Other prominent newspaper editors sided with Greeley: "Murat Halstead of the *Cincinnati Commercial*, Horace White of the *Chicago Tribune*, William Cullen Bryant of the *New York Evening Post*, and Edwin L. Godkin of the *Nation* all swung over to Greeley's camp and adopted his rhetoric about unproductive black workers looting the Reconstruction governments, while they emphasized that white Southerners were helping the South to prosper."[55] Greeley's successor at the paper, Whitelaw Reid, dealt ruthlessly with labor unions during the 1870s, causing one biographer to label him "a leader of anti-union sentiment" (Duncan, 61–62).

After the war, Whitman, like other Republicans, opposed the use of paper currency to pay war bonds, a fundamental part of the party's platform in 1868, but his position on bottom-up labor movements is not easily reconciled with the party's principles. In *Democratic Vistas*, he includes a striking passage on "The Labor Question." While clearly attacking the wealthy elite, the passage also speaks in ominous tones of pending labor disputes:

> The immense problem of the relation, adjustment, conflict, between Labor and its status and pay, on the one side, and the Capital of employers on the other side—looming up over These States like an ominous, limitless, murky cloud, perhaps before long to overshadow us all;—the many thousands of decent working-people, through the cities and elsewhere, trying to keep up a good appearance, but living by daily toil, from hand to mouth, with nothing ahead, and no owned homes—the increasing aggregation of capital in the hands of a few—the chaotic confusion of labor in the Southern States, consequent on the abrogation of slavery—the Asiatic immigration on our Pacific side—the advent of new machinery, dispensing more and more with hand-work— the growing, alarming spectacle of countless squads of vagabond children, roaming everywhere the streets and wharves of the great cities, getting trained for thievery and prostitution—the hideousness and squalor of certain quarters of the cities—the advent of

late years, and increasing frequency, of these pompous, nauseous, outside shows of vulgar wealth—(what a chance for a new Juvenal!)—wealth acquired perhaps by some quack, some measureless financial rogue, triply brazen in impudence, only shielding himself by his money from a shaved head, a striped dress, and a felon's cell;—and then, below all, the plausible, sugar-coated, but abnormal and sooner or later inevitably ruinous delusion and loss, of our system of inflated paper-money currency, (cause of all conceivable swindles, false standards of value, and principal breeder and bottom of those enormous fortunes for the few, and of poverty for the million)—with that other plausible and sugar-coated delusion, the theory and practice of a protective tariff, still clung to by many;—such, with plenty more, stretching themselves through many a long year, for solution, stand as huge impedimenta of America's progress. (*PW*, 2:753)

Robert Leigh Davis has recently suggested of *Democratic Vistas* that "Whitman writes an 84-page political essay that has very little to say about the actual *stuff* of nineteenth-century politics—which is to say, particular parties, leaders, elections, and platforms."[56] The passage above powerfully refutes such a claim, as it takes on three of the most prominent issues of the 1868 presidential campaign—labor, the use of paper currency, and the protective tariff—and stakes out positions on each.

The passage indicates the complexity of Whitman's political views, however: while his critique of paper currency put him fully in the Republican camp, the tariff had long been a source of ire for Democrats, even before the Civil War, and its continued use was seen as exacerbating the South's already significant economic woes. Whitman was clearly divided between the two parties on these issues, and his attitudes about labor are even harder to fathom. Is he lamenting the "ominous, limitless, murky cloud" of impending labor and class struggle, another Republican view, or is he merely describing it as an inevitable, perhaps even regrettable, consequence of the "increasing aggregation of capital in the hands of a few—the chaotic confusion of labor in the Southern States, consequent on the abrogation of slavery—the

Asiatic immigration on our Pacific side—the advent of new machinery, dispensing more and more with hand-work"? This would suggest a more Democratic view of the labor problem, which increasingly saw a world where individual labor and hard work were insufficient to make progress and the rich few were aggregating all the wealth at the expense of the many. Heather Cox Richardson argues that moderate Republican distrust of labor unions and immigrants and fears of government-mandated reallocations of property would eventually combine with conservative Democratic views of the freed slaves as a class not only to allow for the Greeley ticket of 1872, but eventually to help fuel the end of Reconstruction. Whitman removed this passage from *Democratic Vistas* when he incorporated it into *Specimen Days and Collect* in 1882. It is possible that he viewed the explicit political concerns of the late 1860s as out of keeping with the broader themes he was seeking to encapsulate in his work, but, as with his removal of the Lucifer passage from "The Sleepers," this deletion appears to represent another step away from the political struggles that marked the question of race in the post–Civil War era.

In a similar passage entitled "The Tramp and Strike Questions," Whitman returns to the class divide, this time without reference to "the chaotic confusion of labor in the Southern States, consequent on the abrogation of slavery—the Asiatic immigration on our Pacific side," and offering instead a general warning regarding the future:

> The American Revolution of 1776 was simply a great strike, successful for its immediate object—but whether a real success judged by the scale of the centuries, and the long-striking balance of Time, yet remains to be settled. The French Revolution was absolutely a strike, and a very terrible and relentless one, against ages of bad pay, unjust division of wealth-products, and the hoggish monopoly of a few, rolling in superfluity, against the vast bulk of the work-people, living in squalor.
>
> If the United States, like the countries of the Old World, are also to grow vast crops of poor, desperate, dissatisfied, nomadic, miserably-waged populations, such as we see looming upon us of late years—steadily, even if slowly, eating into them like a cancer

of lungs or stomach—then our republican experiment, notwith-standing all its surface-successes, is at heart an unhealthy failure. (*PW*, 2:528)

While this "Part of a Lecture proposed, (never deliver'd)" is undated, the description of three tramps that is attached is dated February 1879. Unlike the earlier passage from *Democratic Vistas*, here Whit-man reduces all of the political and economic issues to what he terms the "Poverty Question" (2:528). His remarks are more abstract and more focused on what he sees as the dangers inherent in the unequal distribution of wealth, combined with an encomium to the "poorest, lowest characters" (2:528). While he qualifies the emergence of a dis-contented lower class—"If the United States . . . are also to grow vast crops of poor"—, the sight of the three tramps—"quite good-looking American men" (2:528)—"made [him] serious," as though they rep-resented the first shoots of such crops as those he saw emerging in Europe.

Regardless of the degree of confluence or divergence between their views on the labor question, Whitelaw Reid, Greeley's successor at the *Tribune*, embraced Whitman, albeit belatedly. The editor remarked of Whitman, "No one could fail then [during the War] to admire his zeal and devotion, and I am afraid that at first my regard was for his char-acter rather than his poetry. It was not till long after 'The Leaves of Grass' period that his great verses on the death of Lincoln conquered me completely" (quoted in *Corr*, 2:316n). While it is difficult to deter-mine exactly when the editor was "conquered," the paper published several of the poet's letters and essays in the 1870s in addition to a lengthy review of the 1876 printing of *Leaves*. In a letter to the editor in 1874 offering an article for publication (which Reid apparently re-jected), the poet told Reid, "When you come to Philadelphia, try to come over & see me" (2:317). The friendly tone suggests the two men had a cordial relationship.

The poet's last publication in the *Tribune* was his tribute "A Death-Sonnet for Custer" published in July 1876, and his disappearance from the pages of the paper preceded another transformation. In the late 1870s, as Reconstruction faded as a legislative agenda, Reid began repositioning his paper to be once again explicitly partisan in an attempt to bolster its circulation. While the years following the war had seen the appeal for national unity driving editorial decisions, the change in the political fortunes of the Republican Party inspired the editor to attempt to reinvent the paper as a party organ. In December, 1877, he made the following appeal to his readers:

> The Republican Party is now in a struggle for its very life. The union of a Solid South and Tammany Hall threatens to grasp the Government & plunge us into repudiation or bankruptcy. The duty of the hour is to unite & strengthen the only party which can resist this danger. . . . You are therefore frankly asked to make a practical effort . . . to extend the circulation of *The Tribune*. (Quoted in Duncan, 58)

As Reid's biographer notes, the editor's reassertion of a political role for his paper was aided by the end of Grant's administration, as well as by the diminished controversy over Reid's activities on behalf of Greeley's campaign. Despite his personal connection with both Greeley and Reid, Whitman did not subscribe to their particular brand of politics in the election of 1872—during the campaign, *Harper's Weekly* referred to Reid as "Whitelie Reid" (Duncan, 45)—noting briefly in a letter to his mother, "I think Grant stock is steadily going up, & Greeley stock down, here & every where" (*Corr*, 2:183). The timing of the poet's increased publication in the *Tribune* in the 1870s, then, coincided with Reid's cross-party positioning, and the end of his publishing with Reid's paper came as it reasserted its partisan nature. Once again for Whitman during the later years of Reconstruction, when political questions crept too near, he retreated.

WHITMAN'S "ACTUAL AMERICAN POSITION" IN PERIODICALS

Given the poet's apparent disengagement from the partisan struggles of Reconstruction and his focus on personal and national healing, it is not surprising that Whitman's most public battle over his reputation as an American poet coincided with the ten-year anniversary of the Civil War's end and came just before his flurry of publishing activity tied to the nation's centennial. It was a time to reflect on the status of both his career and his country. The controversy that swirled around Whitman's anonymous article charging American critics and publishers with neglect, "Walt Whitman's Actual American Position," has been well documented by scholars.[57] While many have focused upon the content of the charges and countercharges and the true status of the poet—charges that centered on the question of whether Whitman was celebrated or neglected by the American public and literary establishment—the incident is perhaps most notable for the range of publications that became involved. Reynolds notes, "It is well known that the article, which Whitman sent to his British friends for reprinting, helped make the poet famous, since it prompted an international press war that hugely increased his visibility" (516). This controversy certainly helped keep Whitman in the public eye, but it also clearly indicates that the poet was already an established media figure by the mid-1870s. In a sense, the fact of the controversy surrounding the article fundamentally undermined its basic premise. How seriously could one take the accusations of neglect if they were so heatedly contested in the press?

Even before this latest uproar, Whitman had personally experienced how quickly newspapers could be employed to achieve, if not respect, at least notoriety. By the late 1860s, Whitman was a newsworthy subject in his own regard. A Washington reporter commenting on "Surface Life at Washington" remarked in 1869:

> Walt Whitman wanders up and down the avenue daily. . . . Whitman never carried his eccentricities of appearance to greater lengths than now. His hair, which the old poet gives free scope, falls below his shoulders, and his head is crowned by an immense, weather-stained hat, broad-brimmed as a Quaker's, and "skewed" all out of shape. His overcoat is rowdy, his gloves are unbuttoned; his aspect is as distract [sic] as a lover's. What a splendid waste of raw material! How much more the poet and the man he would look in a decent coat and a pair of cotton gloves![58]

This picturesque description was printed in the *Springfield Republican* and excerpted the next day in the *New York Evening Post*, suggesting both the keen interest in Whitman and the speed with which that news could now travel. In the story, he is an eccentric part of the "surface life" of the capital, the "old poet" even at the age of fifty, most notable for his dress. While the description itself is suggestive of the poet's self-fashioning as a "rough," it is a testament to Whitman's growing literary celebrity, not to his work as an artist.

Two years after this report, the *New York World* provided an even more compelling example of how news about Whitman could spread. In 1871, the newspaper picked up a dispatch from the Associated Press announcing that "Walter Whitman" had perished in a train accident. As Todd Richardson notes, rather than simply running the announcement and seeking confirmation, the paper immediately leapt to conclusions, publishing a largely complimentary obituary of the poet, one that was picked up by various outlets, sometimes with approval, often with derision. The obituary and its reprints are noteworthy for the relatively ample and what Richardson describes as "remarkably apt" quotations "which demonstrate just how rapidly Whitman's poetry had been assimilated into the reading culture."[59] Whitman's verse, if only in fragments, was getting a broad hearing. When the mistake was discovered, coverage was equally broad, with some editors taking the opportunity to hope that the entire incident would inspire the poet to "mend his ways" or at least his verse, as in this note from the *Troy Press*: "We are not sorry to learn that he still lives, if he will write no more or write more decently. He has not only enjoyed that rare boon of reading his own obituary, but the numerous protests against his filth, which he will also read, may possibly reform him. We hope so."[60] Such statements were in the minority, though, and it is hard to believe that Whitman was not pleased both by the speed and the distance that the news traveled. In 1873, he wrote to his friend Peter Doyle, "I shall get out this afternoon, & over to the Reading room in Philadelphia—(Looking over the papers, I see occasionally very interesting *news*, about myself—a paper in Salt Lake, Utah, had me dead—& the Philadelphia *Item*, about the same time, had me at a public dinner, in Phil. making a speech.)" (*Corr*, 2:257). What Meredith McGill has termed the "culture of reprinting" had long been in existence, of course, but now, with improved technology and infrastructure, the pace of such reprinting had accelerated to a degree that would have dazzled the poet in 1855. "Whitman news" was now traveling fast and far.

Late in life, the poet found in the newspaper business a fitting metaphor for his own writing and publishing of *Leaves of Grass*. In a conversation with Traubel, the poet asked his friend to read to him from his own past correspondence—a common occurrence during their talks—and Traubel read a letter from *Graphic* editor Croly in 1874 commenting on his excessive copyediting, as well as a draft of a letter Whitman wrote to a bookseller offering "data on editions." The poet remarked,

> What a sweat I used to be in all the time . . . over getting my damned books published! When I look back at it I wonder I did n't somewhere or other on the road chuck the whole business into oblivion. Editions! Editions! Editions! like the last extra of a newspaper: an extra after an extra: one issue after another: fifty-five, fifty-six, sixty-one, sixty-seven—oh! edition after edition. Yes, I wonder I never did anything violent with the book, it has so victimized me. (*WWC*, 3:561–62)

Whitman's reference to the "last extra of a newspaper" suggests a view of each edition of *Leaves* as an attempt to get out the "latest news," taking advantage of the available technology to reach out to his readership yet one more time.

The statement also puts more of an emphasis on the process than on the product, describing a cascading assault of one edition after another. And although both Traubel and Whitman got a laugh from the fact that the "poor victim is still making edition after edition" (3:562), the poet's remark provides a fitting commentary on his own contribution to the postwar "paper world." As Whitman worked to incorporate the Civil War into his work and into the narrative of his life and the nation, he had unprecedented access to his American audience, and he repeatedly took advantage of that access, not only through the "extra" editions of *Leaves of Grass*, but through his numerous appearances in periodicals. The frequency and prominence of the poet's publications had profound implications for his attempts to deal with his experiences in the Civil War hospitals and the war's effect on his poetic vision. With his national reputation established, his memories of the war would become strikingly public, part of the record, even as he insisted that they eluded such cold recountings. If Whitman was not quite the American bard he had imagined so many years ago, he at least had the ear of more listeners than ever before. His challenge would now lie in determining what could and should be sung.

3. Whitman and the Elusive Site of Memory

*Will the America of the future—will this vast rich Union ever
realize what itself cost, back there after all?—those hecatombs of
battle-deaths—Those times of which, O far-off reader, this whole
book is indeed finally but a reminiscent memorial from thence by
me to you?—Walt Whitman, "Preface Note to 2d Annex," 1891*

The rise of American periodicals and the continued expansion of the publishing business that followed the Civil
War coincided with a rush to commemorate and then,
as years passed, to document definitively the events that
took place. National monuments were built at a rapidly
increasing pace, first largely in the North, and then even
more commonly in the South and the Midwest.[1] At the
same time, the push for an accurate record of the war, which began during the conflict itself with the use of correspondents, illustrators, and,
of course, through the new medium of photography and the work of
photographers like Alexander Gardner and Mathew Brady, continued
to pick up steam, eventually becoming big business in the 1880s.[2] The
New York Tribune's editor Whitelaw Reid had been part of this wave
early in his career, first rising to prominence as a war reporter before
becoming Horace Greeley's assistant at the *Tribune*. By the end of the
war, book publishers were already announcing the appearance of their
histories, including some that had been planned well in advance of
the war's conclusion. Such foresight initially reflected early Northern
optimism, as this 1866 announcement for Benson Lossing's *Pictorial
History of the Civil War in the United States of America* makes clear:

> The undersigned takes pleasure in announcing that he has made
> arrangements for publishing Mr. Lossing's great work.
> When this arrangement was first made, the end of *armed* re-
> bellion seemed to be near, and it was believed that the space of
> a single volume of a thousand imperial octavo pages would be
> ample wherein to give a complete record of the great event. Since

then, all of the most important battles have been fought, and some of the most momentous events in the civil history of the Rebellion have occurred.[3]

Lossing had become a popular historian following the publication in the 1850s of his pictorial account of the American Revolution, so his turning to the subject of the Civil War was one more sign that Americans were ready to include the war in the historical record of the nation. The driving need for contemporary journalistic accounts of the conflict would be quickly supplanted by the push for documentaries and memorials.

These parallel movements of commemoration and historiography were to some degree motivated by an acute anxiety over the fading memory of events. A writer of a Connecticut regimental history noted in 1873, "So many years have elapsed since the war closed, that the remembrance of many facts and incidents that should have been preserved, has faded away,"[4] and in 1876, a writer for *Harper's* remarked, "The name of 'Mason and Dixon's Line' is one that to the rising generation is fast losing its significance and power, though for the first half of the century it was in every one's mouth . . . as the watch-word and battle-cry of slavery on the one hand and freedom on the other."[5] Constance Fenimore Woolson wrote in her 1876 story of the postwar South, "Rodman the Keeper," "The closely ranged graves . . . seem already a part of the past, that near past which in our hurrying American life is even now so far away."[6] As the nation grappled with the postwar upheaval of Reconstruction and the competing desires to continue hostilities and to "bury the hatchet,"[7] there was a concomitant concern that the true power of the war in the collective memory of the United States might be lost, even in the midst of the unprecedented drive to document it.[8]

THE BLOODLESS ELECTROTYPE PLATES OF HISTORY

As a writer, journalist, and, most significantly, as one who had seen so much of the misery of the war while serving as a nurse in the Union hospitals in Washington, D.C., Whitman was never far removed from concerns regarding the preservation of the history of events. As he wrote in 1874, "Already, the events of 1863 and '4, and the reasons that immediately preceded, as well as those that closely followed them, have quite lost their direct personal impression, and the living heat and excitement of their own time, and are being marshaled for casting, or getting ready to be cast, into the cold and bloodless electrotype plates of History" (quoted in Thomas, "Whitman's Obligations," 52). The poet's fears that the experience of the war would be lost are coupled with an anxiety that the feelings of the war would be sacrificed to the cold permanence of history, signified by Whitman's metaphor of electrotype printing plates. The image is both provocative and revealing: electrotype plates were most remarkable for their permanence and durability, allowing for the production of thousands of identical copies. Whitman objects both to the distance between the inevitable copies and the original—the loss of a "direct personal impression"—and the unchanging nature of those plates: they are "bloodless" and static. Plates had long signaled impersonality to the poet: in 1855, he wrote, "This is unfinish'd business with me . . . . how is it with you? / I was chilled with the cold types and cylinder and wet paper between us" (*Leaves*, 1855, whitmanarchive.org). The printing process is marked by the "cold" in both instances, and, in contemplating the fiery events of the war being "marshaled for casting," the poet decries a history reduced to mere reproduction, a record that expands rather than collapses the gap between the people and the felt experience of the times.

The problem of how best to preserve the "living heat and excitement" of the conflict was not a new concern for Whitman, who contemplated recording his own experiences and publishing them from almost the very beginning of his involvement. In addition to writing newspaper accounts of his days in the hospitals, the poet considered gathering his writings for a book. As Ed Folsom explains, Whitman approached James Redpath about publishing a volume as early as 1863: "He told Redpath the book was called *Memoranda of a Year* and would be 'a book of the time, worthy the time—something considerably beyond mere hospital sketches.' He designed a title page and drafted a circular for the book and sent them to Redpath, suggesting the volume be advertised as 'a book indeed full of *these vehement, these tremendous days*'" (*WMB*, 45). He had likely chosen Redpath because of the success the publisher had found in 1863 with the publication of

Louisa May Alcott's volume *Hospital Sketches*,[9] a work that the poet imagined himself surpassing by producing something that would truly measure up to the magnitude of the times. Whereas Alcott's narrative is fictionalized and at times sentimental in its representation, Whitman saw his own work as doing more than simply reproducing sketches of the events: it would contain them, be full of the passion and the significance of the time, thus eluding the "cold and bloodless electrotype plates of history" and reaching out to his readers in a manner reminiscent of his poetry of 1855, passing not with "paper and types" but instead "with the contact of bodies and souls" (*Leaves*, 1855, whitmanarchive.org). His Civil War writing, like his poetry, would convey more than the types (evoking both printers' types and figural representations) of history. In 1863, then, Whitman was confident in his ability to preserve and present the experience of war, a confidence that Alice Fahs suggests was common at the outbreak of the conflict: "Early wartime poets demonstrated an optimism concerning the power of representation that never entirely disappeared during the Civil War" (62). As time passed, however, Whitman appeared less and less convinced that the essence of what had taken place could be preserved and represented through any text, even his own. He lamented that so much of the truth of the war would be lost even as he employed a variety of strategies in an effort to produce a record distinct from the multitudes that were being published around him.[10]

While the book project he had envisioned early in the conflict would wait until 1875–1876, Whitman did publish excerpts from his memoranda in the *New York Times* between 1863 and 1865.[11] When the imagined book was at last published years later, Whitman's choices of a title demonstrate the way that he wrestled with his text's relationship with (now past) events: while the title page reads simply *Memoranda During the War*, the cover itself reads *Walt Whitman's Memoranda of the War, Written on the Spot in 1863–'65* (*WMB*, 46). The change from "during" to "of" implies a growing distance from the war, but then the subtitle insists on the text's proximity to it, asserting its production in the midst of events. As Timothy Sweet notes, however, the title does more than locate the creation of the text: "Etymologically a memorandum is something that *ought* to be remembered (in the future); it is not so much a description as a prescriptive agenda for memory."[12]

The introduction to the text speaks to this agenda and captures Whitman's unwillingness to accept his work as simply a representation of past events. He begins by sketching the source of the writings in his book, assuring the reader that they are his firsthand impressions, not the product of ten-year-old retrospection: "From the first I kept little note-books for impromptu jottings in pencil to refresh my memory of names and circumstances, and what was specially wanted, &c. In these I brief'd cases, persons, sights, occurrences in camp, by the bedside, and not seldom by the corpses of the dead. Of the present Volume most of its pages are *verbatim* renderings from such pencillings on the spot."[13] In this description of the history of the text, Whitman presents his notes primarily as supplements of memory, before underlining how close he has attempted to remain to the original experience in reproducing the content of those notes. What were originally designed to refresh Whitman's memory while on the spot have become the memories themselves.

Yet, despite the dutiful transcription the poet introduces, he also quickly signals his dissatisfaction with the twice-removed nature of his representation:

> I wish I could convey to the reader the associations that attach to these soil'd and creas'd little livraisons, each composed of a sheet or two of paper, folded small to carry in the pocket, and fasten'd with a pin. I leave them just as I threw them by during the War, blotch'd here and there with more than one blood-stain, hurriedly written, sometimes at the clinique, not seldom amid the excitement of uncertainty, or defeat, or of action, or getting ready for it, or a march. Even these days, at the lapse of many years, I can never turn their tiny leaves, or even take one in my hand, without the actual army sights and hot emotions of the time rushing like a river in full tide through me. Each line, each scrawl, each memorandum, has its history. Some pang of anguish—some tragedy, profounder than ever poet wrote. Out of them arise active and breathing forms. (*MDW*, 3–4)

Although Whitman acknowledges that he can only wish that he could convey the emotion of the memories invoked by his memoranda, he spends a great deal of time describing how his notes play upon his own mind, evoking the experiences of the war themselves. His description presents a memory that is visceral, tangible, almost embodied. The scrawls on the page contain more than anything written by poets could contain—a striking admission for the poet—although Whitman hints at the connection to his own poetry by referring to his notes' "tiny leaves," an echo of his title trope for *Leaves of Grass*, in which poems deriving from some of these notes would eventually appear. As he had promised more than ten years earlier to Redpath, Whitman argues here that in his wartime writings he has somehow captured the essence of those events, at least for himself, for he cannot hold them without "the actual army sights and hot emotions of the time rushing like a river in full tide through me." While he remarks that the notes form "a special history of those years, for myself alone, full of associations never to be possibly said or sung" (*MDW*, 3), this personal response does not preclude his describing his associations to his readers.

These attempts at sharing his reactions with his readers are significantly undermined by the emphasis Whitman places on the material nature of the notes themselves rather than on the words that he has recorded there. Not only in the opening pages, but a number of times afterwards, the poet refers to the bloodstains on his pages, tangible reminders of the events that he struggled to capture in both prose and poetry. In his description of the small notebooks, "folded small to carry in the pocket" (*MDW*, 4), Whitman attempts to impress upon the reader the physical connection his pages hold to wartime events and his place in them—they were close to his body, folded in his pocket as he walked the hospitals—a connection that at last he can only describe, not share. As Sweet notes, "The very presence of the 'blood-stain[s]' prevents Whitman from representing them; their reality thwarts textualization" (48). For Whitman, the written word alone is never enough, offering as it does only "scraps and distortions" of events (*MDW*, 8); yet it is his only recourse, and so, throughout his writing following the war, as he had in earlier poems, Whitman is left to describe his attempts to transcend the signifying nature of language and to provide a more embodied connection between the reader and the text.

In this instance, the goal is not simply an intimate embrace, but the preservation of memory in the face of the calcifying grasp of history. As Thomas notes in "Whitman's Obligations,"

> What the war had really been like is something far different from what could be conveyed by most accounts of the war, certainly those that were offered in the burst of histories that followed the conflict: "What the technists called history" seemed to [Whitman] merely empirical, according to his own definition of empiricism: "an acquaintance with a number of isolated facts, yet not of the subtle relation and bearing of them, the meaning—their part in the ensemble—the instinct of what they prove." (51)

Whitman's recourse to "instinct" is significant, for it speaks to something more primal than what one finds in historical accounts like the "mere hospital sketches" of writers like Alcott. For the poet, these ultimately fail to capture the essence of events, the "hot emotion" that washes over him whenever he returns to his notes. Relying upon and triggering this instinct in his own work was his persistent goal, even though it was one that time and time again he would confess was forever out of his reach.

MEMORY, HISTORY, AND THE TRUTH OF EVENTS

At the heart of Whitman's anxieties regarding his ability to convey the essential truth of the war to his readers is an implicit awareness of a separation between history and memory. In terms that resonate powerfully with the rush to document the Civil War as well as with Whitman's own descriptions of memory and history, critic Pierre Nora distinguishes between the two in this way:

> The "acceleration of history" . . . confronts us with the brutal realization of the difference between real memory—social and unviolated, exemplified in but also retained as the secret of so-called primitive or archaic societies—and history, which is how our hopelessly forgetful modern societies, propelled by change, organize the past. On the one hand, we find an integrated, dictatorial memory—unself-conscious, commanding, all-powerful, sponta-

neously actualizing, a memory without a past that ceaselessly re-invents tradition, linking the history of its ancestors to the undif-ferentiated time of heroes, origins, and myth—and on the other hand, our memory, nothing more in fact than sifted and historical traces. . . . With the appearance of the trace, of mediation, of distance, we are not in the realm of true memory but of history.[14]

When Whitman holds his memoranda in his hands, his description of what takes place demonstrates the "unself-conscious, commanding, all-powerful, spontaneously actualizing" nature of memory that Nora describes, the experiences "rushing like a river in full tide through me" (*MDW*, 4).[15] Mark Feldman sees Whitman's response as demonstrating the "breakdown of the metaphoric exchanges that undergirded . . . Whitman's poetic machinery," arguing, "Whitman's memories of the war were also convulsive: they were unwilled and seem to exactly repeat the original experience. Whitman writes about how he, as well as the soldiers, suffered repeated flashbacks" (5). His "flashbacks" are Nora's "spontaneously actualizing" memories. By connecting his own powerful recollections to those of veterans, Whitman creates a communal sense of memory beyond the personal recollections he experiences when rereading his memoranda.

While Whitman's description of the effects of his war notes attempts to place his work on the side of memory rather than history, he was still forced to grapple with the inescapably textual nature of those memories. By the 1880s, as he turned much more deliberately to offering a historical account of his life, he emphasized still further the limitations of written accounts of the war. When he included material from *Memoranda* in *Specimen Days*, his autobiographical work, he relocated and edited an earlier passage to produce what is now a famous statement on reporting the truth of war: "Future years will never know the seething hell and the black infernal background of countless minor scenes and interiors, (not the official surface-courteousness of the Generals, not the few great battles) of the Secession war; and it is best they should not—the real war will never get in the books. In the mushy influences of current times, too, the fervid atmosphere and typical events of those years are in danger of being totally forgotten" (*PW*, 1:116). Both the limited ability of texts to convey the actual atmosphere of the war, and the "mushy influences of current times,"[16] conspire to work against retaining the memories of the war.

Recently, historian Stephen Cushman argued, "Whitman's statement about the real war not getting in the books is disingenuous when it comes to his own, in which he developed, if not pioneered, new verbal conventions for representing real war."[17] Given the documentary fever of the 1880s that would sweep the popular press, Whitman's passage serves as a caution to readers and writers alike regarding the shortcomings of Civil War writing. Throughout his career, he strained against the limitations of print, and Cushman demonstrates the varied ways that Whitman explored telling the history of the war. He provides three possible readings of Whitman's phrase, but none quite captures the nature of the poet's doubt. The closest is what he terms "epistemological skepticism," but Whitman's concern is not with the "self-referential" nature of language (139) but rather with the printed page's ability to preserve the essence of events, to convey the sights, smells, and emotions of experience: in other words, the memory of the war. In his Civil War writing, Whitman would continually seek to preserve this memory in his work, even as he wrestled with his own doubts about whether his text was up to the task.

His efforts are evident in the passage as it first appeared in print. Despite shared material in *Memoranda* and *Specimen Days*, there is a striking difference between this later passage and what the poet originally wrote in *Memoranda*. The poet concludes his section on the war in *Specimen Days* with his lament that the "real war will never get in the books," and then, almost as an example, he moves from this lament regarding the possibility for a written record of the war to a careful description of one of the very events that he argues texts cannot convey: "I have at night watch'd by the side of a sick man in the hospital, one who could not live many hours. I have seen his eyes flash and burn as he raised himself and recurr'd to the cruelties on his surrender'd brother, and mutilations of the corpse afterward" (*PW*, 1:116). This same passage is offered at the *outset* of *Memoranda During the War*, and here there is no admission that the "real war will never get in the books." With that phrase omitted in the earlier version, Whitman's description of his haunting deathbed memories is offered as testimony that *confronts* the forgetfulness of "current times" rather than demonstrating its inevitability: "I have seen," he tells the reader. Dying in the hospital, the sick man experiences the past events as they "recur" to him, and Whitman relives them with him, then invites the reader to do the same. He does not diminish the reality of what one finds in books like his own; rather, he shows his determination to speak for the truth of events, even if his memory must be supplemented by his handwritten texts. Neither Whitman nor his readers can disentangle the memories from the memoranda, for the memoranda themselves command that he remember. While this episode as presented in *Specimen Days* becomes a final note of caution regarding the historical nature of Civil War accounts, in *Memoranda* it foregrounds his work. He may concede that the war's "interior history will . . . never be written" (*MDW*, 7), another passage that is retained in *Specimen Days*, but the subsequent pages of *Memoranda* complicate this claim, for, if Whitman is not offering an "interior history," what is he offering?

WRITTEN ON THE SPOT
WHITMAN'S *LIEUX DE MÉMOIRE*

Memoranda During the War is in part a resistant historical record, a text that rails against its own textuality in its efforts to transcend it or at least to embed within it the memories that its representative nature simultaneously threatens to supplant. In the process, Whitman's Civil War writings, most importantly the published text *Memoranda During the War*, form what Nora calls "*lieux de mémoire*," "sites of memory." By embodying his experiences of the war in texts—his small, blood-stained notebooks—and then by further embodying his *responses* to those texts in a later more comprehensive text, Whitman consciously attempts to formalize the spontaneous act of memory that occurs to him whenever he handles the documents, or, as Sweet observes, to produce a "prescriptive agenda for memory" (47). Nora describes a similar process taking place in the creation of *lieux de mémoire*, which

> originate with the sense that there is no spontaneous memory, that we must deliberately create archives, maintain anniversaries, organize celebrations, pronounce eulogies, and notarize bills because such activities no longer occur naturally. The defense, by

certain minorities, of a privileged memory that has retreated to jealously protected enclaves illuminates the truth of *lieux de mémoire*—that without commemorative vigilance, history would soon sweep them away. We buttress our identities upon such bastions, but if what they . . . [defended] were not threatened, there would be no need to build them. Conversely, if the memories that they enclosed were to be set free they would be useless; if history did not besiege memory, deforming and transforming it, penetrating and purifying it, there would be no *lieux de mémoire*. (289)

Whitman's Civil War writings coincide with the rush both to memorialize and to historicize the conflict, and the poet is as suspicious of the memorials as he is of the historians: they are insufficient for similar reasons. In "The Million Dead, Too, Summ'd Up," he writes,

And everywhere among these countless graves—everywhere in the many Soldier Cemeteries of the Nation, (there are over seventy of them[18])—as at the time in the vast trenches, the depositaries of slain, Northern and Southern, after the great battles—not only where the scathing trail pass'd those years, but radiating since in all the peaceful quarters of the land—we see, and see, and ages yet may see, on monuments and gravestones, singly or in masses, to thousands or tens of thousands, the significant word UNKNOWN.
(In some of the Cemeteries nearly *all* the dead are Unknown. At Salisbury, N.C., for instance, the known are only 85, while the Unknown are 12,027, and 11,700 of these are buried in trenches. A National Monument has been put up here, by order of Congress, to mark the spot—but what visible, material monument can ever fittingly commemorate the spot?) (*MDW*, 103–4)

All of the efforts to commemorate the events of the war, the poet suggests, are doomed to fail: "Think how much, and of importance, will be—how much, civic and military, has already been—buried in the grave, in eternal darkness!" (8). As Nora argues, it is precisely this notion of memory under threat, this consciousness of the past slipping away despite one's best efforts to retain it, that contributes to the creation of *lieux de mémoire*. The poet's attempts to resist the "purifying" efforts of history render his own writing a site of memory.

In folding his *Memoranda* into his autobiographical *Specimen Days*, Whitman transferred a few paragraphs from the former's introduction into a lengthy discursive note to the introduction of the latter; in doing so, he added this description of the source of his war writings: "Most of the pages from 26 to 81 are verbatim copies of those *lurid and blood-smutch'd* little note-books" (emphasis added; *PW*, 1:2). Whitman's memories may be spontaneous, but his recording of them cannot be; nevertheless, he assures his readers that his representation of events is deliberately uncensored and, in an attempt to retain the spirit of their times, as unmediated as he can manage. Nora notes that *lieux de mémoire* "originate with the sense that there is no spontaneous memory, that we must deliberately create archives" (289), and Whitman's concerted effort demonstrates how the writings, while attempting to preserve the spontaneity of memory, succeed in becoming *lieux de mémoire*.

"A Glimpse of War's Hell-Scenes," the passage that Whitman refers to in setting forth the true experience of war that he later claimed would never be written, provides an example of how the poet uses the stories of others in an attempt to capture the cruelty of war. In it he relates first the attack of Mosby's men on a Union hospital caravan near Upperville, Virginia, and then the detention and execution of a number of the Confederates who were captured by Union cavalry. Whitman does not provide the source for this tale that he believes is emblematic, and he positions himself as a narrator both inside and outside of events. More than simply a historical account, the poet sees in it a fundamental truth about the nature of war, and his representation of the event reflects his unwillingness to serve merely as a historian:

> Those three, and those twelve [corpses of Union soldiers], had been found, I say, by these environing regiments. Now, with revolvers, they form'd the grim cordon of their seventeen prisoners [captured Confederates]. The latter were placed in the midst of the hollow square, were unfasten'd, and the ironical remark made to them that they were now to be given "a chance for themselves." A few ran for it. But what use? From every side the deadly pills came. In a few minutes the seventeen corpses strew'd the hollow

square . . . . I was curious to know whether some of the Union
soldiers, some few, (some one or two at least of the youngsters,)
did not abstain from shooting on the helpless men. Not one.
There was no exultation, very little said; almost nothing, yet every
man there contributed his shot. (*MDW*, 63)

Whitman's point of view as narrator here is more than a little ambiguous. At first he seems a first-person witness, as though he is telling his
own story—"Those three, and those twelve, had been found, *I say*, by
these environing regiments" (emphasis added). The tone is at once
colloquial and affirmative; Whitman is giving the reader his word. The
detail that follows confirms the sense of this as an eyewitness account.
It is quite jarring for the reader, then, when the poet makes it clear
that this is not in fact his own story, but one that he is gleaning from
an unknown interlocutor: "I was curious to know whether some of
the Union soldiers . . . did not abstain from shooting on the helpless
men. Not one." Whitman is the "curious" reporter here—either on the
scene or after the fact—as well as the witness, for the answer to his
query—"Not one"—is disembodied, coming from no other speaker
save himself. In this way, Whitman's prose conflates the documentary
approach of history, the archival description of events, with the personal experience of memory. His memory is not so much of learning
about the event, as he provides no description of what it was like to
hear the story, no description of the hospital setting nor of the original
storyteller, but only of the massacre itself.[19] As in his poetry, "[He was]
the man, [he] suffer'd, [he] was there" (*LG*, 66).

Whitman breaks from his ambiguous point of view at the end of the
section, using parentheses to demarcate clearly his narrative voice in
order to emphasize the emblematic nature of the episode. Here, he
contends, one can get a glimpse of the truth of the war that eludes
most other accounts:

(Multiply the above by scores, aye hundreds—varify [*sic*] it in all
the forms that different circumstances, individuals, places, &c.,
could afford—light it with every lurid passion, the wolf's, the
lion's lapping thirst for blood, the passionate, boiling volcanoes
of human revenge for comrades, brothers slain—with the light

of burning farms, and heaps of smutting, smouldering black embers—and in the human heart everywhere black, worse embers—and you have an inkling of this war.) (*MDW*, 63–64)

The tone and diction is much different from what had preceded it. As Whitman moves to comment upon the signifying function of the event that he has described, his language becomes much more figural and metaphorical. In his attempt to capture the atmosphere of the war, Whitman moves from witness, to journalist, to historian, even as the event itself is transformed from personal memory to shared story until it is finally offered as a specimen of the indescribable character of the war. It is a representation of what is unrepresentable. Furthermore, the poet shifts the burden of memory to the readers by ordering them to extrapolate from the example to gain an "inkling of this war." Sweet remarks of this passage, "The only way to 'verify' a scene, however, is to return to a memory (of an experience), and relatively few readers (none, today) have the capacity to do this. . . . The reader is made responsible for *inventing* his or her own memories of the war by particularizing the represented types supplied in this indirect way" (52).[20] Again, this is in keeping with Nora's description of *lieux de mémoire*, which demand "commemorative vigilance," an effort to retain some sense of memory through latching onto a trace—in this case, Whitman's account of a war episode that was in fact recounted to him, now a trace of a trace. As Thomas notes, the poet had "specific obligations of memory which he felt deeply obliged to honor. He became preoccupied with the responsibility of producing an appropriate personal and national memory out of the war, and was in turn also haunted by the possibility of failure in these respects" (*Lunar Light*, 221). Both his sense of obligation and his concern that he might fail to meet it account for the poet's vigilance in his writing.

In the opening pages of *Memoranda*, Whitman explicitly directs his readers to this Upperville episode as an example of the limits of history and of his own efforts to transcend those limits, but he could have chosen any number of moments in his text. One particularly striking example is "May 12—A Night Battle, over a week since," in which Whitman again critiques the inevitable shortcomings of the rush to historicize the war and demonstrates his own preference for how the truth of the experience must be conveyed: "We already talk of Histories of the War, (presently to accumulate)—yes—technical histories of some things, statistics, official reports, and so on—but shall we ever get histories of the *real* things?" (*MDW*, 22). As Thomas notes, history as it is normally practiced is, for Whitman, defined by "empiricism" ("Whitman's Obligations," 51), the accumulation of data rather than the emotional experience of events. In contrast to the already emerging histories, Whitman offers "just a glimpse . . . a moment's look in a terrible storm at sea" (*MDW*, 23) as representative of "*real* things."

After setting the scene of the night battle, Whitman describes the battlefield as the day ends, and suddenly his point of view shifts dramatically as he transforms himself from a secondhand reporter to a participant in the conflict. The tense shifts from past to present, and his sentence structure also changes to reflect the frenzied commotion that surrounds him:

> The woods take fire, and many of the wounded, unable to move . . . are consumed—quite large spaces are swept over, burning the dead also—some of the men have their hair and beards singed— some, splotches of burns on their faces and hands—others holes burnt in their clothing. . . . . The flashes of fire from the cannon, the quick flaring flames and smoke, and the immense roar— the musketry so general, the light nearly bright enough for each side to see one another—the crashing, tramping of men—the yelling—close quarters—we hear the Secesh yells—our men cheer loudly back, especially if Hooker is in sight—hand to hand conflicts, each side stands to it, brave, determin'd as demons, they often charge upon us—a thousand deeds are done worth to write newer greater poems on—and still the woods on fire—still many are not only scorch'd—too many, unable to move, are burn'd to death. . . . . Then the camp of the wounded—O heavens, what scene is this?—is this indeed *humanity*—these butchers' shambles? (24)

As Whitman reaches the end of this description, the reader is reminded once again that the poet is not speaking from memory but is instead offering a vivid recreation of the scene. First, his retelling circles back to where it began: "still the woods on fire," he writes, once again emphasizing the fate of the men who could not escape the flames. Then, as he does so often in his poetry, he flies to another scene, this time the camp of the wounded. The passage continues with a similarly graphic and disjointed picture of the wounded before racing back to the battlefield once more.

Given the energy that the poet puts into his descriptions, his sudden disclaimer at the end of this sketch is almost disingenuous:

> Of scenes like these, I say, who writes—who e'er can write, the story? Of many a score—aye, thousands, North and South, of unwrit heroes, unknown heroisms, incredible, impromptu, first-class desperations—who tells? No history, ever—No poem sings, nor music sounds, those bravest men of all—those deeds. No formal General's report, nor print, nor book in the library, nor column in the paper, embalms the bravest, North or South, East or West. (26)

Whitman argues repeatedly that signification fails to convey the true essence of the soldiers and their deeds. No representation, presumably even the one that he has *just* provided, is equal to the task of conveying the truth. What history attempts to do through its signifying practices is "embalm" its subject in reports and books.[21] Of course, the arts seem to do no better in his estimation, as Whitman explicitly notes that no poetry or music is adequate to the task, despite his earlier claim that in the battle "a thousand deeds are done worth to write newer greater poems on" (25).

NATURE'S CHEMISTRY AND THE UNKNOWN

Descriptions like the one above repeatedly demonstrate how Whitman refuses to accept his own claim regarding the unrepresentable nature of the war. If conveying the events and heroism of war is impossible, however, how does Whitman see his own writing as distinct from either the reports or sketches offered by other writers? The answer may lie in his final description of the soldiers on the battlefield:

> Likely, the typic one of them, (standing, no doubt, for hundreds, thousands,) crawls aside to some bush-clump, or ferny tuft, on

receiving his death-shot—there, sheltering a little while, soaking roots, grass and soil with red blood—the battle advances, retreats, flits from the scene, sweeps by—and there, haply with pain and suffering, (yet less, far less, than is supposed,) the last lethargy winds like a serpent round him—the eyes glaze in death—none recks—Perhaps the burial-squads, in truce, a week afterwards, search not the secluded spot—And there, at last, the Bravest Soldier crumbles in the soil of mother earth, unburied and unknown. (27)

In contrast to historical representations of the battle, Whitman offers another type of the soldier, a representative of "hundreds, thousands" who are unknown. This is a soldier who evades the official records of history, unnoticed by the burial-squads who might enter his death into those records. For Whitman, such an end does not mean that the death is meaningless, however, and it is significant that he does not equate "unknown" with "forgotten." For, while "none recks" the unknown soldier's death, his passing moves him into the body of the nation: "The Bravest Soldier crumbles in the soil of mother earth."[22]

In a well-known passage in "The Million Dead, too, summ'd up— The Unknown," Whitman highlights the estimated number of casualties not officially buried before commenting on what becomes of "the Infinite Dead—(the land entire is saturated, perfumed with their impalpable ashes' exhalation in Nature's chemistry distill'd, and shall be so forever, and every grain of wheat and ear of corn, and every flower that grows, and every breath we draw,)—not only Northern dead leavening Southern soil—thousands, aye many tens of thousands, Southerners, crumble to-day in Northern earth" (103).[23] In the poet's view, the soldier becomes a part of the national body, is literally consumed by future generations in "every grain of wheat and ear of corn." Feldman argues, "For Whitman, the wounded bodies must remain simply wounded bodies" (21), and that the poet's "optimism and ability to see purpose in death was shaken by [his] experiences of war" (4). This may at times be the case, but, in passages like these, we see Whitman linking the casualties of war with the future health and sustenance of the nation. In this way, the soldiers elude the "embalming" representation of history to become a component of the living present.

This is, in Nora's terms, the realm of memory, "a perpetually actual phenomenon, a bond tying us to the eternal present" (285).[24] Memory is not represented; it is embodied, just as the truth of the soldiers is not captured in the histories, but in the soil: "Ten years and more have pass'd away since that War, and its wholesale deaths, burials, graves. (*They* make indeed the true Memoranda of the War—mute, subtle, immortal.)" (*MDW*, 104). The graves that form the "true Memoranda" are an "actual phenomenon" and available to the present in the soil and in the crops, forming an inescapable command to remember.

The "chemistry" that enables the soldier to become part of the nation (and its embodied national memory) is an essential part of Whitman's poetic project, as he set forth in 1855 in the long poem that would eventually become "Song of Myself": "I bequeath myself to the dirt to grow from the grass I love, / If you want me again look for me under your bootsoles. / You will hardly know who I am or what I mean, / But I shall be good health to you nevertheless, / And filter and fibre your blood" (*Leaves*, 1855, whitmanarchive.org). In the same poem, Whitman also establishes the relationship to historical events that he later employs in his memoranda.[25] The speaker moves from witness to participant to detached poetic "singer" several times, perhaps nowhere as vividly as in the following lines, which resonate with the descriptive technique the poet later employs in the various "Glimpses" he gives his readers in his Civil War prose writing:

> Did you read in the seabooks of the oldfashioned frigate-
> fight?
> Did you learn who won by the light of the moon and stars?
> (*Leaves*, 1855, whitmanarchive.org)

The speaker begins the episode by invoking John Paul Jones's fight in specifically historical terms, highlighting the representational nature of the event. It is "read in the seabooks," and is "oldfashioned," part of the dated historical record learned by students. Then the speaker immediately becomes a participant in the event itself, speaking as if from personal experience, shifting from history to memory[26]:

Our foe was no skulk in his ship, I tell you,
His was the English pluck and there is no tougher or truer,
   and never was, and never will be;
Along the lowered eve he came, horribly raking us.
We closed with him . . . . the yards entangled . . . . the
   cannon touched,
My captain lashed fast with his own hands.
                        (whitmanarchive.org)

"I tell you" is the mark of personal memory that Whitman later employs in the "Glimpses" section of the Civil War memoranda with "I say," locating the speaker and his account in the middle of the events that he is relating. In his poetry, Whitman's "I" is ever-present and often all-encompassing; here, however, it is very specifically located in time and place aboard the *Bonhomme Richard*. The history that was "read in the seabooks" becomes supplanted by the memories of the combatant.

The speaker's emphasis on memory and shared experiences continues through the battle and its aftermath, "the hiss of the surgeon's knife" (*Leaves*, 1855, whitmanarchive.org), until he is spun into other memories and scenes: "Not a mutineer walks handcuffed to the jail, but I am handcuffed to him and walk by his side" (*Leaves*, 1855, whitmanarchive.org). The speaker is overwhelmed by his identification and, as Whitman does in the memoranda, at last separates himself from the events in which he has located himself as a participant, noting, "Somehow I have been stunned. Stand back! / Give me a little time beyond my cuffed head and slumbers and dreams, gaping, / I discover myself on a verge of a usual mistake" (*Leaves*, 1855, whitmanarchive.org). The mistake that the speaker mentions appears to be one of memory: "That I could forget the mockers and insults! / That I could forget the trickling tears and the blows of the bludgeons and hammers! / That I could look with a separate look on my own crucifixion and bloody crowning!" (*Leaves*, 1855, whitmanarchive. org). The speaker critiques his own forgetfulness and separation from events — "that I could look with a separate look" — before regaining his equilibrium through memory: "I remember . . . . / I resume the overstaid fractions, / The grave of rock multiplies what has been confided to it . . . . or to any graves, / The corpses rise . . . . the gashes heal . . . . the fastenings roll from me" (*Leaves*, 1855, whitmanarchive.org). The speaker follows his Christ imagery with an image of the risen Christ, with memory serving literally as the animating force. The speaker remembers and "the corpses rise." This is the "eternal present" of memory that history forecloses.

Of course, Whitman's best efforts to convey the truth of the war, even in glimpses, are confined to textual representation. The poet is acutely aware of this, as his frequent lamentations regarding the limits of text indicate, just as in his poetry he repeatedly demonstrates his awareness that his identity is inextricably linked to the text of *Leaves*:

> Camerado, this is no book,
> Who touches this touches a man,
> (Is it night? are we here together alone?)
> It is I you hold and who holds you,
> I spring from the pages into your arms—
>   decease calls me forth.
>
>   (*LG*, 505)

This is not a denial of the textual nature of the work; rather, it is a gesture of redefinition and investment, an act of will that transforms the book from inert object of the past into an active presence. "Decease" calls Whitman forth from the pages of his book, his physical absence allowing for his textual presence. This gesture is similar to the ways in which Nora argues that *lieux de mémoire* emerge: "*Lieux de mémoire* are created by a play of memory and history, an interaction of two factors that results in their reciprocal overdetermination. To begin with, there must be a will to remember. If we were to abandon this criterion, we would quickly drift into admitting everything as worthy of remembrance" (295). Whitman's continual denunciation of the ability of history and text to convey the truth of the war, followed at almost every occasion by his attempt nevertheless to impart at least some trace of the conflict's reality, reveals the will to remember that transforms the text into a site of memory. Whitman also makes clear what is worthy of remembrance and what is not: it is the personal grief, anger, and suffering of the participants rather than the "general's reports" or "technical things." Where in his prewar poetry Whitman had been seeking a form that would embody his all-encompassing poetic "I," his postwar project transforms and extends the text as he attempts to preserve and give life to the memory not only of his own experiences of the war, but those of the soldiers and the nation, as well.

His desire to transcend the limitations of textuality in order to establish a personal connection with his readers led Whitman to attempt to personalize his editions of *Leaves* through various means, including autographs and statements like the one he included at the front of the 1888 printing: "Authenticated and Personal Book (handled by W.W.)" (quoted in Myerson, 121). This same desire was clearly at work as Whitman prepared *Memoranda*. Joel Myerson notes that the several extant copies of the second issue of 1876 include a "Remembrance Page" that follows the title page and that "most copies are signed by Whitman on the 'Remembrance page'" (190). Following the spaces for "TO" and "FROM," there is a subheading "PERSONAL—Note" followed by a brief note to "Dear Friend" and a concise, two-page biographical sketch. This introduction, then, reinforces *Memoranda*'s nature as a personal reminiscence while placing the events that it describes into Whitman's own history. The entry for 1862 in this short biography reads, "In December of this year went down to the field of War in Virginia. My brother George, reportedly badly wounded, in the Fredericksburgh [*sic*] fight. (For 1863 and '64, see my *Memoranda* following)" (quoted in Myerson, 191). For Whitman, his account of the war is as much autobiography as it is history, just as the stories that he relays of the battles are also part of his own story. This is a personal account sent to a "dear friend," not simply one more historical document reporting events.

WHITMAN'S BODY AND "BLOOD-SMUTCH'D LITTLE NOTEBOOKS"

In the same way that Whitman reinforced his personal connection through *Leaves* by asserting that he had "handled" the books and by signing his name to several copies, he returned on many occasions in his war writings to the blood that stained the original notebooks. Upon folding the memoranda into his autobiography *Specimen Days*, Whitman modified the introduction into a footnote for the new work, again pointing out the "lurid and blood-smutch'd little notebooks" (*PW*, 1:2). In a sign of the poet's unceasing attempts to preserve the immediacy of his memories, even near the end of his life, he wrote in "Preface Note to 2d annex" as he prepared the final volume of *Leaves of Grass*, "Had I not better withhold (in this old age and paralysis of me) such little tags and fringe-dots (maybe specks, stains,) as follow a long journey, and witness it afterward?" (*PW*, 2:736). In the years that followed the war, Whitman saw the physical condition of both his text and his own body as the clearest indicators of what had taken place during the war.

The process through which he transforms his later illnesses into war injuries, nearly rendering himself a veteran, is worth considering in the context of his view of memory. He writes at the conclusion of this "Preface Note":

> Then behind all, the deep-down consolation . . . that this late-years palsied old shorn and shell-fish condition of me is the indubitable outcome and growth, now near for 20 years along, of too over-zealous, over-continued bodily and emotional excitement and action through the times of 1862, '3, '4 and '5, visiting and waiting on wounded and sick army volunteers, both sides, in campaigns or contests, or after them, or in hospitals or fields south of Washington City, or in that place and elsewhere—those hot, sad, wrenching times—the army volunteers, all States,—or North or South—the wounded, suffering, dying—the exhausting, sweating summers, marches, battles, carnage—those trenches hurriedly heap'd by the corpse-thousands, mainly unknown—Will the America of the future—will this vast rich Union ever realize what itself cost, back there after all?—those hecatombs of battle-deaths—Those times of which, O far-off reader, this whole book is indeed finally but a reminiscent memorial from thence by me to you? (*PW*, 2:738)

As the passage begins, Whitman offers a causal link between his experiences in the war more than thirty years prior, as well as his stroke in 1873, and his present weak and brittle body. As he describes his wartime experience, however, its circumference expands dramatically, first moving outward from the fairly specific locale of the "hospitals or fields south of Washington City" to "that place and elsewhere," to "those hot, sad, wrenching times—the army volunteers, all States,— or North or South—," until finally he seems to have experienced the death and loss of the war as it was manifest nearly everywhere: "the wounded, suffering, dying—the exhausting, sweating summers, marches, battles, carnage—those trenches hurriedly heap'd by the corpse-thousands, mainly unknown." His reference once again to the unknown dead reminds the reader of how much of the conflict will not get into the official ledgers and histories.

In the absence of such record and in the face of the march of time, Whitman is dubious whether or not future citizens will fully grasp the nature of the conflict. What he offers the "far-off reader," then, is his own record, both in his decaying condition and in the "body" of his work, as a "reminiscent memorial" of the times. It is an odd phrase, combining the personal tone of a reflection on his past with the more collective function of a public document of commemoration. Thomas notes that, for Whitman, history "depends intimately upon the power, indeed the unique potency of memory" (53) and views this passage as indicative of Whitman as a "sometimes melancholy . . . memorial-iser" (53), fearing the loss of memory in the present moment. As we have seen, this fear is a constant for the poet, and Whitman once more offers two ways to combat it: through his reminiscence, the personal story told to another, and through his war memorial, encompassing much more than his own experience and open to the shared obser-vance of all.

What connects memory and history to the present, however, is the same thing that threatens to sunder them—that is, the text—so the poet continually strives to reconcile his work's purely signifying func-tion with the incommunicable strains of memory, using his own body as a metaphor and site for this reunion. This is evident in the late poem "A Twilight Song" (1890):

As I sit in twilight late alone by the flickering oak-flame,
Musing on long-pass'd war-scenes—of the countless buried
   unknown soldiers,
Of the vacant names, as unindented air's and sea's—the
   unreturn'd,

> The brief truce after battle, with grim burial-squads, and
>   the deep-fill'd trenches,
> Of gather'd dead from all America, North, South, East,
>   West, whence they came up
> [...]
> (Even here in my room-shadows and half-lights in the
>   noiseless flickering flames,
> Again I see the stalwart ranks on-filing, rising—I hear the
>   rhythmic tramp of the armies;)
> You million unwrit names all, all—you dark bequest from
>   all the war,
> A special verse for you—a flash of duty long neglected—your
>   mystic roll strangely gather'd here,
> Each name recall'd by me from out of the darkness and
>   death's ashes,
> Henceforth to be, deep, deep within my heart recording, for
>   many a future year,
> Your mystic roll entire of unknown names, or North or
>   South,
> Embalm'd with love in this twilight song.
>
> (*LG*, 549)

The poet's memories of the war are composed of the unrepresented and unrepresentable: "countless buried unknown soldiers," "the unreturn'd," "vacant," "unwrit," and "unknown names." Given the poet's friendships with soldiers and his correspondence with some after the war, his continual invocation of those who are unknown is significant; where specific soldiers' identities are limited, conveying delineated types of information, the unknown elude this historical boundary and represent far more, even as they exist only in the "room-shadows and half-lights in the noiseless flickering flames." What Whitman offers instead of the history books is the "mystic roll" "henceforth to be, deep, deep within my heart recording." The poet internalizes the unwritten history of the unknown soldiers, even while at the same time it is "embalm'd" (albeit with love) in the poet's text—his "twilight song." The language here contradicts his assertion years earlier in *Memoranda* that "No formal General's report, nor print, nor book in the library, nor column in the paper, embalms the bravest, North or South, East or West" (*MDW*, 26). Here at least his song appears to succeed, if only within the speaker's heart, in preserving what the poet had earlier thought forever lost to history.

LITERATURE AND THE CARNAL
ATTACHMENT TO THE PAST

Whitman creates in his writing a site of memory, an artifact that does not reveal the past so much as it requires the reader to meditate upon it, a text that does not limit meaning (as traditional historiography does), but multiplies it, as Nora describes:

> Contrary to historical objects . . . *lieux de mémoire* have no referent in reality; or, rather, they are their own referent: pure, exclusively self-referential signs. This is not to say that they are without content, physical presence, or history; it is to suggest that what makes them *lieux de mémoire* is precisely that by which they escape from history. In this sense, the *lieu de mémoire* is double: a site of excess closed upon itself, concentrated in its own name, but also forever open to the full range of its possible significations. (300)

One would be hard pressed to find a better description of Whitman's postwar writings than found in the final sentence of this passage. As the poet increasingly connects all of his writing, including *Leaves of Grass*, to the war and his experience of it, a move that would appear to limit its significance, his work also becomes expansive, representing not only his own life and experiences, but those of the unnamed and unrecorded past as well. Late poems like "A Twilight Song" share space with intensely personal poems such as "My 71st Year" and self-reflexive poems like "L. of G.'s Purport," a poem about the poems that compose the book. Even as the poet risks creating a closed circuit (the subject of L. of G. is *Leaves*), however, he opens it outward, creating the doubleness inherent in the *lieux de mémoire*.

Nora argues that it is no surprise to find works of literature serving as the model for the sort of double movement one finds in the *lieux de mémoire*. Literature illustrates the tension between the intellectual act of interpretation and the emotional investment in a reminder of the past, as well as the fear that the former will inevitably take the place of the latter. The history of *lieux de mémoire*

> rests upon what it mobilizes: an impalpable, barely expressible, self-imposed bond; what remains of our ineradicable, carnal attachment to these faded symbols; the reincarnation of history as it was practiced by Michelet, irresistibly putting to mind the recovery from lost love of which Proust spoke so well—that moment when the obsessive grasp of passion finally loosens but whose true sadness is no longer to suffer from what one has so long suffered, henceforth to understand only with the mind's reason, no longer with the unreason of the heart. (300)

Whitman's "carnal attachment" to his own "faded symbols," the notebooks from the war, the poems of *Leaves of Grass* themselves, is clear, of course, but, as the poet himself fears, those bonds cannot adequately be expressed to his readers. As he writes in "The Unexpress'd":

> How dare one say it?
> After the cycles, poems, singers, plays,
> Vaunted Ionia's, India's—Homer, Shakspere . . .
> [. . .]
> All human lives, throats, wishes, brains—all experiences'
>   utterance;
> After the countless songs, or long or short, all tongues, all lands,
> Still something not yet told in poesy's voice or print—something
>   lacking,
> (Who knows? the best yet unexpress'd and lacking.)
>
> > (*LG*, 556)

The notion that "the best" is yet "unexpress'd" resonates with Whitman's belief that the truest stories of the war can never be shared and that the bravest soldiers are those who died unknown, their deeds lost forever to history's recording and signifying mechanisms, represented here in the catalog of modes of human expression. It is not that symbols, then, convey the truth of the past or the emotional life, but that they convey their loss, calling for an intellectual response rather than the "unreason of the heart."

Nora's invocation of Proust is, he concedes, "a very literary reference" (300). He argues that the boundary between history and literature is "blurring" as a result of the death of both "memory-history" and "memory-fiction" (300). While he does not go into great detail regarding what separates "memory-fiction" from other fiction, he does argue that "history has become our replaceable imagination—hence the last stand of faltering fiction in the renaissance of the historical novel, the vogue for personalized documents, the literary revitalization of historical drama, the success of the oral historical tale" (300). Nora does not indicate precisely when he sees such a transition taking place, but his description certainly speaks to the resurgent interest in Whitman's historical writing—as evidenced by the recent Oxford University Press edition of the *Memoranda*—as well as the ongoing interest in histories of the Civil War. As the poet makes clear throughout his work during the Reconstruction period and after, he sees his own writing as bridging the gap between history and literature, attempting to offer a documentary text that will still succeed in containing memory, signifying the unsignifiable.

Whitman's conclusion to the *Memoranda* once again solidifies the connection, suggesting that his work will serve to memorialize what has occurred as other traces fade away:

As I write this conclusion—in the open air, latter part of June, 1875, a delicious forenoon, everything rich and fresh from last night's copious rain—ten years and more have pass'd away since that War, and its wholesale deaths, burials, graves. (*They* make indeed the true Memoranda of the War—mute, subtle, immortal.) From ten years' rain and snow, in their seasons—grass, clover, pine trees, orchards, forests—from all the noiseless miracles of soil and sun and running streams—how peaceful and how beautiful appear to-day even the Battle-Trenches, and the many hundred thousand Cemetery mounds! Even at Andersonville, to-day, innocence and a smile. (A late account says, 'The stockade has fallen to decay, is grown upon, and a season more will efface it entirely, except from our hearts and memories.') The *dead line*, over which so many brave soldiers pass'd to the freedom of eternity rather than endure the misery of life, can only be traced here and there, for most of the old marks of the last ten years have [been] obliterated.

> And now, to thought of these—on these graves of the dead of
> the War, as on an altar—to memory of these, or North or South, I
> close and dedicate my book. (*MDW*, 104)

Once again, the true record of the war, the graves, are "mute" and
"subtle" in contrast to what Whitman can offer in his own memoranda. Whitman's conclusion is situated in the present moment—not
that moment preserved in the bloodstained notebooks, but emerging
from a sunny afternoon ten years distant from the conflict in a process of integration that is echoed in the "noiseless miracles of soil
and sun and running streams" that work upon the burial mounds
of the war dead. In that natural process of decomposition, of compost, the signifying traces of historical memory are slowly giving way;
all legible signs, even of shocking scenes such as Andersonville, are
being effaced by the passage of time, "most of the old marks . . . have
[been] obliterated." What is left of Andersonville after the chemistry
of time and nature has done its work, according to the account Whitman cites, will soon be found only in "our hearts and memories," just
as the chemistry of the poet's text transforms a piece of journalistic
correspondence into part of his own story.[27] In a final ceremonial act,
then, "as on an altar," Whitman offers his own text as a site of memory, invoking those graves that stand as the "true" memoranda even
as he offers the world his own printed version. This act of sanctifica-
tion at the close adds an element of ritual absent from the historical
accounts burgeoning around him and points to what has been lost.
What remains to the poet, and to the reader, is the present ceremony,
the present summer day. This is the final consecration of Whitman's
lieu de mémoire.

4. "By the Roadside" and Whitman's Narrative of Poetic (Re)Awakening

Who are you dusky woman, so ancient hardly human,
With your woolly-white and turban'd head, and bare bony feet?
Why rising by the roadside here, do you the colors greet?
—*Walt Whitman, "Ethiopia Saluting the Colors," 1871*

 As formal Reconstruction came to a close and commemorating the war took precedence over the contentious political debates in the public imagination, Whitman returned once more to the task of the next edition of *Leaves of Grass*, the latest "extra" and a fully refashioned poetic commentary on postwar events. Throughout the 1870s, his creative energies had been more focused on his Civil War prose writing and his contributions to the periodical press, although he did take time in 1876 to compose *Two Rivulets*, a collection of poetry and prose intended, as Ed Folsom describes it, "to cash in on the nation's centennial celebration" (*WMB*, 43). The book's form was probably inevitable, since the poet would repeatedly turn to poetry as well as prose in his efforts to make sense of the conflict and its aftermath. He also released a "Centennial Edition" and an "Author's Edition" of the 1871–1872 edition of *Leaves of Grass* to mark the nation's centennial (*WMB*, 40); however, just as he would later use his autobiographical *Specimen Days* to integrate his war stories into his personal history, his ongoing work of reconstruction demanded a *Leaves of Grass* that fully integrated the cataclysm of the Civil War into his signature text. As we have seen, Whitman continually sought to collapse the distinctions between himself, his book, and even the nation itself. A nation that sought reconstruction, and a recovering poet, required a reconstructed *Leaves*, as well.

ONE, YET OF CONTRADICTIONS MADE

In 1870, Whitman had made what appeared to be a decisive attempt to enfold his war poetry into what he then conceived to be the final edition of *Leaves* (*WMB*, 32). As numerous scholars have observed, one of the most important attributes of the 1871–1872 edition is the poet's full integration of his previous *Drum-Taps* poems into *Leaves of Grass*, in a new "Drum-Taps" cluster and in two other clusters, "Marches Now The War Is Over" and "Bathed in War's Perfume." Where the 1867 edition had literally grafted the war poetry into his body of work, stitching unbound pages of *Drum-Taps* into *Leaves*, he now prepared a "new & improved edition" (quoted in *WMB*, 32) that spread the poems throughout the volume. Folsom and Price suggest that these new clusters demonstrate "Whitman's attempt to fully absorb the Civil War and its aftermath into his book . . . as the war experience bleeds out into the rest of the poems" (*Re-Scripting Walt Whitman*, whitmanarchive.org). Mancuso argues, "This textual multiplication underscores Whitman's assertion that he owed the existence of *Leaves* to the creative energy he found in the war itself" ("*Leaves of Grass*, 1871–72 Edition," 368). While this dispersal of the war poetry may suggest the conflict's power to inspire the poet's creativity, other changes indicate how the poet was still working to create a structure in *Leaves* that could include the war in a unified whole.

In her review of the publishing history of *Leaves*, Amanda Gailey points out that one of the most significant features of the 1871–1872 edition is the inclusion of his pamphlet *Passage to India* (422). Conceived as a separate project, it contained almost a third of the poetry of the previous edition (422), and Whitman had it bound into the second issue of the 1871 edition. Just as he had earlier included the unrepaginated *Drum-Taps* in the 1867 edition of *Leaves*, he now included pages from this smaller work within the whole, "still bearing their own title page and pagination" (*WMB*, 33). The poet appears to desire wholeness and completion, but, as in the earlier edition, the process is still strained, disjointed. Given this strain, it is perhaps not surprising that one of the most jarring notes in the 1871–1872 edition is another cluster that appears only here, the provocatively titled "Songs of Insurrection" cluster. Coming *after* the final cluster of war poetry, "Bathed in War's Perfume,"—a cluster marked by patriotic enthusiasm and what one critic has called Whitman's "fancy flags for public display"[1]—the "Songs of Insurrection" begins with the short new poem "Still Though the One I Sing":

Still though the one I sing,
(One, yet of contradictions made,) I dedicate to Nationality,
I leave in him revolt, (O latent right of insurrection! O quenchless,
    indispensable fire!)

(LG, 13)

Mancuso notes that the cluster as a whole appears to represent a "struggle with [the] question of liberation from domination," arguing that the other poems, largely taken from previous editions and put into new order here, "accented the federalization of America" ("*Leaves of Grass*, 1871–72 Edition," 370). At the same time, however, the parenthetical insertions in this first poem suggest that the "One" still contains within it the seeds of revolution, the fiery potential for the contradictions that lie within to break out into conflict and disunion.

To embody this sense of fracture, Whitman has scattered many of his poems, including several that would later be reassembled into "By the Roadside," into seven different "Leaves of Grass" clusters. These clusters are completely intermingled with the three war clusters, coming before, between, and after them. The 1867 edition had five "Leaves of Grass" sections, and the increased number of these clusters in the 1871–1872 edition suggests that the presence of the war has continued effectively to splinter "Leaves of Grass," fragmenting the volume into self-referential clusters that deny the war poetry pride of place in the book. Both in its form and its content, then, the 1871–1872 *Leaves of Grass* demonstrates that, for both Whitman and the nation, reconstruction was still very much a work in progress.

A POST-RECONSTRUCTION MELANGE?

In the new edition of *Leaves of Grass* that Whitman published in 1881 after years of personal and national struggle, the poet at last arrived at a combination that largely suited him. Gay Wilson Allen refers to it as "essentially the final, definitive *Leaves of Grass*,"[2] and, as Folsom notes, "This would become the authorized final arrangement of his poems, the post-Reconstruction version of his life's work" (*WMB*, 49). By the time Whitman began revising that work for publication in this volume, he had decided that *Drum-Taps*, and indeed the Civil War itself, were now at the heart of his poetic project, just as it was now at the heart of both the nation's history and his own. In speaking of the relationship of the war to his work, Whitman would continually stress the importance of the conflict, at times even anachronistically describing the war as the foundational event of his poetry, as he did when he commented to Horace Traubel late in life, "[The war was] the very centre, circumference, umbilicus, of my whole career."[3] Unlike his treatment in the 1871–1872 edition, the poet now brought all of the war poetry back together again into a central "Drum-Taps" cluster, removing the other two war clusters. At the same time, he removed the "Songs of Insurrection" that followed the war poetry, leaving the war itself as the culminating moment of violence for both the nation and the text.

While the 1881 edition clearly shows a new poetic focus on and synthesis of Whitman's war experiences, critics have long been divided regarding one of the other major additions to the volume, the "By the Roadside" cluster. Because of its placement immediately preceding "Drum-Taps," the cluster demands scrutiny, and indeed, its apparently haphazard assortment of new and old poems on disparate subjects has attracted a range of opinions. In general, however, there has been little in the way of sustained analysis, and few other clusters have inspired such varying opinions. Allen refers to it as a "miscellaneous collection," "merely samples of experiences and poetic inspirations along Whitman's highway of life" (150). Bradley and Blodgett largely echo this view: "What we have here seems at first to be simply poetic miscellany. . . . The group is truly a melange held together by the common bond of the poet's experience as roadside observer" (*LG*, 264n).

Others have taken nearly the opposite position, arguing that what appears to be a disjointed collection of previous works is in fact a carefully composed unity. James E. Miller, while describing the poems in the cluster as "miscellaneous and passing," nevertheless suggests that they are best viewed in the context of *Leaves* as a whole as "transient moments of mystic evolution."[4] Mary Virginia Stark argues most strongly for a unified reading of the cluster, seeing in the poems images of the Union and the coming disunion of the Civil War. Her analysis relies on close readings of Whitman's imagery and a study of the positioning of the poems within the cluster, and her study is suggestive of the kind of structural examination that can be done.[5]

Most recently, Folsom and Price have suggested that the cluster may be read "as a kind of gloss on [Whitman's] conception of what the good life entailed" (*Re-Scripting Walt Whitman*, whitmanarchive.org), drawing on Whitman's 1881 letter to his young friend Harry Stafford. In it, the poet urges his friend not to be drawn into a contentious back-and-forth regarding religion; instead, the poet asserts, *"the good life, steady trying to do fair,* & a sweet, tolerant liberal disposition, shines like the sun, tastes like the fresh air of a May morning, blooms like a perfect little flower by the road-side" (quoted in *Re-Scripting Walt Whitman*). The phrase "by the road-side" forcibly brings the cluster to mind and, given the proximity of the letter to the poet's work on the 1881 edition, Folsom and Price wisely highlight those poems in the cluster that seem to share this optimistic, "tolerant liberal disposition." Given the tumult of the preceding years, one can understand why the poet may have desired to imagine a more measured existence that would avoid emotional extremes.

Some of the poems, like Whitman's prewar "Thought" (1860), do speak to the sense of Whitman's letter to Stafford: "Of Justice—as if Justice could be anything but the same ample law, expounded by natural judges and saviors, / As if it might be this thing or that thing, according to decisions" (*LG*, 276); but several others are much less sanguine, and the effect of reading the cluster as a whole can be disorienting. Whitman's speaker may be the observer by the roadside, and yet such a viewpoint does not free him from the back-and-forth that takes place on the road before him, which is fitting for a cluster that serves as prologue for Whitman's poetic take on the cataclysm of the Civil War.

THE CIVIL WAR AND A BETTER ENSEMBLE

Many of the poems that make up "By the Roadside" were scattered throughout the 1871–1872 edition, both as stand-alone poems and in the short "Leaves of Grass" clusters. Given the size of "Passage to India," then, Whitman's inclusion of very few of these poems in the annexed pages suggests that he always found these poems a much more integral part of *Leaves* than has been traditionally recognized. His decision in 1881 to reassemble this diverse assortment of poems into a single cluster, then, is as significant as his decision to reunify the war poetry into "Drum-Taps." In fact, the seemingly random nature of the poems reassembled in "By the Roadside" now works to convey a sense of crisis for Whitman's poetic persona. As Whitman refashioned *Leaves of Grass* to incorporate the war into his poetic body, he rendered the war's approach poetically in terms of an attempt to stave off chaos through a combination of liberal inclusiveness and aesthetic distance; however, the strategy is frequently undermined by self-doubt and the intrusion of political failure. The result appears chaotic, and part of the difficulty of "By the Roadside" may lie in our tendency to confuse apparent disorder with purposelessness. In repositioning these poems as a prelude to "Drum-Taps," Whitman creates a dramatic narrative of poetic dissolution, one that culminates in the poetic persona's surrender in the face of his inability to deal with the failure of both his poetic self and his nation to contain and reconcile opposition.[6] The "*good life, steady trying to do fair*" is shattered by the Civil War, marking the corruption of compromise in the face of the impending cataclysm.

In the face of this crisis, the persona in effect throws up his hands and, in a distinctively novelistic turn, executes what we might call a "reverse Rip Van Winkle." While Irving's hero unwittingly sleeps through the violent upheaval of the Revolutionary War, only to awaken to a new world order in which the nation has been liberated and he himself is now free from his spousal tyranny, at the end of the "By the Roadside" cluster Whitman's poetic persona determines to sleep *until* the cataclysm comes, in order to flee a world in which the spirit of King George lives again. Only the Civil War itself, it appears, can restore both the nation and his disjointed poetic vision. In "To the States," the final poem of the cluster, Whitman writes: "Then I will sleep awhile yet, for I see that these States sleep, for reasons" (*LG*, 279). The position of this poem is unchanged from the 1871–1872 edition, where it also precedes the "Drum-Taps" cluster, indicating that Whitman had long seen the poem working as a kind of prologue. In 1881, however, the poem is now the culmination of a new combination of works that tells the story of a persona confronted with a growing sense of powerlessness and doubt, evident in the fragmented nature of "By the Roadside." "To the States" announces even more decisively in 1881 that only the martial sounds of "Drum-Taps" will restore and reawaken the speaker. In reconstructing the poems in this cluster in such a fashion, Whitman retells a poetic and national story in which the Civil War plays a necessary and redemptive role.

Whitman had long sought to integrate his war poetry into his larger poetic project of *Leaves*. As Folsom remarks of the 1867 edition,

> Whitman performed his own textual version of healing surgery, suturing the leftover and still-unbound pages of *Drum-Taps* and *Sequel to Drum-Taps* into the back of his new volume, thus binding the poetry of the war into *Leaves of Grass*. This was the first step in Whitman's ongoing experiment with how to bleed the Civil War into *Leaves*. In the 1871 and 1881 editions, he would radically shuffle and cluster his *Drum-Taps* poems so as to make the war integral to (instead of simply appended to) *Leaves of Grass*. (*WMB*, 28–29)

While this reshuffling is dramatic in both the 1871–1872 and the 1881 editions, Whitman emphasized in writing to his publisher James R. Osgood regarding the 1881 edition that what was to make it unique was not its new content, but rather an improved organization: "The text will be about the same as hitherto, occasional slight revisions, simplifications in punctuation &c—the main thing a more satisfactory consecutive order—a better *ensemble*, to suit me—some new pieces, perhaps 30 pages" (*Corr*, 3:224). In comparing his two editions, the poet clearly thought that his new structure was the key element of the 1881 *Leaves*. Whitman repeated this idea a month later in a letter to his friend John Burroughs, stressing that in the new edition, he would "secure now the consecutiveness and *ensemble* I am always thinking of" (*Corr*, 3:231). Whitman's repeated emphasis on a "consecutive order" lends credence to the idea that "By the Roadside" might best be understood through viewing it as a precursor to "Drum-Taps" and argues for a systematic analysis of the poems it contains, not simply as discrete entities but as part of a sequential progression.[7]

Such a reading is made difficult by the wide range of subject matter and dates of first publication for the poems. For modern readers of *Leaves of Grass*, there is no getting around the fact that, whatever edition we may read, many of the poems were first published elsewhere, both in and out of the text, perhaps with other titles and with different lines; and this history demands attention. As we have already seen, Whitman's publications in periodicals were a significant part of both the construction of his public persona and his ongoing efforts to shape his response to contemporary events. In reading "By the Roadside," we must not only understand the ways Whitman influenced and was influenced by the world in which he lived, we must also pay careful attention to one poem's relationship to the next. While the poems Whitman includes speak to the times in which they were written, they also take on new meanings and serve different purposes when placed in different relations with each other. Whitman himself always valued most highly the most current expression of his poetic self, the most recent edition of *Leaves of Grass*,[8] and so we must read the poems in "By the Roadside" as we find them. The tendency to read these works with more of an eye to "where they've been" rather than where Whitman placed them in the 1881 edition has likely contributed to the view of the cluster as more a random assortment of observations than any coherent ensemble. In recombining them as a prologue to "Drum-Taps," Whitman creates a sense of the political and personal tumult that preceded the Civil War.

THE AMERICAN SCENE AND THE COMING CONFLICT

The opening poem of "By the Roadside" demonstrates this forcefully. The cluster begins with one of Whitman's earliest and most strident denunciations of the American political landscape, "A Boston Ballad." As with other poems in the cluster, Whitman had earlier placed this work in a "Leaves of Grass" cluster in the 1871–1872 edition. There, as here, the poem precedes "Drum-Taps." The American scene "A Boston Ballad" describes is so disturbing that it compels the dead patriots of the Revolution to rise from their graves, and the sight of what the nation has become both grieves them and nearly drives them to take up arms once more: "What troubles you Yankee phantoms? what is all this chattering of bare gums? / Does the ague convulse your limbs? do you mistake your crutches for firelocks and level them? / If you blind your eyes with tears you will not see the President's marshal, / If you groan such groans you might balk the government cannon" (*LG*, 265). Their behavior is quite unlike that of their descendants, who are "well dress'd" and "conduct themselves" in an "orderly" manner. Their behavior, it appears, will not "balk the government cannon." In the face of such properly martial behavior, the speaker urges the corpse warriors to retreat back to their graves, leaving the field to the "orderly citizens" and the newly restored corpse of King George that appears at the poem's conclusion.

Written in 1854, the poem expresses Whitman's contempt for the spirit of compromise that led to the imposition of the Fugitive Slave Law in 1850. In provocative language, Betsy Erkkila argues that the poem echoes the fiery rhetoric of William Lloyd Garrison, who burned a copy of the U.S. Constitution the year the poem was written: "'A Boston Ballad' . . . is Whitman's poetic burning of the Constitution."[9] By positioning this strident work at the beginning of the cluster, Whitman introduces a vision of a nation that is torn by conflict between past and present and between the nation's ideals and the compromised complicity of the current generation. He also presents a poetic persona that is identified not by a tone of universal acceptance but by biting irony and critique, a caustic physician diagnosing the nation's ills. The opening poem, then, challenges any notion of this cluster as simply a passive collection of social observations.[10] Indeed, the tone belies the notion that the speaker is lounging "by the roadside." The speaker is mocking in his final judgment of the scene: "Stick your hands in your pockets, Jonathan—you are a made man from this day, / You are mighty cute—and here is one of your bargains" (*LG*, 266).

As Erkkila observes, when we consider the time of its composition, Whitman's text appears to be a reaction to the arrest of Anthony Burns under the Fugitive Slave Law. There are several parallels between the scene Whitman describes and contemporary accounts of the Burns arrest and reenslavement. As Martin Klammer notes, newspapers at the time reported that "more than 20,000 persons lined the streets, jeering the police and cheering Burns."[11] By replacing these supportive crowds with the passive conformists described in the poem, however, the text's historically descriptive elements are supplanted by its social commentary. The absence of any particular reference to Anthony Burns renders it a more sweeping critique, taking as its theme American hypocrisy broadly construed.[12] As a result, Whitman is able to transfer it from its untitled placement in the 1855 *Leaves* to the head of "By the Roadside" and use it to establish the setting in which the speaker's drama of poetic crisis will take place, while at the same time illustrating the attitudes that would lead to the Civil War.

Whitman follows this poem with another exploration of contemporary society. Like its predecessor, this poem is a response to a particular historical moment, as the title makes clear, but it employs language and imagery that is abstract enough to contribute to a larger picture of the prewar United States. In the 1871–1872 edition, Whitman included "Europe, The 72d and 73d Years of These States" in the provocatively titled "Songs of Insurrection" cluster that followed "Drum-Taps," an indication that the poet consistently saw the text as driven by an activist impulse.[13] The work combines a paean to the spirit of democracy and a critique of those who now work against this spirit. While its earlier placement pointed to a continued potential for violent uprising even after the Civil War's end, now the poem looks ahead to the conflict as a consequence of denying the revolutionary impulse:

> And you, paid to defile the People—you liars, mark!
> Not for numberless agonies, murders, lusts,
> For court thieving in its manifold mean forms, worming
> from his simplicity the poor man's wages,
> For many a promise sworn by royal lips and broken and
> laugh'd at in the breaking,
>
> Then in their power not for all these did the blows strike
> revenge, or the heads of the nobles fall;
> The People scorn'd the ferocity of kings.
>
> (*LG*, 267)

In the world Whitman describes, these multifarious villains first defeated in numerous revolutions, including the American, are now re-emergent. As in "A Boston Ballad," the speaker contrasts present corruption with the "corpses of young men," emblematic of the earlier liberatory impulse. The skeletons of the Revolutionary fathers had retreated in the face of present decay; in this poem, they are replaced by the "invisible" signs of liberation, and the speaker is left to scan the horizon for hopeful signs: "Is the house shut? is the master away? / Nevertheless, be ready, be not weary of watching, / He will soon return, his messengers come anon" (*LG*, 268). Both poems place the speaker in the position of viewer, but he is more a "watchman" than merely a passive spectator: he judges the present danger and maintains a look-out for the "master's" return.

THE SPEAKER AS (SELF) CRITIC

Both of these poems thus depict a more active—or at least more judgmental—presence in the opening of the cluster than is generally acknowledged by critics, yet neither presents Whitman's poetic vision as itself redemptive. Neither of these texts is itself a means of liberation or renewal; despite the almost strident tone, they are more symptomatic of a current malaise, more diagnostic than curative. This is a speaker who can identify the illness, who can sound the alarm and look toward future aid, but can provide little himself. Given this apparently limited potential for intervention, it is not surprising that Whitman's speaker makes a similar gesture toward recognition of corruption without suggestion of solution when he urges readers, and himself, to reflect upon their own natures in the poem that follows, "A Hand-Mirror." Just as the government's martial display concealed the decaying spirit of revolution, Whitman's speaker here suggests that the outer human frame hides disease and malignancy. The circumstance is the same whether one wears a "fair costume," is a slave, a drunkard, an "unwholesome eater," or a "venerealee." All are bound together by their internal corrosion:

Hold it up sternly—see this it sends back, (who is it? is it you?)
Outside fair costume, within ashes and filth,
No more a flashing eye, no more a sonorous voice or springy step,
Now some slave's eye, voice, hands, step,
A drunkard's breath, unwholesome eater's face, venerealee's flesh,
Lungs rotting away piecemeal, stomach sour and cankerous,
Joints rheumatic, bowels clogged with abomination,
Blood circulating dark and poisonous streams,
Words babble, hearing and touch callous,
No brain, no heart left, no magnetism of sex;
Such from one look in this looking-glass ere you go hence,
Such a result so soon—and from such a beginning!

(*LG*, 268–69)

Here Whitman's text is itself the looking glass, revealing the true nature of existence, and the picture is not pretty: words are meaningless, human contact carries no sympathy, and the flesh itself is slowly decaying. Coming as it does after the first two poems, the text becomes an anthropomorphic suggestion of the nation itself, "such a result so soon—and from such a beginning!" Both the body and the body-politic have rotted through. Such a reading would certainly have squared with the political corruption of the 1870s when Whitman constructed the cluster; but the poem's placement before "Drum-Taps" indicates that it would also speak to the conditions that brought on the Civil War. This is a telling difference from the 1871–1872 edition, where "A Hand-Mirror" immediately follows the patriotic "Bathed in War's Perfume." What was once a troubling coda to the speaker's martial triumphalism is now repositioned to indicate the decay that precedes the trauma of the war.

The speaker himself is not excluded from these circumstances. As critics have noted, if we imagine Whitman's persona looking into the hand-mirror, then the "you" addressed here is clearly Whitman himself. This is, of course, in keeping with Whitman's general poetic practice, particularly in "Song of Myself," where Whitman's persona speaks to and embraces his soul. In this line of interpretation, Whitman here comments on his own poetic project as well as the project of democracy. The poem was first included in the third edition of 1860, a telling time for Whitman and the nation, and his judgment, then, is directed as much at the life of his own verse and the figure he has struck in print in the years since his first appearance in 1855. Betsy Erkkila notes how the poem highlights a split between the poet's public and private selves,[14] and R. W. B. Lewis has remarked that in this poem and others, "we find Whitman executing what might be called the grand Romantic strategy—the strategy of converting private devastation into artistic achievement."[15] However, the poem's placement in this new cluster demands that we also see its commentary in the context of the social critique that precedes it.[16] In positioning this poem in the cluster, the poet renders his "private devastation" as at least in part a response to the disintegrating public scene just prior to the Civil War. In Whitman's poetic reconstruction of this tumultuous time, he creates a perception of both a failed nation and a failed artistic vision. Despite the early promise, the words have failed, and the speaker expresses his disappointment in himself and his country in the defeated, almost bemused conclusion.

Once again, this is more than simply passive observation; this is diagnosis and judgment. Once again, when readers compare this poetic voice to the one elsewhere in *Leaves*, they cannot help but notice the dramatic departure from the normally welcoming and reassuring voice of Whitman's speaker, as in the poem "Crossing Brooklyn Ferry," first published in 1856 as "Sun-Down Poem": "It is not upon you alone the dark patches fall, / The dark threw its patches down upon me also, / The best I had done seem'd to me blank and suspicious, / My great thoughts as I supposed them, were they not in reality meagre?" (*LG*, 162). This confession of doubt and sin leads the speaker to identify with all who play "The same old role, the role that is what we make it, as great as we like, / Or as small as we like, or both great and small" (*LG*, 163), with the usual throwing wide of arms to embrace both contradictions and those experiences that feel unembraceable. In "A Hand-Mirror," on the other hand, the speaker's harsh self-inspection leads to nothing but bemused, even bitter, evaluation.[17]

THE CORRUPT PRESENT AND
WHAT WILL YET BE SUPPLIED

To follow this withering national and personal critique in "By the Roadside," Whitman chose a poem whose speaker turns to a higher power. Unlike the first three poems, which owed their creation to a prewar impulse dating back as far as 1850 in the case of "Europe," "Gods" is one of the few poems in the cluster that first appeared in *Passage to India* and was then annexed in the 1871–1872 edition of *Leaves of Grass*. There, the text stands alone and follows "Drum-Taps" and all of the other Civil War poetry, being located quite near the end of the volume. By relocating it within "By the Roadside," Whitman makes the poem part of a sequence that shows the diagnosing physician-speaker moving from inspection of society and self to an appeal for spiritual comfort. As he did with the "master" whose return is hopefully awaited in "Europe," the speaker here looks to a savior whose appearance is deferred: "Lover divine and perfect Comrade, / Waiting content, invisible yet, but certain, / Be thou my God" (*LG*, 269).

Once again, this appeal announces a dramatically different persona from the one encountered in other clusters in *Leaves*, different particularly from the Walt Whitman who is the "kosmos" who speaks in "Song of Myself" and is himself the comrade who "stops somewhere waiting" for the reader (*LG*, 89). In appealing to a higher power, the speaker in "Gods" turns elsewhere for aid: as the title suggests, this is a poem of plural deities. The "perfect Comrade" gives way to an appeal to the "Ideal Man," which gives way to a call to "Death . . . Opener and usher," followed by the almost hopelessly vague "Aught, aught of mightiest, best I see, conceive or know," and in turn leads to a net thrown so widely that it strains to encompass all thought and action of human history: "All great ideas, the races' aspirations, / All heroisms, deeds of rapt enthusiasts, / Be ye my Gods" (*LG*, 269). Even this seems inadequate to fill the speaker's restless need for some form of higher power, as he looks to the earth itself and the heavenly bodies for succor:

Or Time and Space,
Or shape of Earth divine and wondrous,
Or some fair shape I viewing, worship,
Or lustrous orb of sun or star by night,
Be ye my Gods.

(*LG*, 269)

The "Or" that begins the first four lines is striking. It replaces the cumulative, democratic cataloguing that is commonly found in Whitman's poetry—often marked with the definite article "The" or the conjoining "And"—with a startling lack of discrimination. This lack of discrimination is distinct from inclusiveness: here the speaker is looking to make a choice, to select a "God," but he will apparently select any of the presented alternatives. The sense of "whatever" that culminates in this final stanza undermines the sense of celebration of the wonders that surround the speaker with something approaching desperation.

Taken as a whole, the four poems form a startling progression, made all the more striking by the way that it departs from the earlier Whitmanian notions of absorption and egoism. This speaker does not look inward and find multitudes, or find "the scent of these arm-pits aroma finer than prayer" (*LG*, 53): "A Hand-Mirror" (and the indefinite article suggests that any mirror might expose the true nature of the speaker's corruption; it apparently requires no magic looking glass) does not reveal a divine inner being, only the "bowels clogged with abomination, / Blood circulating dark and poisonous streams" (*LG*, 269). It is easy to imagine the speaker rushing from the mirror and the disappointing result it reveals to search heaven, earth, and the realms of human potential and possibility for aid. In recasting his poems into a prologue to the war, Whitman opens his new cluster with a cumulative effect of pessimism in both the democratic project, as it was embodied in the United States and in Europe in the years prior to the Civil War, and in the poetic project as demonstrated in *Leaves of Grass*.

Considering this beginning, readers making their way through "By the Roadside" might expect that in the next poem, "Germs," the speaker is either going to return to the bitter tone of the first three poems and explore the contagion that surrounds him, again acting as the physician, or direct his search for inspiration from the macroscopic to the microscopic level. Upon reading the text, we discover that the latter assumption is nearer the mark, although Whitman is employing "germ" in terms of "seed" and "germination." Once again, the speaker turns away from the world as it is to celebrate instead the notion of potentiality. Yet this celebration is oddly truncated, the poet's normally vigorous and wholehearted embrace replaced by a tentative gesture: "Splendid suns, the moons and rings, the countless combinations and effects, / Such-like, and as good as such-like, visible here or anywhere, stand provided for in a handful of space, which I extend my arm and half enclose with my hand" (*LG*, 270). The lack of urgency and commitment in this half-gesture is puzzling: what has become of the firm grasp and warm embrace? In the 1871–1872 edition of *Leaves*, the poem immediately follows "A Hand-Mirror," adding to the sense that the war poetry of "Bathed in War's Perfume" and the other war clusters has not succeeded in truly restoring the speaker. This tentativeness is echoed by the poem that follows it: like "Germs," "Thoughts" was also written in 1860, and the two poems taken together suggest the poet's growing disillusion as signs of war grew more ominous.[18] Their inclusion in "By the Roadside" sets the stage for "Drum-Taps" to follow. Here, in this poetic space before the conflict, hope is placed not in what is, but what will be. He writes in "Thoughts," "Because all I see and know I believe to have its main purport in what will yet be supplied" (*LG*, 270). The reader coming to this postwar addition in "By the Roadside" knows precisely "what will yet be supplied." By placing these poems in the cluster immediately before "Drum-Taps," the heart of the revised *Leaves*, Whitman has made them all become at least in part anticipatory of the Civil War.

IRRECONCILABLE DIVISIONS
AND THE LEARN'D ASTRONOMER

Up until this point, the cluster shows a remarkable degree of cohesion, in spite of the disparate dates of composition and previous placement within *Leaves*. The poet has constructed a narrative of political and social discontent that coincides with a harsh personal judgment. The result is a casting about for alternatives and a weakened extension of the poet's previously robust and all-encompassing embrace of the world as he finds it. Stephen Rachman argues that, following the twinned poems of political commentary that open the cluster, "the rest . . . is largely comprised of brief lyric 'Thoughts' and imagistic snapshots" (93). In his reading, any organization suggested by the first few poems dissipates. Such a view might seem to be supported by the inclusion of "When I Heard the Learn'd Astronomer" as the next poem in the cluster. Many critics have argued that Whitman apparently never knew where his "Astronomer" belonged. It first appeared in 1865 as part of the stand-alone edition of *Drum-Taps*, an odd decision, according to Julianne Ramsey, who argues that the poem is "not by any stretch of interpretation a military poem"[19] (167). Gregory Eiselein agrees, citing the poem as an example of those poems in the original volume of *Drum-Taps* that have "no explicit connection to the war."[20] Opinions such as these are supported by Whitman's decision to remove the poem from the "Drum-Taps" cluster for the 1871–1872 edition, where it appears after all three war poem clusters in "Songs of Parting."

The apparent reluctance to read "When I Heard the Learn'd Astronomer" as first within the context of *Drum-Taps* and then as an integral part of "By the Roadside" is surprising given the language and theme of the work, however. As Ed Folsom notes,

> While the poem's subject is obviously not the Civil War, the tenor of the war times is nonetheless reflected in the speaker's desire to escape a place of fragmentation (where the unified cosmos is broken down and divided into "columns") and to regain a sense of wholeness. Union and oneness, pulling together that which has been separated—these are the subjects of many of Whitman's Civil War poems, and they are the focus of this poem.[21]

The language used by the speaker to describe the astronomer's lecture is strikingly martial, reflecting "the tenor of the war times" that Folsom mentions. Information is not imparted so much as it is deployed as if for battle: "When I heard the learn'd astronomer, / When the proofs, the figures, were ranged in columns before me, / When I was shown the charts and diagrams, to add, divide, and measure them" (LG, 271). Beyond the choice of "columns," the entire structure of the line suggests someone observing the field of combat, considering the divided forces: the speaker finds the proofs and figures "ranged in columns before [him]."

The speaker of the poem retreats in the face of this scientific assault and the enthusiastic reception it receives in the form of "much applause" (LG, 271).[22] Unlike the heavens that make up the lecture's subject, the speaker's response is "unaccountable," and he exchanges the "divisions" arrayed inside the hall for the "mystical moist night-air" where he "Look'd up in perfect silence at the stars" (271). Folsom offers a provocative reading of this poem, suggesting that the speaker has in fact "absorbed" the lecture, as evinced by his statement that he looks up at the stars "from time to time."[23] Folsom writes, "The phrase signals one of the newly formulated concepts that the astronomer would have explained in his lecture: that when we look at the stars, we are not only looking across vast distances of space, but vast distances of time as well."[24] For a poet writing at the end of the war's devastation, we can imagine there would be great appeal in looking "in perfect silence" to a time far removed from his own.

The most prominent action of the poem, however, is the speaker's flight from his fellows in the lecture hall, his turn away from both the oral performance of the lecturer (despite the poet's own acknowledged fascination with public speaking) and the enthusiastic reception of the audience. He exchanges human companionship for solitude as he "wander'd off by [him]self," and the human spectacle within for the celestial spectacle presented outside. He substitutes "perfect silence" for the voices of knowledge and enthusiasm that rendered him "tired and sick," and apparently mutes his own voice as well, at least in that moment of contemplation. This gesture in itself is not unusual in Whitman's poetry: in "Song of Myself," for example, the speaker momentarily seeks respite from the all-encompassing connection and integration: "Enough! enough! enough! / Somehow I have been stunn'd. Stand back! / Give me a little time beyond my cuff'd head, slumbers, dreams, gaping" (LG, 72).[25] Elsewhere, in response to the behavior of people around him, the speaker in "Song of Myself" remarks, "I think I could turn and live with animals, they are so placid and self-contain'd, / I stand and look at them long and long" (LG, 60). Like the speaker in "When I Heard the Learn'd Astronomer," Whitman's persona turns away from the human voices that "sweat and whine about their condition" (LG, 60) to instead simply observe the peace of the natural world.

There are at least two elements of the speaker's reaction to the public in the "Astronomer" poem that make it distinct from these other gestures, however. The first is the almost ethereal, unintentional aspect of it: "How soon unaccountable I became tired and sick, / Till rising and gliding out I wander'd off by myself" (LG, 271). The language lacks the urgency that one finds elsewhere in those passages in Leaves where the speaker seeks distance from the crowd or a moment of respite from the poetic absorption; given the speaker's condition here ("tired and sick"), his movement is strikingly languid and reposed, as well as apparently aimless, his encounter with the heavens a seemingly accidental byproduct of his "wandering." The second noteworthy aspect of the speaker's retreat is a result of the poem's structure and length. Elsewhere in Whitman's poetry, these moments represent temporary retrenchments: in "Song of Myself," for instance, the speaker returns from his contemplation of the animals to a reinvigorated embrace:

Myself moving forward then and now and forever,
Gathering and showing more always and with velocity,
Infinite and omnigenous, and the like of these among them,
Not too exclusive toward the reachers of my remembrancers,
Picking out here one that I love, and now go with him on
    brotherly terms.

(LG, 60)

"When I Heard the Learn'd Astronomer" does not possess this renewal of purpose. As Folsom suggests, the speaker's encounter with
the night sky represents a desire to "regain a sense of wholeness," to
"experience the cosmos again as 'uncountable,' as beyond the clever
adding, dividing, and theorizing of the scientist."[26] The heavens may
represent this for the speaker, just as the animals represent a peaceful
acceptance of being in "Song of Myself," but they do not allow him to
take part or to be anything more than a spectator: he does not "gather"
or embrace anything or anyone here. While the poem may reflect a
longing for union, the reality it describes is one marked by disunion,
of the vast separation between the life inside the lecture hall and the
mystical world of the night.[27] Elsewhere, Whitman's persona serves to
bridge the mystical and the human, the intellectual and the instinc-
tual, even as his all-encompassing "I" speeds from one setting to the
next. This speaker seems capable only of noting the difference. The
time for reunion has not yet come.

WHITMAN'S QUESTIONS AND ANSWERS

"When I Heard the Learn'd Astronomer" represents a
kind of turning point in the cluster: if earlier the speaker was examining society and himself with the eye of a caustic physician and alert
watchman, in this text he turns away from the sight of the astronomer
who clinically examines the heavens. In the larger narrative of poetic
struggle that the cluster describes, the sense of passivity the poem
conveys comes to dominate many of the poems that follow, although
there are moments when the speaker attempts to shake off his lethargy and once again take on his poetic mantle as absorber and singer,
before finally determining to sleep. Whitman constructs "By the Roadside" in a way that resists a sense of wholeness or completion: in re-

organizing *Leaves* to fully integrate the Civil War into its poetic structure, he does not allow for any sustained consolation or unity in the cluster that precedes "Drum-Taps." In his new view, only the war itself can bring such unity. This is a significant departure from the 1871–1872 edition of *Leaves*, in which Whitman scattered his war poetry in three different clusters intermingled with the "By the Roadside" poems, mixing memories of the war with moments of depression, passivity, and self-doubt. By creating "By the Roadside" and bringing together the *Drum-Taps* poems into a single cluster, Whitman replaces the interweaving of 1871 with a sense of narrative progression.

To ensure this sense of progression, poems in "By the Roadside" that are more reminiscent of the exuberant Whitman persona are often accompanied by self-reflection or self-criticism. One can immediately see the impact of the speaker's "perfect silence" in observing the heavens in "When I Heard the Learn'd Astronomer" in the very short poem from 1860 that follows, "Perfections": "Only themselves understand themselves and the like of themselves, / As souls understand souls" (*LG*, 271). The awkward use of the third-person objective pronoun only highlights the sense of alienation that marks the existence of these "perfections," whatever they may be. The foreclosure of understanding and identification—only those like them can be understood—is a dramatic departure from the all-encompassing speaker who elsewhere in *Leaves* "contain[s] multitudes" (*LG*, 88). Given the factionalism that gripped the nation when the poem was written, one might read the first line as critical of the self-assured individuals of "Perfections" who recognize only those like themselves. This is not as great an escape from the divisions of the astronomer as the reader might wish.

In "O Me! O Life!", the longer poem that follows and first appeared in *Sequel to Drum-Taps*, published just after the death of Abraham Lincoln, the speaker questions both the state of the world around him and his reaction to it thus far, demanding

O Me! O life! of the questions of these recurring,
Of the endless trains of the faithless, of cities fill'd with the
    foolish,

Of myself forever reproaching myself, (for who more foolish
    than I, and who more faithless?)
[. . .]
The question, O me! so sad, recurring—What good amid these,
    O me, O life?

(LG, 271–72)

The foundation for this poem has been laid throughout the cluster
in the numerous poems detailing the speaker's discontentment with
both himself and the world around him. The questions raised by the
poem are not only "what good" is to be found in the sorry catalog described in the poem and "what good" is the speaker's life "amid these,"
however. As Whitman indicates in the first three lines, one of the questions raised deals with the speaker's self-reproach, his "foolishness"
and "faithlessness." In what way has this speaker failed to keep his
faith?

The "Answer" that the poem provides implies that the speaker has
failed to fulfill his poetic mission of inclusion and celebration, that he
has allowed his judgment of the "plodding and sordid crowds" that
surround him to negate the simple joy of his existence and his presence in the world (*LG*, 272). More is expected from the speaker than
excoriation or silent observation: "That you are here—that life exists
and identity, / That the powerful play goes on, and you may contribute a verse" (*LG*, 272). The speaker is reminded that life, however it
might manifest itself, is part of the "powerful play," as is the self, the
"identity" that elsewhere the poet has celebrated and sung. With this
recognition comes the responsibility to take action, to "contribute a
verse." While most critics have emphasized the role of Whitman as
observer in this cluster, this poem indicates the presence of a strong
countervoice, one that is more in keeping with the bard who inhabits
the rest of *Leaves of Grass* and one that attempts to prod the persona
from the passivity and negativity that dominate the cluster and to take
part in the "powerful play." In 1871, this poem appeared in a "Leaves
of Grass" cluster that followed all three of the war poem clusters, once
again suggesting that the war has not brought closure to the speaker.
In reading the poem in "By the Roadside" in the 1881 *Leaves*, we antici-

pate "Drum-Taps": the Civil War will lead most powerfully to the poet contributing a verse.

"To a President," the short poem following this moment of self-questioning and eventual affirmation, shows signs of the vigor that informs the early political commentary at the outset of "By the Roadside." Bernard Hirschhorn reminds us that this poem, first included in the 1860 edition, was a reaction to James Buchanan, a politician that the poet frequently scorned for his actions in the years leading up to the Civil War.[28] In placing it here rather than with the other political poems at the beginning of the cluster, the work also signals the speaker's reengagement with the world that he had previously simply lamented. He scolds the president for not heeding "the politics of Nature": "you have not learn'd the great amplitude, rectitude, impartiality" (*LG*, 272). In earlier poems, the speaker had retreated from the division and "partiality" that marked the astronomer's lecture in order to seek the "amplitude" of the heavens, only to suggest that "perfections" could best be understood by themselves. Here, on the other hand, he is unwilling simply to accept or escape from such narrow categorizations, and he uses nature to offer a counter-model. He no longer watches in "perfect silence"; instead, he contributes to the discussion as the speaker in "O Me!" had been urged to do. The president, like the nation prior to the war, needs to learn the benefits of "amplitude, rectitude, impartiality." Given the fierce partisanship and division on the horizon, such a lesson could only come after the war, if at all.

As with "When I Heard the Learn'd Astronomer," however, the poem ends on a strikingly passive note, and the urgency that marks the opening line diminishes by the end of the piece. In "Europe," the speaker is the watchman awaiting the return of the "master," or the resurgence and reappearance of the spirit of liberty that stalks the land. In "To the President," no such active force will appear to counter the "dangled mirages" and partiality offered by the current system. Instead, in the difficult syntax of Whitman's final line, those qualities not befitting America will depart of their own volition: "You have not seen that only such as they [amplitude, rectitude, impartiality] are for these States, / and that what is less than they must sooner or later lift off from these States" (*LG*, 272). "Sooner or later" is certainly different from the assurance in "Europe" that the master "will soon return, his messengers come anon" (*LG*, 268). And what action is the speaker urging the president to take? What is the role of the poet or the people in countering those lesser impulses that diminish the "politics of Nature"? Apparently it is only to wait until these negative forces "lift off from these States" of their own volition.

If this is the only option, then it is no surprise that the speaker in the following poem, "I Sit and Look Out," seems reduced to the mere observation of tragedy and corruption. The sheer impassivity that is conveyed in the poem is striking, and perhaps the fact that it is so at odds with the ways Whitman's persona deals with suffering elsewhere—"All this I swallow and it tastes good . . . . I like it well, and it becomes mine, / I am the man . . . . I suffered . . . . I was there," he wrote in the 1855 *Leaves*[29]—accounts for some of the critical confusion the poem has inspired. In his brief analysis of the poem, David B. Baldwin, for example, remarks: "With rare understatement, [Whitman] conveys his grief that such negative conditions abide and his dismay that he is helpless in the face of them,"[30] and further, "He is dramatizing the fact that he sees the world as it is in its worst condition, that he is pained by what he sees, but that he has no choice but to accept it. The reader participates in that viewpoint."[31] Baldwin's interpretation adds emotional drama that is lacking in the poem itself. Whitman writes, "I sit and look out upon all the sorrows of the world, and upon all oppression and shame" (*LG*, 272), and then goes on to provide a catalogue of the miseries that he "hears," "sees," "marks," and "observes," commenting at the conclusion, "All these—all the meanness and agony without end I sitting look out upon, / See, hear, and am silent" (*LG*, 272–73). While the reader may certainly respond with grief, dismay, and a sense of helplessness, the speaker never suggests these responses; Baldwin's final observation that the "reader participates in that viewpoint" might be better inverted: Whitman's speaker participates in the viewpoint of the reader, who will certainly react with an emotionality that is strangely absent from the piece. One cannot even conclude that the speaker has accepted what he sees, for he refuses any comment at all, choosing instead to remain silent. His silence may well be a form of acquiescence, but he has not absorbed the scene (or "swallowed" it, to use the language of 1855); he only looks out upon it, the diction emphasizing his remoteness and inaction.

George Hutchinson has included this poem in a list of Whitman's "stoical" works, and the poet's preoccupation with stoicism certainly provides one explanation for the speaker's impassivity here. Other aspects of the poem trouble this explanation, however. In his discussion of Whitman and stoicism, Hutchinson writes that defining characteristics of the philosophy include "maintaining imperturbability, acknowledging the kinship of all people, and practicing indifference to one's own experiences of pain, suffering, and death."[32] There is no denying the speaker's imperturbability, certainly, as he retains the language of dispassionate observation no matter how dreadful the vision. What is most troubling about the poem in light of this definition of stoicism is that the speaker practices indifference not to his own suffering, but to the suffering of others; and, if there is kinship, it is one of hardship, and it is not shared equally: "I observe the slights and degradations cast by arrogant persons upon laborers, the poor, and upon negroes, and the like" (*LG*, 273). That last category, "and the like," suggests not universal fellowship but division grounded in class and racial difference; there are those who suffer and those who do not, and this is the situation that the speaker observes silently, resisting commentary other than to note it. As Hutchinson points out, this poem, as well as the other works considered most stoical, was composed in 1860 and "suggests the intensity of Whitman's personal and political disappointments at this time."[33] This is undoubtedly the case, and, by deploying the poem in "By the Roadside," Whitman forwards the narrative of a poetic persona who is increasingly struggling against a kind of paralysis brought on by the social and political ills of the nation. When will the poet cease sitting and get back to the work of singing and absorbing?

This is the question that the speaker asks himself in the next poem, "To Rich Givers." The work's first line sounds the note of acceptance so conspicuously absent from "I Sit and Look Out": "What you give me I cheerfully accept" (*LG*, 273). His new resolution to receive what is offered to him—"A traveler's lodging and breakfast as I journey through the States"—is followed by a question that could easily pertain to poems such as "I Sit and Look Out" and "O Me! O Life!": "why should I be ashamed to own such gifts? why to advertise for them?" (*LG*, 273). This line, when read in context of all that has preceded it, cannot simply be interpreted as a proclamation that the speaker is unashamed; rather, the reading that presents itself is that the speaker *has* been ashamed to receive the gifts offered by the States—at least the States as they are described in the cluster. This is no mere rhetorical question: the speaker is trying to understand his behavior, particularly given what he believes to be his true nature: "For I myself am not one who bestows nothing upon man and woman, / For I bestow upon any man or woman the entrance to all the gifts of the universe" (*LG*, 273). These last lines are clearly a response to the question about shame, and they suggest a speaker trying to convince himself and his audience both that he is not ashamed and that he *should not* be ashamed. Just as in "A Hand-Mirror," this poem is a moment of self-reflection and comparison, one between the speaker's response to his nation and what he views as his poetic nature, and between his response up until now and what his response should be.

OF PICTURES AND THOUGHTS

The degree to which the speaker fails to convince himself to act in accordance with his nature—"I myself am not one who bestows nothing upon man and woman," he reminds us (and himself)—is revealed in the sequence of short poems that follows. More than anything else, these sixteen poems are responsible for the view that this cluster is an assortment of disparate observations. He certainly "bestows" these short poems upon the world, but the diction is more suggestive of Whitman's persona as receiver and observer, the invisible presence made familiar in "Song of Myself," yet without the energetic motion and passionate claims of identification. Throughout these brief vignettes, the speaker "roams," "remembers," "sees," "studies," "glides," and "stands aloof," not verbs that suggest an active engagement with the world beyond the public presentation of the poems themselves. He does not elect to participate in the scenes he describes, and description is the main action of several of the verses, as in the poems "The Dalliance of Eagles," "A Farm Picture," "The Runner," "Beautiful Women," and "Mother and Babe." This last highlights how discreet (and discrete) the persona appears to be in these poems. Here is the entire text: "I see the sleeping babe nestling the breast of its mother, / The sleeping mother and babe—hush'd, I study them long and long" (*LG*, 275). It is worth comparing this poem with a portion of "The Sleepers," which Whitman first wrote in 1855 and included near the end of the 1881 edition of *Leaves*, following the Civil War poems. While the poem begins with the image of the silent observer, the persona soon becomes a more active participant: "I go from bedside to bedside, I sleep close with the other sleepers each in turn, / I dream in my dream all the dreams of the other dreamers, / And I become the other dreamers" (*LG*, 425–26). These shifts from observation to participation to identification are wholly missing from "Mother and Babe" and the other "By the Roadside" poems. The vast majority of these poems were written just prior to or immediately following the Civil War—"Mother and Babe" first appeared in the 1865 edition of *Drum-Taps*—and their placement in the cluster emphasizes the difference between the ways in which this persona interacts with (or fails to react with) the world around him and the persona that is present in *Leaves* after this cluster.

Highlighting this passivity, three of the short verses share the same title, "Thought," while a fourth is titled "Roaming in Thought." The three former all first appeared in 1860, and, along with their titles, the poems themselves all raise questions regarding the attitudes of society, as with the third "Thought" poem: "Of Equality—as if it harm'd me, giving others the same chances and rights as myself— as if it were not indispensable to my own rights that others possess the same" (*LG*, 277). This is hardly a rallying cry, although the syntax forces the reader to slow down and untangle the negation taking place, particularly in the last phrase, "as if it were not indispensable." There is contemplation here, certainly, but without the keen interrogation and firm affirmation one finds elsewhere in *Leaves*. It could be that, at the time of composition, Whitman was still hesitant to support abolition completely for fear of the conflict that was becoming more and more inevitable, recalling the poet's first inclinations in favor of Douglas even over Lincoln and his rather moderate views during this period. These final poems, taken alone, then, lend credence to Stark's observation that, in this cluster, "The persona and nation ebb into self-introspection and observation."[34] Despite occasional exhortations and self-critiques throughout "By the Roadside," the speaker who is physician, watchman, singer, and absorber, seems to have disappeared into thought.

WAITING FOR WAR: WHITMAN'S RIP VAN WINKLE

The cluster does not end with these short verses, however. Whitman concludes "By the Roadside" with "To the States, To Identify the 16th, 17th, or 18th Presidentiad." This poem, first included in the 1860 edition, would seem to bring us back to where the cluster began, with a scathing political critique. Furthermore, it follows "To A President" and precedes "Drum-Taps" in the 1871–1872 edition, as well, suggesting that Whitman had long seen these two poems as offering a final critical word on the nation before turning to the poetry of war. This is certainly the way that scholars have addressed this text. Carl Smeller notes the three presidents referred to in the title, stating, "Whitman takes all three to task, along with the Congressmen and the 'great Judges,' for their political opportunism and corruption. The poem objects as well to the political atmosphere stemming from the Compromise of 1850, which accommodated slavery in the territories at the expense of free soil."[35] Smeller is following Erkkila's lead, noting her observation that the poem is part of "a kind of political jeremiad" (quoted in Smeller, 731). Erkkila also suggests that the poem is a "return to the political invective of his 1850 poems" (*WPP*, 184) with the imagery of sleep "refiguring" the social upheaval "as natural facts in some larger providential design" (*WPP*, 185). Smeller echoes this conclusion as well, arguing that the poem "foreshadows the Civil War as well as Whitman's attempts to rationalize it as part of an inevitable, natural cycle" (732). The poem, these critics argue, is first and foremost preoccupied with a naturalistic metaphor of sleep for social corruption and oppression, and the foreshadowing of the "awakening" to come from the Civil War.

These are undeniably strong elements of this poem; however, what is striking about this poem in the context of the "By the Roadside" cluster is the persistent presence of the speaker. This poem is not only concerned with the state of the nation; it is equally concerned with the state of the persona, once again connecting the poet's interrogation of his poetic practice with his interrogation of the political system. The poem begins not with a denunciation of the presidents mentioned in the title, but with self-questioning: "Why reclining, interrogating? why myself and all drowsing?" (*LG*, 278). Both the question and the tone recall earlier moments of questioning in "By the Roadside," beginning with "A Hand-Mirror," "(who is it? is it you?)" (*LG*, 268), echoed in "O Me! O Life!", "Of myself forever reproaching myself, (for who more foolish than I, and who more faithless?)" (*LG*, 271), and expressed most emphatically in "To Rich Givers": "why should I be ashamed to own such gifts? why to advertise for them?" (*LG*, 273).

Given the poem's placement, the opening question of "To the States" seems to reflect on the contents of the cluster itself, for what has the speaker been doing in these poems if not "reclining, interrogating"? Miller suggests, "The poet himself remains by the roadside and watches."[36] This seems a fair description of what the speaker does, at least in the burst of short verses at the end of the cluster, and in this last poem the speaker suggests that such a practice is not in keeping with his poetic identity: "why myself and all drowsing?" Here is one more example of the poet "[him]self forever reproaching [him]self." How can he be the poet he thought he was and respond to events only by "drowsing"? His tone here is reminiscent of the lament that concludes "A Hand-Mirror": "Such a result so soon—and from such a beginning!" (*LG*, 269).

Elsewhere in the cluster, the speaker meets such moments of self-doubt either with urgings to further action, "the powerful play goes on, and you may contribute a verse" (*LG*, 272); passive observation, "I sit and look out" (*LG*, 272–73); or reminders of poetic identity, "For I myself am not one who bestows nothing upon man and woman" (*LG*, 273). In this final poem, however, the conditions of the nation have at last trumped the speaker's power to respond in any fashion at all, even if only to bear witness:

What deepening twilight—scum floating atop of the waters,
Who are they as bats and night-dogs askant in the capitol [*sic*]?
What a filthy Presidentiad! (O South, your torrid suns! O North,
　　your arctic freezings!)

Are those really Congressmen? Are those the great Judges? is that
    the President?
Then I will sleep awhile yet, for I see that these States sleep, for
    reasons;

(LG, 278–79)

This is no celebratory catalogue; instead, the tone is one of disgusted
disbelief. Rather than seeking some sort of poetic redemption of the
"bats and night-dogs" (and how bad must they be to lie beyond the
pale of a speaker who has elsewhere thrown his arms around all manner of men and women?), the speaker turns away, determined to continue sleeping, taking his cue from the nation that he sees sleeping, as
well. This is the speaker's ultimate surrender to the inertia and disillu-
sionment that he has contended with throughout the cluster, for his
ability to rise from this slumber depends on ominous future events:
"(With gathering murk, with muttering thunder and lambent shoots
we all duly awake, / South, North, East, West, inland and seaboard, we
will surely awake)" (*LG*, 279). By placing this poem immediately before the "Drum-Taps" cluster in the 1881 edition, Whitman makes per-
fectly clear what will be the source of the "muttering thunder" that will
awaken the entire nation. Only the American Civil War can return the
nation to its founding principles and the poetic persona to his alert
and encompassing self.

In this final poem, then, Whitman's persona surrenders to the current forces of poetic and political malaise, looking to future times to
revive his nation and his poetic project. This last gesture completes
the narrative arc in the cluster, and, fittingly, this last poem recalls
another "reclining" American literary figure. In the speaker's resolution to sleep until a revolution occurs in American thought and politics, Whitman in effect reverses the signature episode in Washington
Irving's story "Rip Van Winkle." [37] In Irving's tale, Rip Van Winkle is
a decidedly passive fellow: "He inherited . . . but little of the martial
character of his ancestors," [38] and one given to "drowsing," as Whitman might put it. [39] After his magically induced sleep (a sleep that follows the thunder of the mysterious strangers' nine-pins game in the
mountains), he returns to a country that has just experienced the up-

heaval of the Revolutionary War. Many of his old friends "went off to the wars" (962), leaving the new Rip nearly alone in a new world order: "It was some time before he could . . . be made to comprehend the strange events that had taken place during his torpor. How that there had been a revolutionary war—that the country had thrown off the yoke of old England—and that, instead of being a subject of his Majesty George the Third, he was now a free citizen of the United States" (964). He has slept through the transformation of American politics and emerged a politically (and domestically) liberated man. This liberation does not lead to new action; rather, "he took his place once more on the bench, at the inn door" (964). Rip awakens only to continue drowsing.

Whitman's speaker, of course, lives in an America where the shade of King George once again stalks the land, where the values fought for in the revolution have yielded to a "filthy Presidentiad" of corruption and moral decay. The poetic persona that emerges in "By the Roadside" is one that begins as a fierce critic of his country and of himself, resisting and decrying his own tendencies to merely lounge and observe, but who ultimately succumbs to the torpor that consumes him and "these States" in the years prior to the war. Unlike Rip, whose sleep coincides with the sound of distant thunder, only the thunder of the Civil War will awaken Whitman's persona and reenergize his poetic project and the people: "South, North, East, West, inland and seaboard, we will surely awake" (*LG*, 279). As Erkkila notes, "The firing on Fort Sumter by the Palmetto Guard of South Carolina on the morning of April 12, 1861, brought the awakening of the nation for which Whitman longed in his 1860 poem 'To the States'" (*WPP*, 195). By placing this poem at the end of this key cluster, immediately prior to "Drum-Taps," Whitman firmly establishes the war as the pivotal event not only for national redemption, but for his poetic redemption as well. While Rip Van Winkle's awakening is defined by continued inaction, Whitman's speaker will arise from his slumber with renewed purpose, marked by calls to action and expressions of comfort and empathy, identification, and healing.

Such a reading points us to another instance in which Whitman employs the phrase "by the roadside," his much-remarked-upon poem

"Ethiopia Saluting the Colors." The poem, written in 1867, was first published in "Bathed in War's Perfume" in the 1871–1872 *Leaves of Grass* before Whitman folded it and the other war poems into the "Drum-Taps" cluster in the 1881 edition. The poem describes an encounter between a Union soldier marching with Sherman and a slave woman by the side of the road:

> Who are you dusky woman, so ancient hardly human,
> With your woolly-white and turban'd head, and bare bony feet?
> Why rising by the roadside here, do you the colors greet?
>
> ('Tis while our army lines Carolina's sands and pines,
> Forth from thy hovel door thou Ethiopia com'st to me,
> As under doughty Sherman I march toward the sea.)
>
> *Me master years a hundred since from my parents sunder'd,*
> *A little child, they caught me as the savage beast is caught,*
> *Then hither me across the sea the cruel slaver brought.*
>
> No further does she say, but lingering all the day,
> Her high-borne turban'd head she wags, and rolls her darkling
>   eye,
> And courtesies to the regiments, the guidons moving by.
>
> What is it fateful woman, so blear, hardly human?
> Why wag your head with turban bound, yellow, red and green?
> Are the things so strange and marvelous you see or have seen?
>   (*LG*, 318–19)

The woman, "hardly human," we are twice told, rises by the roadside as the troops march past. Neither of the speaker's questions is answered directly: in response to his query of who she is and why she rises, she offers instead a narrative of her dehumanization, the story of how she was "caught . . . as the savage beast is caught." She offers no further evidence of her identity beyond her enslavement in the US, but spends all the day responding to the troops passing her by, leaving the speaker with more questions: "What is it fateful woman, so blear, hardly human? / Why wag your head with turban bound, yellow, red and green? / Are the things so strange and marvelous you see or have seen?" As she responds to the troops passing on the road, she becomes a "fateful woman," her actions cast as a response to her visions of what she sees and has seen, the encounter itself almost predestined.[40]

Unlike the "perfect little flower by the road-side" that Whitman describes in his 1881 letter to Stafford, this woman is transformed by what she sees by the roadside; she is not merely an observer, removed from both sides. The coming of the troops inspires action on her part, and, with the poem's invocation of Ethiopia, the reader is reminded of how the past and the future of the United States is inextricably linked with Africa, even if that linkage is vexed by misunderstanding, the soldiers marching on while "Ethiopia" is left to linger all the day. In "By the Roadside," the cluster leading up to the pivotal Civil War poems, then, Whitman creates a "consecutiveness and *ensemble*," to use his phrase, that forms his poetic and national Reconstruction narrative. A nation and a poet, fragmented and self-doubting, cannot remain detached from events. Both must finally and forcefully strive to live up to their ideals. In the poetic story that Whitman tells in the heart of his reconstructed work *Leaves of Grass*, the coming of the Civil War will rally the country and the poet from their drowsing repose, restore their unity of purpose, and put them both back on the march. The title of the cluster reminds us, however, that the hoped-for outcome of the march, a fully inclusive nation living at peace, still lies down the road.

5. Whitman's General

I feel about literature what Grant did about war.
He hated war. I hate literature. I am not a literary West Pointer.
—*Walt Whitman to Horace Traubel, 1888*

The dramatic changes in the partisan press after the war matched the considerable upheaval in the post–Civil War political landscape in the United States. While the Democratic Party was clearly in disarray following the war, the Republican Party was also split between its more radical and moderate members, and the failed impeachment of Andrew Johnson brought the fault lines into stark relief. As Walt Whitman wrote to Moncure Conway in 1868, "Our American politics, as you notice, are in an unusually effervescent condition—with perhaps (to the mere eye-observation from a distance) divers[e] alarming & deadly portending shows & signals. Yet we old stagers take things very coolly, & count on coming out all right in due time" (*Corr*, 2:15). In spite of Whitman's apparent nonchalance, he was watching events with considerable interest after the war, and his concerns were both national and personal. While the armed conflict was concluded, the fate of the restored Union still seemed very much in doubt, with riots in the South, Johnson's pardon of a large number of Confederates and their prompt attempts to return to political power, and seething tension and animosity all around. In Congress, debates regarding impeachment of the president, enfranchisement, and amending the Constitution roiled the capital. At the same time, Whitman's own career prospects were in at least some doubt: his position as a clerk in the attorney general's office was now up in the air as he awaited the new appointments that would come with the change in administration. As numerous critics have noted, Whitman was highly attentive to all of these developments, and his correspondence bears this out, as his letters to family and friends make frequent reference to political developments and his employment situation.

With so much at stake, one might expect the poet to be a fervent supporter of Ulysses S. Grant, the candidate whose heroism during the war and whose campaign slogan "Let Us Have Peace" would seem to have made him an ideal subject for Whitman's loyalty and enthusiasm. As his letters home during the war indicate, the poet followed the general's career closely upon his taking command of the Union army, and he often spoke of his confidence in him. While his enthusiasm is not wholly lacking in his correspondence during the 1868 election, it is muted, and he occasionally appears to hedge his bets, as he does in his letter to Conway: "According to present appearances the good, worthy, non-demonstrative, average-representing Grant will be chosen President next fall. What about him, then? As at present advised, I shall vote for him non-demonstrative as he is—but admit I can tell much better about him some five years hence" (*Corr*, 2:15). Given that his assessment came during the same month that the New York Republican Convention nominated the general for the presidency, one would expect Whitman might express his strongest support for the candidate. His relative reticence and willingness to withhold his own opinion until history offered its own judgment is noteworthy.

Perhaps Whitman took his cue from Grant himself, who did little to campaign for his spot on the ticket: "The movement for his nomination was becoming irresistible even without any word from Grant."[1] No doubt the poet would have found such humility admirable in a national figure like Grant, and, when speaking of the general, he would later express his admiration for Grant's "plain" nature, a key factor in his growing appreciation for the man as the years went by. In fact, Whitman's published writing, private correspondence, and conversations late in life all demonstrate how the poet's views on Grant shifted over time, culminating in both admiration for and a surprising amount of identification with the general turned president. While the poet's affection and reverence for Lincoln are well known, far less has been said about his feelings for and writings about Grant.[2] Specific study of Whitman's statements about the general and president offers further insight into the poet's engagement with politics and his own professional position in Washington during the early years of Reconstruction. It also provides an illustration of Whitman's beliefs regarding the heroic nature of the average American. Even more tellingly, his conversations about Grant in the late 1880s show how he saw in the general and his critics a symbol of his own poetic battles against the canons of tradition.

GRANT THE DICTATOR

When Grant was promoted to the rank of lieutenant general and came east to take command of Union forces in 1864, hopes were high for victory.[3] A string of Union triumphs and Grant's success out west contributed to this optimism, and Whitman expressed his confidence in the character of the new leader in a letter to his mother, Louisa Van Velsor Whitman:

> As I told you in a former letter Grant is determined to bend every thing to take Richmond & break up the banditti of scoundrels that have stuck themselves up there as a "government"—he is in earnest about it, his whole soul & all his thoughts night & day are upon it—he is probably the most in earnest of any man in command or in the government either—that's something, ain't it, Mother—& they are bending every thing to fight for their last chance—calling in their forces from southwest &c. (*Corr*, 1:211)

Whitman's remarks are noteworthy for their emphasis not on Grant's skill but on his earnest nature, as in his remark that Grant is more in earnest than "any man in command or in the government." This is not likely a comment upon his relative merit compared to Lincoln so much as it reflects the poet's enthusiasm regarding the new commander. He is a man willing to "bend every thing" to meet his objective, a determination that Whitman would repeatedly refer to as one of Grant's most admirable traits. After the vacillations of earlier generals, the poet was clearly taken with the straightforward commitment of the new leader.

Like a familial wire service reporter, Whitman spent the remaining months of the war reporting back to his mother on Grant's progress and, often, expressing his unwavering confidence in the general's plans. His brother George served under Grant in the battle at Vicksburg, and Whitman and his family had a very personal investment in the campaign that the general undertook in assuming command of the Union army (Loving, 272, 280–81). In a letter the following week, the poet linked the general to his beloved president through his faith in the two of them: "Others may say what they like, I believe in Grant & in Lincoln too—I think Grant deserves to be trusted, he is working continually—no one knows his plans, we will only know them when he puts them in operation" (*Corr*, 1:213). Here, again, his support is not premised upon anything having to do with military skill—he admits that "no one knows [Grant's] plan"—what matters most to Whitman is that the man "deserves to be trusted." It is the steadiness of his determination that gains this trust, and, in pairing Grant with Lincoln, the poet appears to suggest that the Union has at last found a general as devoted to its preservation as its president.

The degree to which Whitman trusted the new commander is evident in a letter the poet wrote home two weeks later:

> Whether there is anything in this story or not, I cannot tell—the city is full of rumors & this may be one of them—the government is not in receipt of any information to-day—Grant has taken the reins entirely in his own hands—he is really dictator at present—we shall hear something important within two or three days—Grant is very secretive indeed—he bothers himself very little about sending news even to the President or Stanton—time only can develope [*sic*] his plans—. (*Corr*, 219–20)

One would be hard pressed to find Whitman using the word "dictator" in any other context without scorn,[4] but here it is simply used to suggest the degree to which Grant has things "in his own hands." This letter was written on the day after the opening of the Battle of the Wilderness, the beginning of which was marked by considerable confusion and casualties from friendly fire in woods south of the Rapidan River. It is likely that Whitman and his mother were hearing as many tales of defeat as they were of victory, yet the poet kept his faith as the battle dragged on. He wrote again almost a week later, "Dearest Mother, I hope you & all are well—you must keep a good heart—still the fighting is very mixed, but it *seems steadily turning into real successes* for Grant—the news to-day here is very good—you will see it in NY papers—I steadily believe Grant is going to succeed, & that we shall have Richmond—but O what a price to pay for it" (*Corr*, 1:223). The price was high indeed; as James McPherson notes, "From May 5 through May 12 the Army of the Potomac lost some 32,000 men killed, wounded, and missing—a total greater than for all Union armies *combined* in any previous week of the war. As anxious relatives scanned the casualty lists, a pall of gloom settled over hundreds of northern communities" (732). As Whitman saw the consequences of Grant's unshakable determination and willingness to press forward in spite of casualties, the price for victory could never be far from his mind, and it would continue to haunt him long after the war. The casualties, not the battles won—not even the capture of Richmond—would become the focus of his postwar writings on the conflict, even as Grant's nature, more than his prowess, would become the most important element in his remarks on the general.

In the hot summer of 1864, however, such reappraisals were far in the future. For now, Whitman continued to follow Grant's campaign closely, sending frequent reports home and to friends, as in a letter to Charles Eldridge on July 9, 1864: "As to me, I still believe in Grant, & that we shall get Richmond" (*Corr*, 1:237). As it had in May, Whitman's expression of confidence came at a bleak time: Grant's Army of the Potomac continued to suffer horrific casualties in battles like Cold Harbor—"Some 65,000 northern boys were killed, wounded, or missing since May 4" (McPherson, 742)—while Sherman's army had been fought to a standstill in its march on Atlanta; in all, McPherson notes, "The months of July and August 1864 brought a greater crisis of northern morale than the same months in 1862" (760). In the face of all of this death and doubt, Whitman's continued faith in Grant and his refusal to criticize or second-guess him is noteworthy.

Following his brother George's capture by Confederate forces in September 1864, Whitman's feelings about Grant may have changed for a time as a result of the Union's unwillingness to pursue prisoner exchanges. He wrote a letter to the *New York Times* assailing the refusal to exchange prisoners and singling out Secretary of War Edwin Stanton and General Benjamin Butler, although he did not set his aim specifically on Grant.[5] In addition, the poet tried to work through private channels to secure his brother's release. In February 1865, he wrote a letter to John Swinton, the editor of the *New York Times*, "from the deep distress of my mother whose health is getting affected, & of my sister" (*Corr*, 1:252), asking him to write a letter to Grant seeking a special exchange for George. Swinton complied, and on February 13

Grant's military secretary sent Swinton a reply stating that Grant had approved the exchange (*Corr*, 1:253n);[6] George was finally freed February 22. While Whitman biographer Jerome Loving suggests that Whitman felt resentment toward Grant for Union policies on prisoner exchange, the apparent speed with which Grant had a letter sent in response to Swinton's appeal—which included much of the language from Whitman's own letter to the editor—may also have helped to cement his respect for the general.[7]

Certainly, following the Union victory several months later, Whitman's feelings about Grant seem to have reached an apex that they would not reach again until much later, and his portrayal of him as the conquering hero is far different from his later image of Grant the politician. On May 23 and May 24 Grant's Army of the Potomac marched with Sherman's Army of Georgia in the Grand Review "200,000 strong . . . in a pageantry of power and catharsis" (McPherson, 853) that Whitman witnessed firsthand. He wrote to his mother on May 25:

> I saw Gen. Grant too several times—He is the noblest Roman of them all—none of the pictures do justice to him—about sundown I saw him again riding on a large fine horse, with his hat off in answer to the hurrahs—he rode by where I stood, & I saw him well, as he rode by on a slow canter, with nothing but a single orderly after him—He looks like a good man—(& I believe there is much in looks)—I saw Gen. Meade, Gen. Thomas, Secretary Stanton, & lots of other celebrated government officers & generals— but the *rank & file* was the greatest sight of all. (*Corr*, 1:261–62)

The description of Grant as the "noblest Roman of them all" is far different from "average-representing Grant" and an exceptional moment in Whitman's writings on the man. Quite likely the poet was still grieving the loss of Lincoln, assassinated a little more than a month earlier, and was swept up in the pageantry of the occasion. While emphasizing Grant's looks—"(& I believe there is much in looks)"—he also contrasts Grant and the other leaders with "the *rank & file* . . . the greatest sight of all." His feelings about Grant in the future would largely be driven by the extent to which he saw Grant as part of the "rank and file" rather than as a member of the elite.

Given Whitman's high opinion of Grant at war's end, his relatively lukewarm endorsement of him as a candidate is rather surprising. Grant himself did little actual campaigning, of course, so while his opponent Seymour sought to build his national profile through public appearances, Grant stayed largely above the fray, leaving his reputation and the newspapers to do the work for him. This seems to have been enough for Whitman and his mother. As the poet wrote to her in June of 1868, "So you like the ticket, Grant & [Schuyler] Colfax, do you, mother? Well, I do, too" (*Corr*, 2:35). Of the Democrats, he observed, "How do you all like the nomination of Seymour and Blair? It is a regular old Copperhead Democratic ticket, of the rankest kind—probably pleases the old democratic bummers around New York and Brooklyn—but every where else they take it like a bad dose of medicine" (*Corr*, 2:36). Whitman's willingness to separate the larger Democratic Party from its standard-bearers is noteworthy, but, given his confidence in the general during the war, his support of Grant seems a foregone conclusion. What is lacking is any kind of intensity or excitement. As election day approached, he wrote to his friend Peter Doyle from New York, where he had traveled to visit family and friends while on leave:

> There is great excitement here over the returns of yesterday's elections, as I suppose there is the same in Washington also—the Democrats look blue enough, & the Republicans are on their high horses. I suppose Grant's success is now certain. As I write, the bands are out here, parading the streets, & the drums beating. It is now forenoon. To-night we will hear the big guns, & see the blazing bonfires. . . . I have been debating whether to get my leave extended, & stay till election day to vote—or whether to pair off with a Democrat, & return (which will amount to the same thing.) Most likely I shall decide on the latter, but don't know for certain. (*Corr*, 2:58–59)

For a poet who repeatedly celebrates American democracy and pageantry, this is a rather tepid response to an important political moment. His ambivalence about going to the trouble to cast his own ballot only heightens the impression that Whitman felt no true excitement at the prospect of a Grant presidency. Indeed, a few days later he wrote Doyle to inform him that he had resolved "to pair off with a friend of mine here who was going to vote for Seymour, and return on time" (*Corr*, 2:67).[8]

Of course, for all of his confidence in Grant as a general, Whitman had some clear policy differences with the Republican platform. He disagreed with Grant on one of the key issues of the time, the tariff. For Whitman, ever a proponent of free trade and enemy of monopoly, the Republican Party's unwillingness to roll back tariffs established in 1860 could certainly have been a barrier to his full endorsement. As one Grant biographer describes the situation after the war, "Politicians of the Republican school sought to secure control of the Southern votes, and industrial magnates laid dark plots to preserve the war-created tariff. Eventually, the marriage of the protective tariff and the bloody shirt enabled the industrial areas to dominate and control."[9] While this is putting the matter rather dramatically, it indicates how the issue of tariffs was of a piece with discussions of economic reconstruction and the political debate over how to rebuild the South. While the Democratic Party platform of 1868 emphasized tariff reform, the issue is not even mentioned in the Republican platform prior to the election. Whitman was suspicious of the emerging labor movement and the portents of class struggle increasingly linked to the Democrats,[10] but he was no proponent of trade restrictions, and the obstacle that these appeared to pose for reunification would have been an additional reason for his disapproval.

Even more pressing for Whitman was the subject of African American suffrage and the fate of the freed slaves. In writing of the election, he commented to Conway, "The Republicans have exploited the negro too intensely, & there comes a reaction. But that is going to be provided for" (*Corr*, 2:15). In his careful reading of Whitman's postwar writing and its relationship with the debates over amending the constitution, Luke Mancuso has noted this phrase and suggested that Whitman was ambivalent about the division being stoked by the political unrest and the question of state and federal sovereignty. This may be true, but it is difficult to place too much blame on the Republicans in a campaign where the Democrats employed the slogan "This

Is a White Man's Government"[11] in what historian David W. Blight has called "one of the most explicitly racist presidential campaigns in American history" (101). Betsy Erkkila has suggested that Whitman's reference to "good, worthy, non-demonstrative, average-representing Grant" in his letter to Conway about the presidential campaign indicates that "like many in the country, Whitman hoped for a retreat from the more radical premises of Republican reconstruction and a restoration of balance through the election of Ulysses S. Grant" (*WPP*, 245). This may indeed have been the case, but Whitman's hesitation regarding Grant in the same letter suggests that he was not certain that Grant's election would produce this sort of outcome, and press reports from the time may have added to his doubts.

In keeping with tradition, Grant himself did not campaign, but his actions as commanding general during Johnson's administration had led the *Hartford Courant* to note in August 1867, "Grant is a Radical all over."[12] As one biographer notes,

> Grant and Stanton took an active interest in [the First Reconstruction Act]. . . . The Reconstruction Act reflected Grant's view that more effort was required to protect Southern blacks. Military government seemed the only solution. It was deplorable to consider such a possibility, he told Stanton, but the failure of local authorities in the South to investigate and punish crimes against the freedmen "constitutes what is practically a state of insurrection." Grant said military rule would provide relative security "to all classes of citizens without regard to race, color, or political opinions, and could be continued until society was capable of protecting itself." (Smith, 432)

This put him significantly at odds with President Johnson, although it would be a few more months before events in the South brought their disagreement into the open. Grant opposed the president's attempts to replace commanders in the South with men more in line with his pro-Southern views on Reconstruction and on the way to deal with the freed slaves. By the time he became candidate for president, then, the Radical Republicans were convinced that the former Democrat shared their views. For Whitman, whose own views on suffrage were conflicted, Grant's strong advocacy and alignment with the Radicals in Congress may have presented another obstacle to a wholehearted endorsement of the man he had praised as a military leader.

Whitman's interest in the next president of the United States was of personal importance at this time as it meant that he was going to gain a new employer. The details of his employment in Washington are well known. With his friend William O'Connor's help, he had begun working for the Lincoln administration's Department of the Interior in January 1865.[13] Following his dismissal at the request of Interior Secretary James Harlan,[14] Whitman was rehired in the attorney general's office in July. He served under three different attorneys general during the Lincoln and then the Johnson administrations, and, when the time came for the election, he was carefully evaluating his job prospects. His most recent employer, William Evarts, who defended Johnson during impeachment proceedings, had been the disappointment he expected when he wrote to his mother in July 1868: "We have a new Attorney General, Mr. Evarts, as I suppose you have seen by the papers—He hasn't made his appearance here yet—but is expected soon—I only hope he will be as agreeable for a boss as the others have been—but somehow I don't believe he will" (*Corr*, 2:37). Regardless of his cautious hopes concerning what Grant would do for the nation, he was hopeful about the more immediate changes the election would have for his situation: "I shall be glad when Grant comes in, & a new Attorney Gen'l appointed—if I weather it out till then—though I am well enough off, at present, & probably safe—I don't think there is any show for Mr. Evarts remaining here after Grant comes in—" (*Corr*, 2:70-71).

When Grant finally announced his appointments, a process that he kept more secret than was customary, thus angering party officials in Washington, the poet's response was mixed. On the one hand, the pick for attorney general obviously pleased him and suggested that his situation would improve tremendously. He wrote his friend Abby Price on April 7, 1869, "My situation in the office continues the same—The new Attorney General, Mr. Hoar, treats me very kindly—He is from Concord, Mass. & is personally intimate with Emerson" (*Corr*, 2:80). The connection to Emerson was clearly an unexpected bonus, and historians generally see the appointment of Ebenezer R. Hoar as a true bright spot in what has been perceived either as a tremendously flawed cabinet, or, more recently, as a mediocre one. One biographer notes, "A genial New Englander, Hoar was a social and literary delight. He was also a close friend of Senator Charles Sumner's and a member of Harvard University's board of overseers. Hoar brought a world of erudition and learning to the cabinet" (Smith, 469); while another describes him as "a distinguished lawyer and a figure of exemplary rectitude" (Perret, 385).

Grant's other selections were not so unquestionably positive, a fact that Whitman noted. In the same letter to Price, he asks, "*What do you think of Grant*—his doings—especially some of his diplomatic appointments—Washburn, for instance?" (*Corr*, 2:81). The circumstances surrounding Elihu Washburn's incredibly brief tenure as secretary of state are murky at best. His name was submitted to Congress on March 5, and he stepped down on March 10, claiming poor health. The next day he was appointed minister to France, a position he held for more than eight years (Smith, 470–71). It seems clear that Grant never intended Washburn to remain Secretary of State, but scholars disagree regarding the motives for the entire episode. While Grant's cabinet generally provoked criticism, in part because he had assembled it without consulting Washington insiders, his appointment of Washburn was held up to particular scorn: "His nomination was a signal for bitter attacks. He was coarse and illiterate—a demagogue unfit for the position!" (Hasseltine, 146). Such critiques were prominent in the Democratic *New York World*, and the fact that Whitman was still pondering the implications of Washburn's appointment a month later suggests that, for the poet, it raised significant questions regarding the president's judgment.

Grant had selected his cabinet by trusting his own instincts and seeking out those with whom he felt comfortable, not by consulting traditional political power brokers (Smith, 468). Whitman appears to have been uncomfortable with this approach in 1869, and he maintained that feeling for twenty years; in a discussion regarding the recently deceased postmaster of New York, Whitman asked, "I don't know why, anyhow, such offices do not always go to men simply for moral, business reasons," and, when Traubel suggested that such concerns were "secondary," Whitman answered with indignation, "Secondary? They do not enter at all. It is not a question of fitness but of whether the fellow who is appointed is a good friend of the fellow who appoints him. Even General Grant would appoint men simply on the ground that he liked them! I think Washington and Jefferson—especially Jefferson—looked above all at the necessities of the service, and sought for those necessities the best man to be found. But the period of such ideals is past" (*WWC*, 5:61–2). Whitman's language here suggests that Grant's approach to appointments is a comedown from what might otherwise have been a lofty position. Despite his later appreciation for the general, the poet's distrust of Grant's political nominees from his time as president stayed with him, a sign that the "period of . . . ideals" represented by the nation's founders had passed.

Events during Grant's first term could only have confirmed Whitman's views. One historian notes,

> In contrast to his wartime determination and resourcefulness, as president he often appeared to lack leadership and vigor. His appointments, with but few exceptions, were nondescript: tested incompetence was frequently rewarded, whereas excellence brought suspicion and often dismissal. . . . Nor did Grant's policies enjoy success. The enactment of a new tariff in 1870 alienated reformers. The plan to annex Santo Domingo during 1870 was ill-conceived—the nation had enough problems without annexing more territory. Also, Grant disappointed many southerners in their hope that reconstruction would cease.[15]

Whitman's disapproval of tariffs has already been discussed, but Grant's policy decisions were the least of his problems during this period. Eventually Grant's vice president, Schuyler Colfax, would be implicated in one of the greatest political scandals of the period, the Credit-Mobilier case, involving kickbacks from the Union Pacific Railroad in exchange for favorable policy decisions (Smith, 552). Grant's own brother-in-law became embroiled in a conspiracy to corner the gold market in 1869, and Grant himself was often seen together with the two main conspirators, Jay Gould and Jim Fisk (Smith, 483–85). While Grant acted to stop the conspiracy, the result of the Gold Panic was an economic slump that lasted several months, well into 1870 (Smith, 490). Loving notes that the poem "'Nay, Tell Me Not To-Day the Publish'd Shame' expresses dismay and disappointment over the main topic of the day, the Credit Mobilier scandal" (353). While scholars have begun reassessing the legacy of Grant's presidency, there is no doubt that at the time his performance was a disappointment given the (perhaps unrealistically) high expectations that greeted him. There is a reason that the fact that Whitman "liked and defended Grant" was considered newsworthy to a correspondent for the *New York Evening Mail* in October of 1870 (quoted in *Corr*, 2:116n).

In spite of the scandals, Whitman stuck with Grant, and, while in Washington, seems to have worked to cultivate the kind of nodding familiarity with the president that he had enjoyed with his beloved Lincoln. He wrote to his mother in December of 1871, "I saw Grant to-day on the avenue walking by himself—(I always salute him, & he does the same to me.)" (*Corr*, 2:147). He would remember these meetings much later in life in conversations about Grant with Traubel, but by then he had already revised his assessment of Grant significantly. In these years, his salute seems more an attempt at connection than a verification of the man's democratic nature. Such a connection had implications for Whitman's job prospects as well as his vision of a president who tipped his hat to the people. In 1874, he sent copies of some of his Civil War writing for the *New York Weekly Graphic* to the president. A draft of the letter reads, "I take the liberty of sending (same mail with this) some reminiscences I have written about the war, in Nos. of the N. Y. Weekly Graphic, & thinking you of all men can best return to them, in the vein in which they are composed. I am not sure whether you will remember me—or my occasional salute to you in Washington. I am laid up here with tedious paralysis, but I think I shall get well & return to Washington" (*Corr*, 2:280–81). Whitman was still recovering from the effects of a stroke that he had suffered more than a year before, and, although he had hired a replacement to cover for him in Washington, he had been out of the office almost the entire time other than occasional brief visits, after the initial paralysis.

While it is unclear exactly which essays he sent to Grant, one selection that was published only a month earlier contains this swelling tribute to Grant:

The present! Our great Centennial of 1876 nigher and nigher at hand—the abandonment, by tacit consent, of dead issues—the general readjustment and rehabilitation, at least by intention and beginning, South and North, to the exigencies of the Present and Future—the momentous nebulae left by the convulsions of the previous thirty years definitely considered and settled by the re-election of Gen. Grant—the Twenty-second Presidentiad well-sped on its course—the inevitable unfolding and development of this tremendous complexity we call the United States—our Union with restored, doubled, trebled solidity seems to vault unmistakably to dominant position among the governments of the world in extent, population, products, and in the permanent sources of naval and military power. (*PW*, 1:310–11)

Given the nature of Grant's presidency and the 1872 campaign that saw Republicans split in their support of the incumbent, Whitman's declaration that his reelection has "definitely considered and settled" all the difficulties of the previous thirty years is hard to take. And, as he points out, Grant's second term was already "well sped on its course" by the time he refers to it here, so it is strange that he reaches back to the election as a turning point. The overall tone is more reminiscent of his praise for the general following the Union victory than of anything he had written of Grant in the years since, and, taken in the context of his letter to Grant a short while later, it is hard not to see in this piece a degree of self-interested puffery.

Subsequent events seem to confirm this, or at the very least pro-vide another example of the poet employing a newspaper article in an effort to shore up his position. Whitman did get a response to his first letter to Grant, but it was not the kind of personal connection he likely sought. A little more than a week later, the president's secretary wrote that Grant "wishes me to assure you of the appreciation of the polite attention, and his best wishes for your speedy recovery" (*Corr*, 2: 280–81n). An even more striking example of Whitman's apparent attempts to gain the good graces of the president is his poem "A Kiss to the Bride." Published a little more than two months later in the *New York Daily Graphic* on May 21, 1874, the same day the paper reported the wedding of the president's daughter Nelly, and again two days later, the poem is a strikingly specific occasional poem for the marriage, and it was not reprinted again until 1897 in "Old Age Echoes." The poem begins with innocuous salutations and warm wishes for the future, but Whitman's poetic persona can't seem to resist taking part in the nuptials, and one can only imagine what Nelly or her father might have thought upon reading the poem's final lines:

> Dear girl—through me the ancient privilege too,
> For the New World, through me, the old, old wedding greeting:
> O youth and health! O sweet Missouri rose! O bonny bride!
> Yield thy red cheeks, thy lips, to-day,
> Unto a Nation's loving kiss.
>
> (*LG*, 578)

In demanding that the "bonny bride" present her "red cheeks" and lips to the speaker for the nation's channeled kiss, Whitman may not have aided his efforts to build a rapport with the president.

While there is no record of a response from Grant to the poem, almost exactly a month later, when Whitman apparently learned that Congress had ordered the Department of Justice to make substantive cuts to staff, he wrote the president again, appealing directly that he be allowed to keep the position that he himself had not filled for almost two years: "Would it be convenient to the President to personally request of the Attorney General that in any changes in the Solicitor Treasury's office, I be not disturbed in my position as clerk in that office—all my duties to the government being & having been thoroughly & regularly performed there, by a substitute, during my illness. I shall probably get well before long" (*Corr*, 2:306). Along with his letter he included a newspaper clipping that provided Whitman's own anonymous remarks on his health, which one critic suggests might have been published to sway the president (*Corr*, 2:306n). His appeal fell upon deaf ears, and he was terminated at the end of the month. Later, Whitman cut the passage about the reelection of Grant and the "Twenty-Second Presidentiad" from the reprinted essay in *Memoranda During the War*, published 1875–1876, and in 1882 removed its interpolation into *Specimen Days and Collect*, leaving his tribute to Grant's second term to languish. As Loving notes, Whitman was scarcely well enough to take up his work in Washington at any rate (358), so it is hard to blame the Grant administration for the change, but the episode seems to represent a low moment in Whitman's feelings about the president, one that would linger until his final reassessment of his feelings regarding the man who helped to save the Union.

THE UNWAVERING DEMOCRAT

Perhaps because he did not return to Washington to work or live, or perhaps because he became consumed with attention to his various publishing ventures in 1875 and 1876, including his *Memoranda* and the Centennial Edition of *Leaves of Grass*, Whitman does not appear to have taken a great deal of interest in the presidential politics of 1876. Still wrestling with illness, he may also not have been personally inclined to comment on these matters in his correspondence or writings; Loving suggests that Whitman in fact might have seen his works of this period, the 1876 edition and his collection of poetry and prose, *Two Rivulets*, as "deathbed editions" (373). By 1879, however, the poet had recovered enough to travel West to see the country and visit his brother Jeff, and his journey coincides with a renewed interest in current events. In September of that year, he wrote a laudatory essay on the former president, and, although the work was not published until its inclusion in *Specimen Days* in 1882, after the campaign was over, the date on which he wrote it suggests that it might almost be seen as an endorsement of Grant's possible run for a third term in office. The language of the piece also demonstrates how Whitman was reconciling his two views of Grant—as the "average" man and the national leader and legend. Originally titling it "A Very Utilitarian Hero," Whitman seems to have felt that the title went too far in emphasizing the former, for he retitled the piece "The Silent General" (*PW*, 1:226n). Because it reveals a great deal about the poet's evolving attitude, it is worth examining in its entirety:

> So General Grant, after circumambiating the world, has arrived home again—landed in San Francisco yesterday, from the ship City of Tokio [*sic*] from Japan. What a man he is! what a history! what an illustration—his life—of the capacities of that American individuality common to us all. Cynical critics are wondering "what the people can see in Grant" to make such a hubbub about.

They aver (and it is no doubt true) that he has hardly the average of our day's literary and scholastic culture, and absolutely no pronounc'd genius or conventional eminence of any sort. Correct: but he proves how an average western farmer, mechanic, boatman, carried by tides of circumstances, perhaps caprices, into a position of incredible military or civic responsibilities, (history has presented none more trying, no born monarch's, no mark more shining for attack or envy,) may steer his way fitly and steadily through them all, carrying the country and himself with credit year after year—command over a million armed men—fight more than fifty pitch'd battles—rule for eight years a land larger than all the kingdoms of Europe combined—and then, retiring, quietly (with a cigar in his mouth) make the promenade of the whole world, through its courts and coteries, and kings and czars and mikados, and splendidest glitters and etiquettes, as phlegmatically as he ever walk'd the portico of a Missouri hotel after dinner. I say all this is what people like—and I am sure I like it. Seems to me it transcends Plutarch. How those old Greeks, indeed, would have seized on him! A mere plain man—no art, no poetry—only practical sense, ability to do, or try his best to do, what devolv'd upon him. A common trader, money-maker, tanner, farmer of Illinois—general for the republic, in its terrific struggle with itself, in the war of attempted secession—President following, (a task of peace, more difficult than the war itself)—nothing heroic, as the authorities put it—and yet the greatest hero. The gods, the destinies, seem to have concentrated upon him. (*PW*, 226–27)

Grant's tour of the globe was a sensation. He traveled for more than two years, departing Philadelphia in May 1877 to return where he started in December 1879; according to one biographer, "He visited more countries and saw more people, from kings to commoners, than anyone before" (Smith, 606–7). This seems like grandiose overstatement, but even if it is a claim that is difficult to verify, it likely appeared true at the time, thanks in no small part to the constant companionship of a reporter for the *New York Herald*.[16] American readers welcomed his frequent dispatches and watched with great attention as their former president walked the world stage as a military hero.

The image clearly captured Whitman's imagination as it did the rest of the nation's. Yet even as he pictures the president making "the promenade of the whole world," likening him to Greek heroes, he insists that at bottom there is nothing special about him. Instead Grant merely symbolizes the "capacities of that American individuality common to us all." This was to be Whitman's new formula for encompassing Grant. During the military parade at the conclusion of the war, he had praised Grant as "the noblest Roman of them all," only to then assert that the "*rank & file* was the greatest sight of all" (*Corr*, 1:261–62). Now, rather than making a contrast, the poet saw the former president as fulfilling both roles: "A common trader, money-maker, tanner, farmer of Illinois—. . . nothing heroic, as the authorities put it—and yet the greatest hero." And although Whitman alludes to Grant's failings, it is his average nature in extraordinary circumstances that ultimately carries the day: "A mere plain man—no art, no poetry—only practical sense, ability to do, or try his best to do, what devolv'd upon him." In his capacity both to stand for the plain man even while performing the work of heroes, moving in the orbit of world leaders with his cigar in his mouth all the while, Grant truly contains multitudes. It is no surprise that Whitman asserts "I am sure I like it": the poet had long imagined himself in a similar fashion, bowing before no king or emperor as his words traveled the globe, lifting his hat to no one. In this context at least, Grant appears to have become "one of the roughs, a kosmos" (*LG*, 52n). Truly, "The gods, the destinies, seem to have concentrated upon him," confirming both his metaphysical and "plain" appeal.

The poet's enthusiasm certainly seems fitted to the presidential campaign that Grant became embroiled in soon after his return to the United States,[17] regardless of the fact that Whitman did not publish this piece until after the general election. He did, however, express many of the same sentiments in a poem entitled "What Best I See in Thee, [General Grant in Philadelphia, December—, 1879]" and later addressed "To U.S.G. return'd from his World's Tour" when published in the 1881 edition of *Leaves of Grass*. The poem, first published in the Philadelphia newspaper *The Press* on December 17, "bears the characteristics of his genius," according to the editors, and is only one small part of the paper's extensive coverage of the general's return, for which "no expense or pains have been spared to make it worthy of the occasion."[18] Whitman's poem is not particularly set apart on the page or placed next to other reportage on Grant, but instead is located between a selection of humorous headlines from regional newspapers and the obituaries. Such an unassuming placement is fitting for the tone of the poem itself. Because its first appearance differs in language, capitalization, and formatting from its revised form in the 1881 edition of *Leaves*, the following is included here to indicate how the poem first appeared in the newspaper:

> What best I see in thee,
> Is not that where thou mov'st down history's great highways,
> Ever undimm'd by time shoots warlike victory's dazzle;
> Or that thou sat'st where Washington, Lincoln sat, ruling the land in peace;
> Or thou the man whom feudal Europe feted, venerable Asia swarm'd upon;
> But that in war and peace, and in thy walks with kings,
> These average prairie sovereigns of the west, Kansas, Missouri, Illinois,
> Ohio's, Indiana's millions, comrades, farmers, soldiers, all to the front,
> Invisibly with thee walking with kings with even pace the round world's promenade,
> Were all so justified.[19]

The speaker of the poem quickly negates all of the standard measures of greatness, rejecting them as rationales for "what best" he sees in Grant. Yet even as he appears to rule out Grant's military victories, his presidency, and the very world tour that is the occasion for the poem in the first place, he reinstates them. Grant's greatness does lie in those episodes, but not solely; the speaker sees beside Grant "invisibly with thee walking" all of those "average" Americans, "comrades, farmers, soldiers."[20] In rising to such heights of fame, Grant has simultaneously "justified" those who live and work unknown. The term is a crucial one for Whitman, emerging several times in his poems and signaling the emergence of or proof of the true quality of America, as in "By Blue Ontario's Shore":

Rhymes and rhymers, pass away, poems distill'd from poems
   pass away,
The swarms of reflectors and the polite pass, and leave ashes,
Admirers, importers, obedient persons, make but the soil of
   literature,
America justifies itself, give it time, no disguise can deceive it
   or conceal from it, it is impassive enough.

(LG, 350)

In Grant's "even pace" as he walks with kings, he embodies Whitman's ideal of the democratic American.

Both Whitman's essay and his poem effectively serve to recast Grant as a kind of poetic proxy. Grant was to politics and the military as Whitman was to poetry. While he had spoken in passing of the "average-representing Grant" in 1868, it was only in the waning days of the 1870s that he finally saw the full potential of what this could mean. As he remarked to Traubel not long before his death, "There was Grant, I think him the best—he typifies so many things— towers, tops, stands ever alone!" (WWC, 8:326). There is again the apparent contradiction: the general is clearly an encompassing figure who "typifies so many things"—he is literally a "typical American" for Whitman—yet at the same time he is eminent and alone.

Again and again when commenting on Grant, Whitman would emphasize the general's democratic nature while simultaneously holding him up as superlative. In talking with Traubel, he adds an interesting detail to his story of saluting the president as he walked the streets of Washington, one that emphasizes not only the man's humility but his "common" nature:

> I was still in Washington while Grant was President. I saw a good deal of him about the city. He went quite freely everywhere alone. I remember one spot in particular where I often crossed him—a little cottage on the outskirts of Washington: he was frequently there—going there often. I learned that an old couple of whom he was very fond lived there. He had met them in Virginia—they received him in a plain democratic way: I would see him leaning on their window sills outside: all would be talking together: they

seeming to treat him without deference for place—with dignity, courtesy, appreciation. (*WWC*, 1:257–58)

These exchanges between the president and the elderly couple[21] impressed the poet so much that he referred to them again three years later, only a few months before his death: "He cavorted the whole earth around, yet was as simple on his return as when he started. He must have taught those who met him, away from America, a lesson— a lesson of our life here. Perhaps of all there have been, Grant most expresses the modern *simple*—is thoroughly unadorned. I have told you of the old folks, the old couple, I knew him to visit in Washington. It was a profound lesson to me, to others. And he never forgot them, however high his place. I have seen him three or four times, leaning at the doorsill, or into the window, talking—seeming to enter into their life" (*WWC*, 9:144). Here is the relationship between the president and the people that Whitman spoke of in the 1855 preface: "The President's taking off his hat to them [the citizens], not they to him" (*PW*, 2:436n). While in the first rendition of the story the poet emphasizes the "plain democratic reception" he received from the elderly couple, the second makes it clear that Grant's "high place" never interfered with his "unadorned" nature. The last phrase is even more telling for the poet whose persona presents itself as moving in and out of private places and lives of Americans across the country: Grant not only speaks with these people, he "enter[s] into their life."

Only once more would Whitman return to his vision of Grant as primarily the conquering hero, emphasizing his grandeur more than his simplicity, and that was the occasion of Grant's final illness and death. As Loving details, *Harper's Weekly* commissioned Whitman to write a poem in April 1885, when it appeared the general was dying. (He survived until July 23rd.) Eventually entitled "Death of General Grant," this is only Whitman's second poetic description of the man although, as we have seen, he wrote about him in prose articles during the 1870s. In his poem, Whitman does all that he can to lift up Grant to the level of those other war heroes, "the lofty actors" who have left "that great play on history's stage eterne" (*LG*, 519). Loving refers to the work as "one of Whitman's better poems of occasion [that] captured the autumnal mood by which both the poet and his era were now defined" (434). This is an astute assessment, and it emphasizes why the poem ultimately is not an accurate gauge of the poet's sentiments regarding Grant. In the version first published in *Harper's*, "As One by One Withdraw the Lofty Actors," the poet added a stanza in recognition of the fact that the general still lived, and there he references "the hero heart" (*LG*, 519). In the rest of the piece, however, the speaker emphasizes the times and the part that Grant played in them:

> As one by one withdraw the lofty actors,
> From that great play on history's stage eterne,
> That lurid, partial act of war and peace—of old and new
> contending,
> Fought out through wrath, fears, dark dismays, and many a long
> suspense;
> All past—and since, in countless graves receding, mellowing,
> Victor's and vanquish'd—Lincoln's and Lee's—now though with
> them,
> Man of the mighty days—and equal to the days!
> Thou from the prairies!—tangled and many-vein'd and hard has
> been thy part,
> To admiration has it been enacted!
>
> (*LG*, 519)

Without the historical context, this poem could refer to any number of Civil War generals. Beyond the title, of course—and even that was originally the first line of the poem, not a specific reference to the general—the only possible clue to Grant's identity is the reference to "Thou from the prairies," and while Whitman would often find great significance in Grant's origins, here the speaker does nothing to elaborate upon it. And the poem almost completely obscures Grant's two terms in office, the only possible, highly oblique reference being to "That lurid, partial act of war and peace." More than a tribute to Grant upon his passing, the poem serves as a comment upon the passage of the Civil War into history.

In his personal recollections, Whitman would often forego the heroic language to instead repeatedly emphasize Grant's humility rather than his greatness. In looking back, he would even revise his view of the great military parade after the Union victory. Grant is no longer the noble Roman, or not simply that:

> No, no, Grant was quite another man. Even that day, where was he? Off in his corner—in his place, no doubt—but making nothing of it, at most. Probably going by some obscure way to rejoin them later on. Out of all the hubbub of the war, Lincoln and Grant emerge, the towering majestic figures. There were others: Seward, Sumner, Phillips—such—elegant, refined, scholarly—the gift of college, the past, book-keen, great men: these: then, by contrast, Lincoln, Grant! Don't that tell everything? . . . Grant savored of our soil—was Saxon—Sherman Norman. Grant hated show—liked to leave things unsaid, undone—liked to defy convention by going a simple way. (*WWC*, 8:6–7)

Whitman's Grant lives in these conversational remarks much more vividly than in his poem of a few years earlier. The general that Whitman would come to embrace, even more than in those heady days at the end of the great cataclysm of the war, was the simple man who, like Lincoln, simultaneously towered above the rest.

GRANT THE CREATIVE GENIUS

In coming to see Grant as the representative American, the one who towers in the world as a result of his simple, democratic nature, Whitman left behind his doubts regarding the man as president and his apparent resentment for his dismissal from the Justice Department to accept him fully into his pantheon of the greatest Americans. In doing so, he simultaneously came to identify with him in new ways. While Grant's figure in the world tracks with Whitman's poetic persona, in his final years Whitman himself would more and more come to see his own struggles and achievements as a writer as paralleling the career of the general. Like Grant, he was no "literary West Pointer," following the accepted track to prominence, and he came to see his experience under the fire of critics as comparable to the criticism of Grant and even Napoleon in a military context:

> Napoleon, as a general, came up against the same class [of critics]—yes, is a good case in point. When he set to and whacked

away at the enemy, the tacticians, the traditionists, the canonites, all cursed him: "God damn him! he is violating all the laws, the customs, of soldiering we were taught in the schools!" but then the fellow who was getting licked would come on and cry: "That's true; that's all true; but, God damn him, he's knocking hell out of us anyway!" The canon proves that the poet is not a poet—but suppose he *is* a poet anyway, what can be said for the canon? . . . And that's the method of the critics everywhere. Why—there was Grant—see how he went about his work, defied the rules, played the game his own way—did all the things the best generals told him he should not do—and won out! Suppose the poet is warned, warned, warned, and wins out? (*WWC*, 1:445–46)

In spite of the emphasis on the military, the passage itself is, of course, only nominally about either Napoleon or Grant. Whitman himself is the subject, the general plotting his own course in defiance of canons (and cannons), only to win out in the end. As he remarked on another occasion, "All genius defies the rules—makes its own passage—is its own precedent. But I can see how all this is emphasized in Grant: it is part of him. I more and more incline to acknowledge him" (*WWC*, 8:12). This is the inevitable conclusion of Whitman's evolving views on Grant: in defending his genius, and "acknowledging" him, a gesture that seems fraught with import as the poet describes it, Whitman upholds his own genius in defying the rules.

His good friend Traubel encouraged such a perspective. Traubel reported the following exchange regarding Whitman's medical treatment:

[W.:] "And in this, therefore, as in literary matters, in writing, I listen (listen intently) to all the critics have to say—then pursue my own convictions, 'whim' you may call it, after all." I said: "You listen to your friends as General Grant used to hold his councils of war." W.: "How is that?" "Out of politeness, merely, having determined upon a course of action before anybody has a chance to offer you any advice." W. laughed. "Do they say Grant did that?" I said: "They don't say it: Grant has said it himself." W. was very merry over this: "Horace, I shouldn't wonder but I'm treed: yes, I guess you've got the facts in the case." (*WWC*, 4:376–77)

A keen observer of the poet, Traubel knew how to speak to him, and it is likely that his Grant reference was deliberately chosen to elicit precisely this reaction. The two men had an almost identical discussion more than a year later. Traubel reported that Whitman said:

> "And I like to hear what all the fellows have to say—all. It is a part of the scheme, to be heard, weighed, perhaps accepted. I like it all. Then at last I stand by my own stubborn guns, for somewhere in me is the last unbendingness which must have its way." And when I laughed and said I had written something of this sort in my paper, and spoke of Grant as of similar habit, he assented, "Yes, I have heard it of Grant, too—and how much it explains which would otherwise be inexplicable!" (*WWC*, 7:253)

In the end, Grant offered the aging Whitman a way to look at himself, his unorthodox style, his trials, and his accomplishments. Of another occasion, Traubel writes, "I reminded him of a remark he made to me years ago one noon-day on the boat: 'If Grant is not himself poet, singer, artist, he at least contains within himself the eligibility, the subject-force, of song, art.' He listened intently. 'Repeat that,' he said. I did so. Then he said: 'Yes, I should stand by that'" (*WWC*, 2:191). If the simple facts of the case precluded labeling Grant a poet, then Whitman was sure that he had the stuff of poetry: this could help explain him. In his essay "Walt Whitman at Date," Traubel writes, "When I once asked Whitman what three or four names of absolute greatness he thought America had so far offered, he answered interrogatively: 'What would you say to Washington, Lincoln, Grant, and Emerson?'" (*WWC*, 8:562). The list, like so many of Whitman's catalogs, is revealing. There is the Founding Father and eminent aristocrat; the sweet, sad savior of the Union and its martyr; there is the nation's intellect and its inspiration; and there is Grant, the towering plain man, Whitman's General.

6. Reconstructing His Story

The Secession war? Nay, let me call it the Union war. Though whatever call'd, it is even yet too near us—too vast and too closely overshadowing—its branches unform'd yet, (but certain) shooting too far into the future—and the most indicative and mightiest of them yet ungrown.
—Walt Whitman, from "Death of Abraham Lincoln," 1879

Whitman saw his *Memoranda* as an effort to preserve the truth of the Civil War by honoring the blank spaces, the undocumented struggles, and the unknown dead, at the same time the country was preoccupied as never before with filling in the gaps. This was not simply a matter of documenting the battles and campaigns. As Drew Gilpin Faust writes, "In the absence of arrangements for interring and recording overwhelming numbers, hundreds of thousands of men—more than 40 percent of deceased Yankees and a far greater proportion of Confederates—perished without names" (102). Unlike in previous conflicts, however, the situation was not simply accepted as one of the consequences of warfare. While it would not be until World War I that the U.S. armed services would present their members with dog tags for identification purposes, the Civil War marked a turning point in how the nation would seek to identify and honor its war dead (103). Faust carefully documents the numerous organizations formed to track down and identify the casualties of the conflict, most notably the Sanitary Commission and the Christian Commission; and, as she demonstrates, Whitman himself was a part of the effort in his service writing letters in the hospitals.

At the same time, however, in ascribing "the significant word UNKNOWN" to the unidentified, Whitman does more than illustrate the emerging importance of identifying U.S. soldiers and the efforts that would make the unknown soldier more of a rarity; he is literally working to make the word "unknown" signify, to represent something about the lost and the war itself that those named bodies and their engraved markers cannot. This is of course part of the work of memory, eluding the "cold electrotype plates of history," but it also demonstrates the connection between Whitman's postwar project and the march to memorialize and construct monuments to the fallen. Here Whitman's work is of a piece with that of the Sanitary Commission. If he cannot identify the names of the fallen, he can paradoxically attempt to make the fact that their names are unknown itself representative.

On its face, this is an odd endeavor for the poet who celebrates the "chemistry" of "This Compost" (1856, 1881) that transforms the bodies of the deceased into "sumptuous crops" (*LG*, 370). There is a tension between the poet whose persona assures readers that when he is sought, he can be found beneath their bootsoles (*LG*, 89) and the poet who expresses an ongoing interest in his own history and literary legacy. If the 1881 edition of *Leaves of Grass* reveals the effects of the war and Reconstruction on Whitman's poetic project, then his autobiography *Specimen Days* is perhaps most representative of his efforts to reconcile the war with his personal history. On the most fundamental level, this can be seen in the inclusion of his *Memoranda* in the larger text, indicating how his war experiences and his reflections on their aftermath have become incorporated into his life and body of work. As George Hutchinson notes, "The book attempts to link Whitman's life history to national and natural history" ("*Specimen Days*," 678). Yet the integration is not an entirely easy one, for if the *Memoranda* sought to find meaning in the "significant word UNKNOWN" by releasing it from history, Whitman's incorporation of it back into his personal history means placing the gaps into a larger narrative and unity, and even, in places, attempting to fill in those blank spaces himself.

In turning to the work of crafting his own story, he turns to the raw material of his personal archive: "Diary-scraps and memoranda, just as they are, large or small, one after another" (*PW*, 1:1). No wonder that he remarks, "If I don't do anything else, I shall send out the most wayward, spontaneous, fragmentary book ever printed" (*PW*, 1:1). While at first glance it is difficult to contest the notion that the work is fragmentary—after all, it encompasses genealogy, the war years, previously published articles, diary entries from his time spent at Timber Creek in New Jersey, recovering from his stroke, and his trip West in 1879, to mention only a few of the work's myriad subjects—his unifying trope of "specimen" suggests that the work is representative of something larger: "the middle range of the Nineteenth century in the New World; a strange, unloosen'd, wondrous time" (*PW*, 1:3). Just as the inclusion of the "By the Roadside" cluster transforms the "Drum-Taps" cluster into the culmination of a personal poetic drama as well as a national one, *Specimen Days* transforms *Memoranda* in a similar fashion, reconstructing the poet's life narrative.[1]

GENEALOGY

In setting forth upon his autobiographical project, Whitman offers an image of historical research as a means of illuminating progress and development. In his "Answer to an Insisting Friend," he writes,

> You ask for items, details of my early life. . . . You say you want to get at these details mainly as the go-befores and embryons of "Leaves of Grass." Very good; you shall have at least some specimens of them all. I have often thought of the meaning of such things—that one can only encompass and complete matters of that kind by exploring behind, perhaps very far behind, themselves directly, and so into their genesis, antecedents, and cumulative stages. (*PW*, 1:3–7)

This is clearly a historical turn, and the poet proceeds to provide a description of his family tree, immediately offering a counterpoint to the *lieu de mémoire* he constructed in his earlier *Memoranda*. In "Genealogy—Van Velsor and Whitman," he offers archival traces in place of ritual. Although the entry itself is quite brief, the poet is intent on preserving the details of his history, even referencing "Savage's 'Genealogical Dictionary'" as a source for his own historiography. Here he embraces the kind of precise documentation that he had earlier sought to circumvent in his writing; however, his "pedigree-reminiscences" (*PW*, 1:5), a term that emphasizes verifiable review, soon give way to the uncertain signifiers of the family cemetery. In the process, the final resting places of the Whitman and Van Velsor families join those unknown graves that preoccupy the poet's writings of the war years:

I now write these lines seated on an old grave (doubtless of a century since at least) on the burial hill of the Whitmans of many generations. Fifty and more graves are quite plainly traceable, and as many more decay'd out of all form—depress'd mounds, crumbled and broken stones, cover'd with moss—the gray and sterile hill, the clumps of chestnuts outside, the silence, just varied by the soughing wind. There is always the deepest eloquence of sermon or poem in any of these ancient graveyards of which Long Island has so many; so what must this one have been to me? My whole family history, with its succession of links, from the first settlement down to date, told here—three centuries concentrate on this sterile acre.

The next day, July 30, I devoted to the maternal locality, and if possible was still more penetrated and impress'd. I write this paragraph on the burial hill of the Van Velsors, near Cold Spring, the most significant depository of the dead that could be imagin'd, without the slightest help from art, but far ahead of it, soil sterile, a mostly bare plateau-flat of half an acre, the top of a hill, brush and well grown trees and dense woods bordering all around, very primitive, secluded, no visitors, no road (you cannot drive here, you have to bring the dead on foot, and follow on foot). Two or three-score graves quite plain; as many more almost rubb'd out. (*PW*, 1:6–7)

The gravesites that Whitman discovers at these "burial hills" are reminiscent of those that littered the countryside following the Civil War, "depress'd mounds" "out of all form." While many of the graves of his father's family are "traceable," many others have been obscured by time. Still, Whitman insists that his whole family history is told here. If this is the case, then it is a dramatically different history than the "pedigree-reminiscences" invoked by his genealogical research. The same is true at the Van Velsor plot, where many of the graves are "almost rubb'd out." Here the "deepest eloquence" of the graveyard is not unlike that found in those passages in *Memoranda* where Whitman evokes all that cannot be represented in printed histories, even those carved upon the stones of his ancestors.

While such reflections seem to run counter to the documentary impulse described earlier in the autobiography, this passage is also notable for the emphasis placed on the word "sterile." The word appears more frequently here than in any other Whitman text. Indeed, Whitman's family cemeteries appear to be the most sterile places described in his entire body of printed works. At the same time, however, Whitman himself is "penetrated and impress'd" by the site of the burial grounds, particularly by the "maternal locality." This suggestive sexual language may indicate that while the burial grounds themselves are lifeless, Whitman as the descendant preserves a fecundity that is oddly excluded from the resting place of the family dead, where even the trees are confined to the borders. Perhaps the poet sees himself as the source of maternal power now absent on his mother's side.

His language is all the more remarkable when compared to other prominent descriptions of graves in Whitman's work, most notably the early poem that would become "Song of Myself." As Desiree Henderson has recently pointed out, the poet's response to the well-known query in that work, "what is the grass"—the "beautiful uncut hair of graves"—can be linked to the popular emphasis in the nineteenth century on images of idyllic cemeteries.[2] While Whitman's descriptions of his family burial plots contain elements of this image of the cemetery as a rural retreat, the emphasis on their lifelessness is at odds with the "beautiful" regeneration of the "hair of graves." These resting places are not the parklike settings that, as Henderson points out, captured the imagination of so many writers, including Whitman.[3] In his family plots, new growth seems absent: in other words, the "compost" of the Whitman and Van Velsor family has not made its contribution. It is likely the absence of both new life and clear signifiers of the past that leaves the poet with only "inferr'd reminiscences." It is his poetic imagination, then, his inferences, that grant meaning to this important place in his family history and stand as the primary life-affirming product of those in the grave. His own work is the fertile burial space of the Whitman family.

His creative action in *Specimen Days* mirrors his poetic work in the 1881 edition of *Leaves*. In "As at Thy Portals Also Death," a poem first published in this edition, Whitman reflects on the death of his mother years before:

> As at thy portals also death,
> Entering thy sovereign, dim, illimitable grounds,
> To memories of my mother, to the divine blending, maternity,
> To her, buried and gone, yet buried not, gone not from me,
> (I see again the calm benignant face fresh and beautiful still,
> I sit by the form in the coffin,
> I kiss and kiss convulsively again the sweet lips, the cheeks, the
>   closed eyes in the coffin;)
> To her, the ideal woman, practical, spiritual, of all of earth, life,
>   love, to me the best,
> I grave a monumental line, before I go, amid these songs,
> And set a tombstone here.
>
> (LG, 497)

Whitman's biographers have long noted the poet's attachment to his mother, describing how the poet sat through the night beside his mother's casket,[4] an experience he replicates in this poem's long parenthetical inclusion. As in his autobiographical writing on his mother's family burial ground, Whitman here offers reminiscences both of his loss and of the woman herself, "buried and gone, yet buried not, gone not from me." What is most radical about this poem is that rather than insisting upon a living memory, a vision of Whitman's mother living on in his verse, it instead supplies a poetic reburial. The mother's grave shall not be forgotten or obscured, because the poet has relocated it: "I grave a monumental line, before I go, amid these songs, / And set a tombstone here." What the poem offers is not eternal life in art, but a guarantee that the burial place will not be lost; unlike those obscured, sterile graves on the hill, here his mother's tombstone will be forever legible in *Leaves of Grass*.[5]

Whitman's actions in this poem echo those of another Whitman following the war, although one of no relation. The chief quartermaster of the Military Division of the Tennessee, Edmund B. Whitman, was tasked at the end of the war with locating the burial places of Union

dead and responding to the general order that called for "an evaluation of the appropriateness of each site and a judgment as to whether
bodies should be left in place or removed to a 'permanent cemetery
near'" (Faust, 219). This other Whitman took to his task with a will,
traveling the theater of the Tennessee Division and recommending
sites for national cemeteries (228); in the process, he was ultimately
responsible for reinterring numerous bodies: "Whitman reaped what
he described as a 'Harvest of Death,' reporting that by 1869 he had
gathered 114,560 soldiers into twenty national cemeteries within his
assigned territory. . . . Ultimately each reburied soldier would also be
marked by a name—if it was in fact known—for in 1872 Congress at
last yielded to Quartermaster Meigs's insistence upon such commemoration" (235). In relocating his mother's tombstone to *Leaves*, the poet
Whitman engaged in a similar task of retrieval and preservation.

RECONSTRUCTING HIS STORY

In *Memoranda*, Whitman offered his text as a *lieu de mémoire* in place of cold history, speaking in a way that the "mute" and
"subtle" graves could not (*MDW*, 104). With the recasting of *Memoranda* in *Specimen Days*, however, he does something more overtly
historical. As Murray notes, Whitman "straightened the war chronology" in *Specimen Days*, "starting his diary with Ft. Sumter in April
1861 and ending with the Grand Review of troops in May 1865" (560).
The poet omits the poetic description of the transformation of battle-
grounds and burial grounds that is part of the original work's conclusion: "From ten years' rain and snow, in their seasons—grass, clover,
pine trees, orchards, forests—from all the noiseless miracles of soil
and sun and running streams—how peaceful and how beautiful appear to-day even the Battle-trenches, and the many hundred thousand
Cemetery mounds!" (*MDW*, 104). In the process of enfolding the text
into *Specimen Days*, the poet inserts the section with the now famous
title "The Real War Will Never Get in the Books." Where in *Memoranda*
the poet ended with an apparent celebration of the unknown graves
slowly being transformed by natural processes, a transformation that
eliminates the clear signifying function of history, here the poet seems
to lament that the truth of the war will be forgotten "in the mushy influences of current times" (*PW*, 1:116). There is a new anxiety about

forgetting in this passage that is not present in the earlier form of the *Memoranda*. This is despite his claim that it is best for future years not to know the true horrors of the war.

Even as he suggests that it is best that events cannot be captured in books, even that they *should* not be, he still insists on doing it himself in his autobiography: "The preceding notes may furnish a few stray glimpses into that life, and into those lurid interiors, never to be fully convey'd to the future. The hospital part of the drama from '61 to '65, deserves indeed to be recorded" (*PW*, 1:117). There is quite a bit of self-justification in this statement, of course, for he has already extensively recorded "the hospital part of the drama." But unlike the attitude he records in the *Memoranda*, Whitman cannot now bring himself to accept that many details will be lost. He closes his writings on the war years in *Specimen Days* with the following pessimistic conclusion: "Think how much, and of importance, will be—how much, civic and military, has already been—buried in the grave, in eternal darkness" (*PW*, 1:118). As in his description of his family plot, the national graves seem by 1882 somehow insufficient, yielding "eternal darkness." Rather than preserving memory, they are burying traces of both "civic and military" life.

Whitman's work then becomes an inadequate supplement, an attempt to stave off this darkness by offering glimpses that might illuminate what is lost. In "Final Confessions—Literary Tests" near the end of *Specimen Days*, he claims that his autobiography is divided between a retelling of the past and firsthand narratives:

> The synopsis of my early life, Long Island, New York city, and so forth, and the diary-jottings in the Secession war, tell their own story. My plan in starting what constitutes most of the middle of the book, was originally for hints and data of a Nature-poem that should carry one's experiences a few hours, commencing at noon-flush, and so through the after-part of the day—I suppose led to such idea by my own life-afternoon now arrived. But I soon found I could move at more ease, by giving the narratives at first hand. (*PW*, 1:293)

Again there is the sense of *Specimen Days* as a fragmented work, the earlier pieces serving to "tell their own story," suggesting that they are removed from the larger, more contemporary text that Whitman has constructed. In fact, however, the pieces that the poet cites as products more of the present and somehow more organic — "so afraid of dropping what smack of outdoors or sun or starlight might cling to the lines, I dared not try to meddle with or smooth them" (*PW*, 1:293) — are as much historical documents as the earlier pieces. While not addressing historicity specifically, his "One or Two Index Items" that precedes the "Collect" portion of the book makes this clear. He writes, "Several of the convalescent out-door scenes and literary items, preceding, originally appear'd in the fortnightly 'Critic,' of New York" (*PW*, 2:360). Just as he reached back to his *Memoranda* and to texts like Savage's genealogy for the early material, then, Whitman continued this practice throughout much of the rest of *Specimen Days*. In transferring his nature writings from his journals and from the subsequent periodical publications, Whitman continues the same historical work of the early portions of the text. His earlier texts do not tell their own story of his genealogy or of the war: all of his writing is refigured in the service of his story. What had once been memoranda of the war are now more truly seen as memoranda of Whitman's war, one component of the documentary of his life.

NATIONAL MEMOIRS

This reconstruction of the conflict in the context of his autobiography and his advancing years was part of a larger movement in American culture that gained steam in the 1880s. As we have seen, efforts to document the war were undertaken from the moment of its onset, but this decade proved to be the period when historical accounts of the war truly flourished, aided by such publishing events as the *Century*'s blockbuster series of first-person accounts and memoirs. As he made preparations for the project, the magazine's editor, Robert Underwood Johnson, approached Whitman about contributing to the series, despite his distaste for the poet's work:

> My dear Sir: We are making preparations for a notable series of papers on the Battles of the War to be written by participants — general officers — including Grant, McClellan, Rosecrans, Beauregard, Longstreet, Joe Johnson and others. These we desire to sup-

plement by short pithy papers on different phases of the War. At Mr. Gilder's request I write to ask if you would not write us a short, comprehensive paper on Hospital Nursing in Washington and on the field—something human and vivid. We should like about four thousand words.

The object of the supplementary papers is to give the life, the spirit, the color, of the War, which may be left out by the generals.

Of course, we should like the paper to cover different ground from what you have before written if possible—at least to cover it in a different way. (*WWC*, 2:218)

One can only imagine how Whitman's eyes must have rolled at the idea of preparing a "short, comprehensive" piece on the subject of the hospitals that would simultaneously be "human and vivid." At the same time, however, the urge to supply "supplementary papers" that would provide a fuller account than those offered by the leading military actors was one that Whitman had himself addressed in his own writing, even as he acknowledged the inevitable impossibility of such an undertaking.

Many of the generals that Johnson alludes to in his letter went on to publish pieces in the *Century* as well as entire autobiographies during this decade, but it was Whitman's general, Grant, who produced the benchmark for all other memoirs of the period. His *Personal Memoirs of U.S. Grant* met with huge success, and it made the war "Grant's war" in a fashion similar to the way in which *Specimen Days* made *Memoranda of the War* into memoranda of Whitman's war. When Johnson initially approached Grant about his autobiography, the general demurred: " 'It's all in Badeau,' he told Johnson, referring to Adam Badeau's three-volume *Military History of U.S. Grant*, which had recently been published" (Smith, 622). He had already told his story. The collapse of his business and the subsequent financial distress in which he found himself induced him to change his mind, as he admits in the preface to the first volume.[6] Of the work's contents, he notes, "The comments are my own, and show how I saw the matters treated of whether others saw them in the same light or not" (Grant, 1:9). As if to highlight the individual nature of his account, Grant includes as an appendix his official report of 1865 to Edwin M. Stanton, Secretary of War. This is not a history of the Civil War; it is solely his view from the field.

Despite the fact that the work encompasses two volumes, it is also oddly truncated. This is no doubt due to Grant's severe illness at the time of composition, but the absence of his years as president and afterward as a prominent international figure is striking in a work purporting to be a memoir. Similarly, as Martin Murray has commented, Whitman's decision to ignore almost completely the ten years following the war in his own autobiography is also remarkable: "Those years had been remarkably rich ones personally and professionally, and Whitman's decision to overlook them is pregnant with meaning" ("*Specimen Days*," 560). Murray suggests that the poet's intention in omitting reference to the professional setbacks and successes of this period is to "present a more approachable character, with whom a reader might identify and who might emulate the essential verities that Whitman's autobiography seeks to promote" (561). While this might be the case, the elision also allowed the poet to avoid the political complications of the period and to represent the war as the fulcrum of the book. Similarly, Hutchinson argues of the omission, "The decade 1865–1875 was very lonely and depressing for the poet, not easy to integrate into the story he is trying to construct of his life course and the nation's" ("*Specimen Days*," 680–81). Both of these critics note the way that the work puts forth a particular personal and national narrative that does not create a space for the contentious years of Reconstruction, an omission that Grant replicates in his own autobiography. Both Whitman and Grant begin with a family genealogy but spend the majority of time discussing their experiences during the war, making it the defining feature of their life stories.

In the conclusion of his memoir, Grant reflects on his illness, and although his work does not contain the same story of recovery that occupies the final third of *Specimen Days*, the general sees in his condition and in the compassionate response of people, North and South, evidence of a brighter future for the nation:

> I feel that we are on the eve of a new era, when there is to be great
> harmony between the Federal and Confederate. I cannot stay to
> be a living witness to the correctness of this prophecy; but I feel

it within me that it is to be so. The universally kind feeling expressed for me at a time when it was supposed that each day would prove my last, seemed to me the beginning of the answer to "let us have peace." (2:553)

As Murray remarks of Whitman, the poet "was interested not just in his own healing, but that of his countrymen" (562). Hutchinson makes a similar point regarding Whitman's discussion of his recovery: "Inasmuch as this section of the narrative begins in May 1876 . . . Whitman symbolically connects his own rejuvenation with that of the nation in the centennial celebrations" ("*Specimen Days*," 679). A similar statement might be made of Grant, who saw the seeds of true national unity revealed through his terminal illness. Although his autobiography was published several years after Whitman's, his work represents a further step in the ongoing process of recovery.

ABRAHAM LINCOLN AND WHITMAN
THE PUBLIC HISTORIAN

It is no coincidence that at around the same time Whitman turned to writing his eclectic autobiography, he was also reinventing himself as a kind of public historian. He first delivered his public lecture "Death of Abraham Lincoln" in April 1879 and continued to deliver it annually until 1890. Whitman's account of the president in this lecture is pointedly historical; the poet even employed his friend Peter Doyle's account of the assassination to offer his audience what appears to be his own first-person report of the event. Gregory Eiselein notes of the poet's treatment in the speech, "Whitman's handling of Lincoln's death in the lectures diametrically reverses the musical, ethereal, often abstract, heavily symbolized style of 'Lilacs.' In his lecture . . . Whitman depicts the scene of the murder with dramatic immediacy, as if he were an eyewitness. The narration is suspenseful, detailed, and focuses on specifics (sometimes minutiae)."[7] The lecture is much like *Specimen Days* in miniature, collecting excerpts from other publications, some dating back to 1874, including *Memoranda of the War*, and combining them with new material to create a historical account connected to his own life. Whitman preserved a newspaper report on the event that speaks to the poet's new role:

"A New Departure"

One of the events of the week has been the new departure made by "Walt Whitman" in coming before the public as a lecturer and reader of his own poems. . . . It was not Abraham Lincoln as an incident or an accident that Mr. Whitman discussed, but Abraham Lincoln in his relation to the historical conditions which preceded him, which surrounded him, and of which he became the central figure. It was a clear, wise, and instructive summing up of all the facts which paved the way for the memorable tragedy which furnished the blood in which nationality was again cemented. He drew the picture of the central figure of that terrible time with something of the breadth, something of the force, of Michael Angelo, presenting him both in life and in death, in that larger aspect of his relation to historical events, and to the country at large, in its past, present and future, and little upon his individuality, except as it illustrated the great points by which the drama of emancipations was begun [line missing]

I have dwelt upon this feature in the lecture because it marks the difference so strongly between Walt Whitman's method of looking at his subject and that of an ordinary lecturer, who goes to work to make an hour's talk out of a great man. It is the philosophy of history instead of a crude and probably biased opinion of a person and his work. It is a study from a social instead of a personal point of view, the latter of which is always unreliable, because tinged with the author's prejudices or partialities.[8]

The poet's apparent success in following the "philosophy of history" is evident in the reviewer's emphasis on how Whitman employs the facts to place Lincoln in context. Given the poet's affection for the president, it is also noteworthy that the review highlights how Whitman has produced a social "study" rather than simply a personal and "probably biased opinion" of his subject.

While it is apparent from reading the work that the poet relies a great deal on his own impressions and opinions in his lecture, his practice of carefully weaving his own story into both Lincoln's and the nation's story likely contributed a great deal to the impression that his portrayal of his subject was impartial. This process is clearly evident in his description of first viewing President Lincoln in New York, which he had published earlier in the *New York Weekly Graphic* (*PW*, 2:497n). He describes the encounter in a context representative of his own history as linked to that of the nation:

> Almost in the same neighborhood I distinctly remember'd seeing Lafayette on his visit to America in 1825. I had also personally seen and heard, various years afterward, how Andrew Jackson, Clay, Webster, Hungarian Kossuth, Filibuster Walker, the Prince of Wales on his visit, and other celebres, native and foreign, had been welcom'd there—all that indescribable human roar and magnetism, unlike any other sound in the universe—the glad exulting thunder-shouts of countless unloos'd throats of men! But on this occasion, not a voice—not a sound. (*PW*, 2:500)

In comparison to the poet's earlier published accounts of this event, Floyd Stovall notes of these and subsequent passages, "These lines are quite different from the corresponding passage in *TR* [*Two Rivulets*] and in *NYWG* [*New York Weekly Graphic*]" (*PW*, 2:500n). The most significant difference here is the way that Whitman connects Lincoln's arrival to one of the most crucial events in the story of his own life (that of meeting Lafayette when he was a boy) and his own observation of any number of other prominent figures. Although the passage begins with Whitman twice asserting his role as firsthand observer, his "I" quickly gives way to the procession of national figures and the contrast between their appearance and that of the late president. In creating a comparison meant to highlight the ominous beginnings of Lincoln's presidency, Whitman also renders Lincoln one more pivotal character in his, and the nation's, narrative.

Critics have often written about the connection between the poet and the president, and it is worth considering these lines from the speech, unpublished by Whitman in any of his previous work, referring to the president's place in American history: "The final use of a heroic-eminent life—especially of a heroic-eminent death—is its indirect filtering into a nation and the race, and to give, often at many removes, but unerringly, age after age, color and fibre to the personalism of the youth and maturity of that age, and of mankind" (*PW*, 2:508). The language is an unmistakable echo of the poet's famous line from the 1855 preface — "The proof of a poet is that his country absorbs him as affectionately as he has absorbed it" (*LG*, 729) — as well as the 1855 poem later entitled "Song of Myself": "You will hardly know who I am or what I mean, / But I shall be good health to you nevertheless, / and filter and fibre your blood" (*LG*, 89). In reaching back to these early lines, Whitman places Lincoln into his poetic history, as well. The president achieves that to which the poet himself had long aspired. Eiselein notes, "Lincoln's death becomes a metaphor for the bloody war itself and the climax of a lofty tragic drama that redeems the Union. Whitman's lecture turns Lincoln's assassination into the ceremonial sacrifice that gives new life to the nation."[9] This is undoubtedly the case; yet, as these lines from his earlier work remind us, Lincoln's death held similar significance for Whitman's poetic project, particularly once he had reconstructed it with the Civil War at its center. The "heroic-eminent life" is shared by both the poet and the president, and the latter's death becomes a key moment in the life of Whitman and the nation. The lecture's conclusion, then, fittingly refers to the assassinated Lincoln as simultaneously "Dear to the Muse" and "thrice dear to Nationality" (*PW*, 2:509). Lincoln is critical to both poetry and politics, a fusing of nation and art that Whitman himself had hoped to embody. His tribute to Lincoln is his reprise of the task he set for himself so many years ago in 1855.

WHITMAN'S PICTURE-GALLERY

In a little house I keep pictures suspended, it is not a fix'd house,
It is round, it is only a few inches from one side to the other;
Yet behold, it has room for all the shows of the world, all
    memories!
Here the tableaus of life, and here the groupings of death;
Here, do you know this? this is cicerone himself,
With finger rais'd he points to the prodigal pictures.
           "My Picture-Gallery," 1881 (*LG*, 401–2)

Following the Civil War, Whitman, like all Americans, confronted a radically changed and wounded nation. This was literally brought home to him in the exhausted personage of his brother George and in the influx of freed slaves in Washington.[10] Professionally, he faced not only the political upheaval brought on by the changes in administration, but he also had to adjust to his new literary reality: the proliferation of publishing venues, their new reach, and the speed with which news traveled, combined with his own new celebrity. Added to this were personal struggles, including the loss of his mother and his own declining health. In the midst of this remarkable period of transition, he turned to the task of sifting through his own experiences of the war in order to give voice to them in poetry and prose and to order the "prodigal pictures" of the hospital scenes into a form that would "justify" them and the role that he played in them.

The self-referential image of the speaker in "My Picture-Gallery" as a "cicerone" pointing the way through a gallery of memories of "tableaus of life" and "groupings of death" in his own mind ("a little house") provides some insight into how Whitman viewed his task in those years following the war, although the poet began experimenting with these lines even before 1855 (*LG*, 401–2). In the wake of the war and its aftermath, he both organized and interpreted events for readers and for himself, not simply once, but repeatedly. In "As I Ponder'd in Silence," a poem first published in the 1871 edition of *Leaves of Grass* and retained as the second poem in the 1881 edition, the speaker describes "Returning upon my poems, considering, lingering long" (*LG*, 1), only to be confronted by a "Phantom" that demands, "*Know'st thou not there is but one theme for ever-enduring bards? / And that is the theme of War*" (*LG*, 2). Given his continual reconsiderations of his experiences during the war and his own reexamination of his poetry in its light, it is no surprise that the poet came to see the war as the pivotal event of his life.

It is also not surprising that scholars examining Whitman and Reconstruction have found the task so daunting, and not simply because of the sheer magnitude of personal and public events that Whitman grappled with during these years. Following the "finger rais'd" to examine the scenes from those war years that Whitman repeatedly sets before us, it is easy to get lost in those dramatic pictures and to overlook the guide himself. At the same time, in looking at those exhibits that crowd his internal picture gallery, Whitman and, by extension, his readers, are again and again confronted with the blank spaces within and between the images, the graves UNKNOWN, the struggles and deaths that elude the written record of history.

Luke Mancuso noted as recently as 1998, "The Reconstruction Whitman remains the Whitman who has yet to be fully scrutinized by Whitman scholars and readers alike" ("Reconstruction," 577). Given the complexity of this period, this is undoubtedly a gap that will persist; however, the fact that scholars and readers have not succeeded completely in coming to terms with this aspect of the poet and his work cannot be ascribed to a critical failing or omission. The "Reconstruction Whitman," no less than the Whitman who declared long before the Civil War that he contained "multitudes," is uniquely plural and, yes, contradictory. He is the public employee and the literary professional, the public intellectual and the outcast, the symbolic mourner and the careful historian, in every case toiling in the shadow cast by the nation's terrible conflict. As Whitman concludes in "As I Ponder'd in Silence," the war rages on in his book even as the nation seeks peace, taking on new life in his verse and new meaning in his recollections:

> I too haughty Shade also sing war, and a longer and greater one than
>   any,
> Waged in my book with varying fortune, with flight, advance and
>   retreat, victory deferr'd and wavering,
> (Yet methinks certain, or as good as certain, at the last,) the field the
>   world,
> For life and death, for the Body and for the eternal Soul,
> Lo, I too am come, chanting the chant of battles,
> I above all promote brave soldiers.

(LG, 2)

Ultimately, as with so much else of critical importance in the poet's verse, the final victory, the accomplished reconciliation, awaits the future.

Notes

1. WALT WHITMAN'S RECONSTRUCTION

1. Allan Nevins, *The Organized War to Victory* (New York: Konecky and Konecky, 1971), 366.

2. Ibid., 365.

3. For a concise description of the complex Reconstruction era, see Eric Foner and Olivia Mahoney, *America's Reconstruction: People and Politics after the Civil War* (Baton Rouge: Louisiana State University Press, 1997). This work includes numerous images and photographs that help to portray many of the important figures and events of the period.

4. Ibid., 134.

5. The commemoration of the 150th anniversary of the outbreak of the Civil War has brought the ongoing challenges of reconstruction into stark relief, with a "secession ball" in South Carolina and events across the nation highlighting the ways in which the war continues to be a source of tension and conflict more than a century later.

6. Luke Mancuso, *The Strange Sad War Revolving: Walt Whitman, Reconstruction, and the Emergence of Black Citizenship, 1865–1876* (Columbia, SC: Camden House, 1997). Hereafter cited parenthetically.

7. W. Wynn Thomas, *The Lunar Light of Whitman's Poetry* (Cambridge, MA: Harvard University Press, 1987), 217. Hereafter cited parenthetically.

8. Passages from the 1855 *Leaves of Grass* are taken from *The Walt Whitman Archive*, edited by Ed Folsom and Ken Price, ⟨http://whitmanarchive.org/published/LG/1855/whole.html⟩. Hereafter cited parenthetically as *Leaves*, 1855, whitmanarchive.org.

9. Frank Luther Mott, *A History of American Magazines*, 5 vols. (Cambridge, MA: Harvard University Press, 1938), 3:5. Hereafter cited parenthetically.

10. Amanda Gailey, "The Publishing History of *Leaves of Grass*," in *A Companion to Walt Whitman*, ed. Donald D. Kummings (Malden, MA: Blackwell, 2006), 424. Hereafter cited parenthetically.

11. Walt Whitman, *Leaves of Grass*, Comprehensive Reader's Edition, edited by Harold W. Blodgett and Sculley Bradley (New York: New York University Press, 1965), 163. Hereafter *LG*.

12. Walt Whitman, *Prose Works 1892*, ed. Floyd Stovall, 2 vols. (New York: New York University Press, 1963–1964), 1:115. Hereafter *PW*.

13. Thomas likewise notes, "In his own body Whitman bears the lurid stigmata of that war's sacrifice, as in his mind he has borne the burden of his memory" (*Lunar Light*, 231).

14. He appears to have considered this project quite seriously. The Harned Collection in the Library of Congress contains several items, including sample lines, a cast of characters, and some preliminary research on the Crusades. Thomas Biggs Harned Collection of the Papers of Walt Whitman, Manuscript Division, Library of Congress, Washington, D.C.

15. Reel 4, Harned Collection, LOC.

16. Ibid.

17. Thomas F. Haddox, "Whitman's End of History: 'As I Sat Alone by Blue Ontario's Shore,' *Democratic Vistas*, and the Postbellum Politics of Nostalgia," *Walt Whitman Quarterly Review* 22 (Summer 2004), 4.

2. PERIODICALS, POLITICS, AND THE NEW PAPER WORLD

1. Alice Fahs, *The Imagined Civil War: Popular Literature of the North and South, 1861–1865* (Chapel Hill: University of North Carolina Press, 2001), 42–43. Hereafter cited parenthetically.

2. Until fairly recently, it has not been easy to read Whitman's original periodical publications. Now, however, the online Whitman archive (⟨http://whitmanarchive.org⟩) has presented nearly all of the known periodical publications, including images of the pages on which they appear.

3. Charles G. Steffen, "Newspapers for Free: The Economies of Newspaper Circulation in the Early Republic," *Journal of the Early Republic*, 23, no. 3 (Autumn 2003): 381–419.

4. Reel 3, Harned Collection, LOC.

5. Ibid.

6. Ted Genoways, "Civil War Poems in 'Drum-Taps' and 'Memories of President Lincoln,'" in *A Companion to Walt Whitman*, ed. Donald D. Kummings (Malden, MA: Blackwell, 2006), 526–27.

7. David C. Smith, *History of Papermaking in the United States* (New York: Lockwood, 1970), 64. Hereafter cited parenthetically.

8. Dard Hunter, *Papermaking: The History and Technique of an Ancient Craft* (New York: Dover, 1978), 382.

9. Quoted in Ann Zwinger and Edwin Way Teale, *A Conscious Stillness: Two*

Naturalists on Thoreau's Rivers (New York: Harper and Row, 1982), 178–79. I am grateful to Wayne Franklin for making me aware of this anecdote.

10. As Smith notes, "The Civil War, with its great drain on paper and men, was the catalytic agent in discovering these new fibres" (130).

11. Philip Gaskell, *New Introduction to Bibliography* (New York: Oxford University Press, 1972), 206.

12. Ibid., 67.

13. Ibid., 114.

14. Quoted in Joel Myerson, *Walt Whitman: A Descriptive Bibliography* (Pittsburgh: University of Pittsburgh Press, 1993), 25. Hereafter cited parenthetically.

15. Quoted in Ed Folsom, *Whitman Making Books / Books Making Whitman: A Catalog and Commentary* (Iowa City, IA: Obermann Center for Advanced Studies, 2005), 24. Hereafter *WMB*.

16. Gaskell, 256.

17. Ibid.

18. Ronald J. Zboray, "Antebellum Reading and the Ironies of Technological Innovation," *American Quarterly* 40, no. 1 (March 1988): 66–67.

19. Richard B. Kielbowicz, *News in the Mail: The Press, Post Office, and Public Information, 1700–1860s* (New York: Greenwood, 1989), 181.

20. James Playsted Wood, *Magazines in the United States*, 2nd ed. (New York: Ronald Press, 1956), 100.

21. Susan Belasco, "Walt Whitman's Poetry in Periodicals," in *The Walt Whitman Archive*, ed. Ed Folsom and Kenneth M. Price. ⟨http://www.whitmanarchive .org/periodical/general_introduction/index.html⟩.

22. The poem was titled "Proud Music of the Sea-Storm" when first published in the *Atlantic* (*LG*, 402n).

23. Ed Folsom and Kenneth Price write, for example, "One can glimpse Whitman's emotional state in 'Prayer of Columbus' . . . which depicts Columbus—a mask of Whitman himself—as a battered, wrecked, paralyzed, old man, misunderstood in his own time" ("Walt Whitman," ⟨http://www.whitmanarchive .org/biography/walt_whitman/index.html#goodgray⟩).

24. ⟨http://whitmanarchive.org/published/periodical/poems/per0013⟩.

25. In an interview with the *St. Louis Post-Dispatch*, for example, Whitman is queried not only about prominent literary figures like Bret Harte and about the state of American poetry, but he is given prompts like this: "And how about religion?" (to which he responded, "I could only say that, as she develops, America will be a thoroughly religious nation") and "Politically?" and "How about

Canada?" (quoted in Robert R. Hubach, "Three Uncollected St. Louis Interviews of Walt Whitman," *American Literature* 14 (May 1942): 146–47).

26. *New York Daily Graphic*, December 7, 1874, 265. Newspaper Collection, American Antiquarian Society.

27. Ibid.

28. *New York Daily Graphic*, December 19, 1874, 357. Newspaper Collection, American Antiquarian Society.

29. See issues of *Daily Graphic* for December 21–23, for example. Newspaper Collection, American Antiquarian Society.

30. Horace Traubel, *With Walt Whitman in Camden* (New York: Rowman and Littlefield, 1961), 3:560. Hereafter *WWC*. The two men appear to have been friends as well as colleagues. On visiting New York in 1878, the poet took an evening boat trip in a vessel owned by Croly. See *PW*, 1:169.

31. Walt Whitman, *The Correspondence, 1868–1875*, ed. Edwin Haviland Miller (New York: New York University Press, 1961), 2:204n. Hereafter *Corr*.

32. David W. Levy, "David Goodman Croly," in *American National Biography*, ed. John A. Garraty and Mark C. Carnes, 24 vols. (New York: Oxford University Press, 1999), 5:756.

33. Jerome Loving, *Walt Whitman: The Song of Himself* (Berkeley: University of California Press, 1999), 352.

34. Quoted in Julius Marcus Bloch, *Miscegenation, Melaleukation, and Mrs. Lincoln's Dog* (New York: Schaum, 1958), 42.

35. See Bloch for a discussion of how the pamphlet was promoted by Croly and employed by Democrats to attack Republicans.

36. David G. Croly and George Wakeman, *Miscegenation* (1864; Upper Saddle River, NJ: Literature House, 1970), 18–19. Hereafter cited parenthetically.

37. Katherine Nicholson Ings, "Between Hoax and Hope: Miscegenation and Nineteenth-Century Interracial Romance," *Literature Compass* 3/4 (2006), 650. Ings examines the ways that the authors employ pseudoscientific language and how that language intersects with literary representations of interracial relationships. She also notes some of the approving responses to the pamphlet by reformers like the Grimke sisters (650).

38. David W. Blight, *Race and Reunion: The Civil War in American Memory* (Cambridge, MA: Belknap Press of Harvard University Press, 2001), 101. Hereafter cited parenthetically.

39. Foner and Mahoney, 88.

40. Quoted in David S. Reynolds, *Walt Whitman's America: A Cultural Biography* (New York: Vintage, 1996), 373. Hereafter cited parenthetically.

41. A number of critics have looked closely at Whitman's writings on race, beginning in 1955 with Leadie M. Clark's *Walt Whitman's Concept of the American Common Man* (New York: Philosophical Library, 1955) and with increasing frequency over the past twenty years. Karen Sanchez-Eppler has attempted to bridge the gap between Whitman's poetic ideals and those expressed in the novel, arguing, "In miscegenation Whitman finds an extremely potent instance of mediation, a blatant demonstration that otherness can be reconciled, that the opposites of black and white can meet and blend." *Touching Liberty: Abolition, Feminism, and the Politics of the Body* (Berkeley: University of California Press, 1993), 59.

42. Debra Rosenthal, *Race Mixture in Nineteenth-Century U.S. and Spanish American Fictions: Gender, Culture, and Nation-Building* (Chapel Hill: University of North Carolina Press, 2004), 68.

43. Ed Folsom, "Lucifer and Ethiopia: Whitman, Race, and Politics Before the Civil War and After," in *A Historical Guide to Walt Whitman*, ed. David S. Reynolds (New York: Oxford University Press, 2000), 82.

44. Levy, 757.

45. Carl Bode, "Columbia's Carnal Bed," *American Quarterly* 15, no. 1 (1963), 58–59.

46. Levy, 756. The magazine championed a strikingly elitist form of positivist thinking. See Gillis J. Harp's *Positivist Republic: Auguste Comte and the Reconstruction of American Liberalism, 1865–1920* (University Park: Pennsylvania State University Press, 1995), 44–46.

47. Gerald J. Baldasty, "The Nineteenth-Century Origins of Modern American Journalism," *Proceedings of the American Antiquarian Society* 100, no. 2 (October 1990): 413–14. Hereafter cited parenthetically.

48. Baldasty, *The Commercialization of News in the Nineteenth Century* (Madison: University of Wisconsin Press, 1992), 122–25. Hereafter cited parenthetically.

49. Croly, a "futurist," did not leave behind the question of race entirely. In fact, his later text *Glimpses of the Future* (1888), published shortly before his death, argues exactly the opposite thesis from the one advanced in the hoax *Miscegenation*. He writes, "I presume the race of mulattoes is dying out. . . . The white race is dominant and will keep their position, no matter how numerous

the negroes may become." Quoted in Werner Sollors, *Interracialism: Black-White Intermarriage in American History, Literature, and Law* (New York: Oxford University Press, 2000), 1. The comment is further evidence, if any were needed, that the views expressed in the early pamphlet were anything but sincere.

50. Ed Folsom and Kenneth M. Price, *Re-Scripting Walt Whitman: An Introduction to His Life and Work* (Malden, MA: Blackwell, 2005). ⟨http://www.whitman archive.org/criticism/current/arc.00152.html⟩. Hereafter cited parenthetically.

51. Hy B. Turner, *When Giants Ruled: The Story of Park Row, New York's Great Newspaper Street* (New York: Fordham University Press, 1999), 60.

52. Ibid., 80.

53. Quoted in Bingham Duncan, *Whitelaw Reid: Journalist, Politician, Diplomat* (Athens: University of Georgia Press, 1975), 44. Hereafter cited parenthetically.

54. Heather Cox Richardson, *The Death of Reconstruction: Race, Labor, and Politics in the Post–Civil War North, 1865–1901* (Cambridge, MA: Harvard University Press, 2001), 99.

55. Ibid., 102.

56. Robert Leigh Davis, "*Democratic Vistas*," in *A Companion to Walt Whitman*, ed. Donald D. Kummings (Malden, MA: Blackwell, 2006), 544.

57. For a discussion of this episode as well as a careful survey of the attitudes of American editors during this period, see Robert Scholnick's "Whitman and the Magazines: Some Documentary Evidence," *American Literature* 44, no. 2 (1972): 222–46.

58. Quoted in Gary Scharnhorst, "Rediscovered Nineteenth-Century Whitman Articles," *Walt Whitman Quarterly Review* 19 (Winter/Spring 2002): 183.

59. Todd Richardson, "Walt Whitman's 'Lively Corpse' in 1871: The American Press on the Rumor of Whitman's Death," *Walt Whitman Quarterly Review* 15 (Summer 1997): 2.

60. Quoted in ibid., 10.

3. WHITMAN AND THE ELUSIVE SITE OF MEMORY

1. Thomas J. Brown provides a revealing table that shows that, while the state of Virginia erected ten monuments to Confederate soldiers between the years of 1863 and 1879, thirty-four were erected from 1880 to 1899 (Brown, *The Public Art of Civil War Commemoration* [Boston: Bedford/St. Martin's, 2004], 24).

2. For a discussion of the proliferation of "records" of the war, see Fahs, 50–55.

3. George W. Childs, "Important Announcement! (Wait and Get the Best.) Lossing's Pictorial History of the Great Rebellion." Publisher's Prospectus (Philadelphia: George W. Childs, 1862[?]), 2. American Antiquarian Society stacks, Z780 C537 1862.

4. Malcolm McGregor Dana, *The Norwich memorial: The Annals of Norwich, New London County, Connecticut, in the Great Rebellion of 1861–1865* (Norwich, CT: J. J. Jewett, 1873), iii–iv, Making of America database, University of Michigan, ⟨http://name.umdl.umich.edu/ac11756.0001.001⟩.

5. Rev. Tryon Edwards, "Mason and Dixon's Line," *Harper's New Monthly Magazine* (September 1876): 549, Making of America database, Cornell University Library, ⟨http://cdl.library.cornell.edu/cgi-bin/moa/moa-cgi?notisid=ABK4014-0053-75⟩.

6. Constance Fenimore Woolson, "Rodman the Keeper," in *Constance Fenimore Woolson: Selected Stories and Travel Narratives*, ed. Victoria Brehm and Sharon Dean (Knoxville: University of Tennessee Press, 2004), 127.

7. A writer for the *New York Times* noted in an 1869 article entitled "Shall the Hatchet Ever Be Buried?" that "Decoration Day" could never become a national holiday because "it is an appeal to the patriotism of one section at the expense of the pride and feeling of the other section. . . . It is a method of reminding the North that it is a conqueror, and the South that it is conquered. It is an attempt to convert even the graves of the dead into testimony affecting the history of millions who are living." The author laments that the practice of memorializing the Union dead brings back "bitter memories of conflict, scattering afresh the seeds of hate." "Shall the Hatchet Ever Be Buried?" *New York Times*, June 14, 1869, 4.

8. The move to document the Civil War would reach a crescendo in the public imagination in the 1880s. The decade would see not only the start of the U.S. War Department's publication of its seventy-volume *The War of the Rebellion: A Compilation of the Official Records of the Union and Confederate Armies*, but also the *Century* magazine's acclaimed series on the war and Mark Twain's two-volume edition of Grant's memoirs. With his lectures on the death of Lincoln and the publication of *Specimen Days*, Whitman became increasingly involved in this historical effort, as the concluding chapter demonstrates. All of these efforts were extensions of the impulse to capture and preserve the record of the war before it disappeared.

9. Martin G. Murray notes the connection to Alcott's work in *"Specimen Days,"* in *A Companion to Walt Whitman*, ed. Donald D. Kummings (Malden, MA: Blackwell, 2006), 555.

10. In his study of Whitman's *Memoranda*, Mark Feldman sees Whitman questioning the efficacy of poetry as a means of representing the war and searching for a "representational form that would preserve the convulsiveness of the period" ("Remembering a Convulsive War: Whitman's *Memoranda During the War* and the Therapeutics of Display," *Walt Whitman Quarterly Review* 23 (Summer/Fall 2005): 2). Hereafter cited parenthetically.

11. Murray, 555.

12. Timothy Sweet, *Traces of War: Poetry, Photography, and the Crisis of the Union* (Baltimore: Johns Hopkins University Press, 1990), 47. Hereafter cited parenthetically.

13. Walt Whitman, *Memoranda During the War*, ed. Peter Coviello (New York: Oxford University Press, 2004), 3. Hereafter *MDW*. Because the *Collected Works* only includes *MDW* as it appears in *Specimen Days*, many passages are omitted or truncated, with the full phrasings appearing only in footnotes or appendixes. Coviello's edition, which reprints the first edition of 1875–1876, is used here for ease of reference, but readers should refer to *Prose Works* 1 of the *Collected Works* for full editorial commentary.

14. Pierre Nora, "Between Memory and History: Les Lieux de Mémoire," trans. Marc Roudebush, in *History and Memory in African-American Culture*, ed. Geneviève Fabre and Robert O'Meally (New York: Oxford University Press, 1994), 285. Hereafter cited parenthetically.

15. Luke Mancuso explores how Whitman's *Drum-Taps* poems create *lieux de mémoire* "as an antidote to concrete sites of postwar fragmentation." ("Civil War," in *A Companion to Walt Whitman*, ed. Donald D. Kummings [Malden, MA: Blackwell, 2006], 300). Mancuso emphasizes Nora's use of the term "to account for the cultural divide that separates us from a collective sense of traditional identity and social values" (300), a divide that Whitman's poetic imagery addresses. In *Memoranda*, the poet explores the gap between what Nora describes as the archival nature of history and the more embodied and communal nature of memory.

16. Whitman included this strange phrase both in 1875–1876 in *Memoranda* and in *Specimen Days* a few years later: it may refer to the growing tide of calls for national unity, the failures of Reconstruction, or to the counter-historical narratives of Confederate apologists, and perhaps all three at once.

17. Stephen Cushman, "Walt Whitman's Real War," in *Wars Within a War: Controversy and Conflict over the American Civil War*, ed. Joan Waugh and Gary W.

Gallagher (Chapel Hill: University of North Carolina Press, 2009), 141. Hereafter cited parenthetically.

18. In *Specimen Days*, Whitman qualifies this assertion: "There are now, I believe, over seventy of them" (*PW*, 1:115). One of the distinctive elements of *Specimen Days* is Whitman's care for precision and his caution in making assertions. Both point to his awareness of the autobiography as his contribution to his own historical record.

19. Sweet sees in this episode a demonstration of why Whitman might find historical representation problematic: "Perhaps if we knew the 'interiors' of the war we would criticize its prosecution, weighing the ends against the means. As it is, Whitman's repeated interrogations of the possibility of historical representation shield the means from a too scrupulous examination" (51).

20. Sweet refers to this passage as it appears in *Specimen Days*, where Whitman has replaced the word "varify" with "verify." In either case, the reader is made to take action, employing his or her imagination to invent scenes in "all the forms that different circumstances, individuals, places, &c., could afford"— as in "varify," or, in Sweet's sense, to invent scenes against which Whitman's can be compared and "verified."

21. Sweet notes that "the metaphor of embalming specifically criticizes the textual mode of representation in general by suggesting that texts preserve only the empty form of experience" (46). For his part, Thomas sees something more positive in Whitman's image: "It was particularly important that he should seek out [the unknown soldiers dying on the battlefield] in imagination so as to 'embalm' them in memory, and so at least to preserve them from the devouring worm of oblivion" (*Lunar Light*, 216). Both readings appear plausible, as the passage represents yet another instance where Whitman expresses his grave doubts regarding print's ability to represent exactly that experience he is attempting to capture in his own text.

22. Cushman is particularly critical of this passage, describing it as "literary fraud" (147). His criticism would seem to point to Whitman's concern with the "cold types" of history. For the poet, the point of the scene would not be whether or not this particular event took place in exactly this way—that is the question for the historian. Rather, he is concerned with all of those who are unaccounted for, who elude the record, for which this soldier is a "type." Cushman notes a modern reader who finds this scene moving, and writes that the reason for her emotional response "could not include the reality or authenticity of Whitman's

account. The only reality present in Whitman's account is the reality of poetic form" (145; 146–47). Whitman sought to use his writing to make his readers feel something of the war beyond the arguments over battles and tactics, and at least as far as concerns the reader that Cushman mentions, he appears to have succeeded.

23. This final statement is quite literally true, for, as many Southerners complained at the time, once the national cemeteries were organized, many bodies of Northern soldiers were exhumed and relocated to the federally sanctioned resting places, while the bodies of most Confederate soldiers who died in the North had to be retrieved by family members or private citizens and brought South, if they could be found at all. See Drew Gilpin Faust, *This Republic of Suffering: Death and the American Civil War* (New York: Knopf, 2008), 236–39. Hereafter cited parenthetically.

24. Feldman sees the continual presence of the war for Whitman as evidence of its continued "convulsiveness": "For Whitman the war continued to be convulsive. As late as 1888, when asked if he thought back to the days of the war, he replied, 'I do not need to. I have never left them. They are here, now'" (20). For Nora, this presence of the past is part of what marks the separation of memory from history, and it is the continual assertion of that presence, the willful effort to make the past present, that defines the *lieux de mémoire*.

25. Feldman sees the prose writings as marking a much more decisive break from the attitudes that mark Whitman's prewar poetry (2); however, the continuity between the two is not solely limited to ideas of generative rebirth, but both the poetry and the *Memoranda* demonstrate the same desire to transcend textual representation to establish a link between the reader and the past that is different from the signifying modes of history and traditional poetic forms.

26. In postwar editions, the poet revises these lines to emphasize the historical nature of his presentation: "Would you hear of an old-time sea fight? / Would you learn who won by the light of the moon and stars? / List to the yarn, as my grandmother's father the sailor told it to me. / Our foe was no skulk in his ship I tell you (said he)" (*LG*, 69). In the prewar editions, Whitman omits this narrative element entirely, allowing his speaker to speak for himself as a participant and witness. In this case, Whitman's prose seems to allow him to relive an experience more fully than the revised poetry does.

27. While the exact source of the article that Whitman quotes is unknown, Whitman preserved an article very similar to it years later from the November 3rd, 1880, *Philadelphia Ledger*. The correspondent writes, "The Andersonville

prison pen has just been visited by a correspondent, who found oaks fifteen feet high growing upon part of it, while near the southern limit was a thrifty cotton field. The caves in which the men burrowed are all gone. On the north hill, which sent its slope down to the south, the rains of fifteen years have carried away their roofs and have washed the earth away until they have gullied ravines thirty feet across at the top and as deep, with crumbling, precipitous sides. On the south hill, facing the north, the caves are marked only by the depressions of the ground where the roofs have fallen. The hollows have not entirely filled, and probably never will, now that they are covered with the meager grass and weeds of Southern Georgia. The stream which was such a horrible agent of death is now a clean brook about four feet wide and ten inches deep. The sides, which, when trodden by the feet of tens of thousands of men daily, were a soggy quagmire, are gaining solidity, though still swampy, and in some places impassable." Reel 4, Harned Collection, LOC.

4. "BY THE ROADSIDE" AND WHITMAN'S
NARRATIVE OF POETIC (RE)AWAKENING

1. William B. Ness, "Bathed in War's Perfume: Whitman and the Flag," *Prospects* 27 (2002): 266.

2. Gay Wilson Allen, *The New Walt Whitman Handbook* (New York: New York University Press, 1975), 147.

3. Quoted in George Hutchinson, "The Civil War," in *Walt Whitman: An Encyclopedia*, ed. J. R. LeMaster and Donald D. Kummings (New York: Garland, 1998), 124.

4. James E. Miller, *Walt Whitman* (New York: Twayne, 1962), 82.

5. Like James Miller, Stark sees the cluster as working in tandem with others; however, her readings of images at times seem forced, as when she argues that the picture of "The Runner" "with lightly closed fists and arms partially rais'd" (*LG*, 275) "could be read as weapons 'partially rais'd' for the approaching war." Stark's reading demonstrates the difficulties in specifically connecting the variety of poetic subjects treated in "By the Roadside" with "Drum-Taps" and the overwhelming subject of the Civil War. See Mary Virginia Stark, "Clustered Meaning in Walt Whitman's *Leaves of Grass*: An Exploration of the New Clusters in the 1881 Edition." Ph.D. dissertation, University of Iowa, 1990.

6. Stephen Rachman makes a suggestive comment along these lines in his brief commentary on the cluster, noting, "The road in this cluster helps Whitman to claim for his *Leaves* continuity between his political and poetic struggles

while traveling between the great movements of his poetic career." ("By the Roadside," in *Walt Whitman: An Encyclopedia*, ed. J. R. LeMaster and Donald D. Kummings [New York: Garland, 1998], 93).

7. In his foundational reader-response text, "Interpreting *The Variorum*," Stanley Fish notes that in most critical analysis, the actual experience of reading, moving from one line to the next, from one poem to the next, is often overlooked in exchange for the process of consulting "dictionaries, grammars, and histories." "Interpreting *The Variorum*," *Modern Criticism and Theory: A Reader*, ed. David Lodge and Nigel Wood, 2nd ed. (Harlow, UK: Pearson Education, 2000), 291.

8. I make this argument in detail in a chapter on Walt Whitman in *Negotiating Copyright: Authorship and the Discourse of Literary Property Rights in Nineteenth-Century America* (New York: Routledge, 2006).

9. Betsy Erkkila, *Whitman the Political Poet* (New York: Oxford University Press, 1989), 63. Hereafter *WPP*.

10. Blodgett and Bradley describe the speaker in the cluster as a whole as a "roadside observer—passive, but alert and continually recording" (264). While this description certainly fits the speaker later in the cluster, the speaker in these first poems seems much more invested in what is being described.

11. Martin Klammer, "A Boston Ballad (1854)," in *Walt Whitman: An Encyclopedia*, ed. J. R. LeMaster and Donald D. Kummings (New York: Garland, 1998), 69.

12. Klammer argues that the absence of reference to Burns reveals his true feelings about the Fugitive Slave Law and the actual target of his critique: "By eliding the fugitive slave from the narrative, Whitman suggests that the Fugitive Slave Law should be resisted not to protect the freedom and rights of blacks, but to protect the freedom of Northern white communities from an invasive federal power whose tyranny is as heinous as the return of British monarchs" (70). While this reading certainly holds true to the time of the poem's original composition and publication, it is the poem's broader critique that allows Whitman to shift it throughout *Leaves* and allows him to use it as the set piece for the drama enacted in "By the Roadside."

13. The inclusion of the poem in this cluster and in "By the Roadside" contradicts David B. Baldwin's assertion in "Europe, the 72d and 73d Years of These States" that "Whitman turned away from specific political topics as he filled out *Leaves of Grass* through the years." See *Walt Whitman: An Encyclopedia*, ed. J. R. LeMaster and Donald D. Kummings (New York: Garland, 1998), 213. For Whitman, the act of placing poems like this one in particular clusters was itself a

poetic and political act even if it did not involve the literal creation of a new poem.

14. Betsy Erkkila, *Walt Whitman Among the French* (Princeton, NJ: Princeton University Press, 1980), 185.

15. R. W. B. Lewis, *Trials of the Word* (New Haven, CT: Yale University Press, 1965), 24.

16. Other critics have suggested that this is an intensely personal poem, arguing for a psychological reading that reveals the poet's sense of shame stemming from his repressed homosexual desire. See Jay Losey, "A Hand-Mirror," in *Walt Whitman: An Encyclopedia*, ed. J. R. LeMaster and Donald D. Kummings (New York: Garland, 1998), 265.

17. One can note a similar gesture in "This Compost," which, like "Crossing Brooklyn Ferry," appears first in the 1856 edition as well as in the 1881 edition. In this work, the speaker hesitates to make contact with a world that has been forced to ingest so much "foul liquid and meat" (*LG*, 368). The language of corruption is quite similar to that in "A Hand-Mirror," yet here the speaker's disgust gives way to the wonder of the "chemistry" that allows the earth to create "such exquisite winds out of such infused fetor" (*LG*, 369). Such a dramatic transformation seems foreclosed to the speaker in "A Hand-Mirror."

18. In the 1871–1872 edition, this poem immediately follows "A Hand-Mirror," once again suggesting that the war, even as expressed in the poet's most positive term, has not brought complete reconciliation.

19. Julianne Ramsey, "A British View to an American War: Whitman's 'Drum-Taps' Cluster and the Editorial Influence of William Michael Rossetti," *Walt Whitman Quarterly Review* 14 (Spring 1997): 167.

20. Gregory Eiselein, "Drum-Taps," in *Walt Whitman: An Encyclopedia*, ed. J. R. LeMaster and Donald D. Kummings (New York: Garland, 1998), 193.

21. Ed Folsom, "When I Heard the Learn'd Astronomer," in *Walt Whitman: An Encyclopedia*, ed. J. R. LeMaster and Donald D. Kummings (New York: Garland, 1998), 769.

22. Gay Wilson Allen reminds us that this poem has often been misread as an indication of Whitman's distaste for scientific inquiry. See Allen, 182.

23. Folsom, 769.

24. Ibid.

25. Even more provocatively, Whitman wrote in the 1860 edition of the poem, then titled simply "Walt Whitman," "O Christ! This is mastering me! / Through the conquered doors they crowd. I am possessed" (*Leaves of Grass*, 1860

ed., in *The Walt Whitman Archive*, ed. Ed Folsom and Kenneth M. Price, ⟨http://whitmanarchive.org/published/LG/1860/poems/2⟩, 80). He removed this line and all variations of it from the 1881 edition of "Song of Myself" and never again restored it. It is interesting to note the apparent inability of the speaker in these lines to assimilate properly or to bar those who would enter through the "conquered doors" to "possess" him.

26. Folsom, 769.

27. Guy Rotella insists that, despite the obvious contrasts in the poem, "what unites the several opposites, what contains them in the familiar Whitmanian embrace, is the consciousness of the speaker, who partakes of them all." ("Cummings' 'kind)' and Whitman's Astronomer," *Concerning Poetry* 18, nos. 1–2 [1985]: 42). It is true, of course, that both the public world of the lecture and the solitary space of the night are "joined" in the poem, but we are left with the fact that the second portion of the poem does nothing to address the first. The speaker's condition drives him from one setting to another. In an earlier formalist analysis, Bernth Lindfors makes much of the difference in tone between the descriptions of the crowded lecture hall and the night air: "Each line prefaced with 'When I,' gives the impression of increasing impatience and anger. Each wave of emotion is followed by a larger, stronger wave until, the poet leaving the lecture hall and wandering away, peace is restored." ("Whitman's 'When I Heard the Learn'd Astronomer,'" *Walt Whitman Review* 10 [March 1964], 21). While hardly denouncing science in the way some have supposed, the speaker still demonstrates a striking inability to reconcile the two environments he describes, an inability that he himself cannot comprehend.

28. Bernard Hirschhorn, "To a President," in *Walt Whitman: An Encyclopedia*, ed. J. R. LeMaster and Donald D. Kummings (New York: Garland, 1998), 726.

29. Walt Whitman, *Leaves of Grass*, 1855, in *The Walt Whitman Archive*, ed. Ed Folsom and Kenneth M. Price, ⟨http://whitmanarchive.org/published/LG/1855/whole.html⟩, 39.

30. David B. Baldwin, "I Sit and Look Out," in *Walt Whitman: An Encyclopedia*, ed. J. R. LeMaster and Donald D. Kummings (New York: Garland, 1998), 298.

31. Ibid., 299.

32. George Hutchinson, "Stoicism," in *Walt Whitman: An Encyclopedia*, ed. J. R. LeMaster and Donald D. Kummings (New York: Garland, 1998), 692.

33. Ibid.

34. Stark, 119.

35. Carl Smeller, "To the States, To Identify the 16th, 17th, or 18th Presidentiad," in *Walt Whitman: An Encyclopedia*, ed. J. R. LeMaster and Donald D. Kummings (New York: Garland, 1998), 731.

36. James E. Miller, Jr., *A Critical Guide to Leaves of Grass* (Chicago: University of Chicago Press, 1957), 216.

37. While there is no way of being certain that Whitman read this story, he was evidently familiar with it. In an 1885 article recalling early New York theater and later reprinted in *November Boughs* (1888), the poet recalled seeing "Hackett as Falstaff, Nimrod Wildfire, Rip Van Winkle, and in his Yankee characters" (*PW*, 2:592).

38. Washington Irving, "Rip Van Winkle," in *The Norton Anthology of American Literature*, ed. Nina Baym (New York: W. W. Norton and Company, 2007), 954.

39. In a conversation with Traubel, Whitman describes Irving in terms that could equally apply to the author's famous protagonist: "Irving . . . suggested weakness, if he was not weak: was pleasant, as you say, but without background. I never enthused over him" (*WWC*, 2:532).

40. Luke Mancuso emphasizes the way that the poem reinforces the continued racial tensions following the war: "The black woman reaches out to the flag in a gesture of inclusion, interracial comradeship, and political citizenship; the soldier's inability to recognize her finds its analogue in the historical agitation in 1871–1872 over the inability of the white majority to cede its social authority over African Americans." ("*Leaves of Grass*, 1871–72 Edition," in *Walt Whitman: An Encyclopedia*, ed. J. R. LeMaster and Donald D. Kummings [New York: Garland, 1998], 370). William Ness notes that, when combined with the earlier poems in the "Bathed in War's Perfume," the poem speaks to an imperialist movement "leaving those mysterious, suspect, half-noble, half-ludicrous black folks to their roadside musings" (262). In alluding to this poem in his new cluster "By the Roadside" in 1881, Whitman perhaps points toward both the inevitable success of the war and the barriers to communication that may remain after its conclusion.

5. WHITMAN'S GENERAL

1. Geoffrey Perret, *Ulysses S. Grant: Soldier and President* (New York: Random House, 1997), 378.

2. The exceptional reference work *Walt Whitman: An Encyclopedia*, edited by J. R. LeMaster and Donald D. Kummings, offers an interesting case in point.

There are numerous references to Grant throughout the encyclopedia, yet Grant himself does not receive an independent entry, nor do any of Whitman's writings about Grant.

3. James M. McPherson, *Battle Cry of Freedom: The Civil War Era* (New York: Ballantine, 1988), 718.

4. In thinking about Whitman's later identification with Grant, however, it may be worth recalling the poet's demand for "races of orbic bards, with unconditional uncompromising sway. Come forth, sweet democratic despots of the west!" (*PW*, 2:407).

5. See Loving, 282. In a letter to his mother, Whitman notes, "I see Gen. Butler says the fault of not exchanging the prisoners is not his but Grants" (*Corr*, 1:252); but he does not seem to put much stock in this claim, perhaps because, as Miller notes, the *New York Times* published an editorial on the speech describing it as "exceedingly able, defiant and mischievous" (252n). There is no reason to think that Whitman would have been inclined to side with Butler rather than Grant in the dispute.

6. It is unclear what role Swinton's letter played in actually accomplishing this release since, as he wrote to Whitman on February 5th, the general had apparently already agreed to a general prisoner exchange. Swinton did send the letter in any case. See *WWC*, 2:426.

7. Despite Swinton's reply to Whitman noting the published reports of an impending exchange, Miller notes, "Swinton endorsed the envelope: 'W.W. 1865 Asking me to help his captured brother. Successful" (*Corr*, 1:253n). Despite this notation and the letter from Grant's secretary, it is likely that George was part of a general prisoner exchange that did occur on February 22, 1865, as Loving observes (283).

8. Loving remarks that Whitman did not vote at all in the 1884 election and that the poet commented to Traubel, "I always refrain—yet advise everybody else not to forget" (430).

9. William B. Hesseltine, *Ulysses S. Grant, Politician* (New York: Frederick Ungar, 1957), 48.

10. In *Democratic Vistas*, the poet writes of "The Labor Question," noting "the immense problem of the relation, adjustment, conflict, between Labor and its status and pay, on the one side, and the capital of employers on the other side—looming up over These States like an ominous, limitless, murky cloud, perhaps before long to overshadow us all" (*PW*, 2:753.) Whitman removed this passage when he enfolded *Democratic Vistas* within *Specimen Days and Collect* in 1882.

11. Foner and Mahoney, 88.

12. Quoted in Jean Edward Smith, *Grant* (New York: Simon & Schuster, 2001), 442. Hereafter cited parenthetically.

13. Dixon Wecter notes that while the official records indicate the January 1 starting date, "he did not set to work until several weeks later." "Walt Whitman as Civil Servant," *PMLA* 58 (December 1943): 1094.

14. This is an infamous episode in Whitman's life and career. For a full account, see, among other places, Loving, 290–92.

15. William Gilette, *Retreat From Reconstruction, 1869–1879* (Baton Rouge: Louisiana State University Press, 1979), 56.

16. The reporter, John Russell Young, sent Whitman a letter from China in 1883 noting that he had heard the poet was in poor health and wishing him well. Whitman called him "the higher type of newspaper man" (*WWC*, 3:311).

17. Two of Grant's most recent biographers take almost diametrically opposed positions regarding the question of whether or not Grant actually wanted to be president again. Smith suggests that he did (614–15), while Perret takes Grant's frequent assertions that he did not desire the presidency to be definitive (462–63).

18. *Philadelphia Press*, December 17, 1879: 8. Available on the Walt Whitman Archive (⟨http://www.whitmanarchive.org/published/periodicals/poems/per.00146.html⟩).

19. In revising this poem for inclusion in the 1881 edition of *Leaves*, Whitman removed the reference to Lincoln, perhaps to remain consistent with the idea of Grant sitting where "Washington sat, ruling the land in peace," a claim that obviously cannot be made about Lincoln. At the same time, this change denies Grant the metonymic link of his presidency to that of Whitman's most beloved hero.

20. In another interesting revision, the version in the 1881 *Leaves* removes the word "average" from the description of the "prairie sovereigns of the West." See *LG*, 485.

21. In his biography of Peter Doyle, Martin G. Murray describes Doyle's recollection of himself and Whitman observing Grant as he "strolled from the White House to visit Mrs. Magruder, widow of a well-respected local physician" (11). Perhaps this is one of the visits that Whitman is recalling. See "Pete the Great: A Biography of Peter Doyle," *Walt Whitman Quarterly Review* 12 (Summer 1994): 1–51; also available on the *Walt Whitman Archive* ⟨http://www.whitmanarchive.org/criticism/current/anc.00155.html⟩.

6. RECONSTRUCTING HIS STORY

1. George Hutchinson notes, "By piecing the fragments together and bathing them in an informal tone of reminiscence, Whitman creates a casual mood that conveys authenticity yet veils the seriousness of his structure and the carefully constructed nature of his pose" ("*Specimen Days*," 679). As with "By the Roadside," Whitman reconstructs earlier publications to fashion a new narrative.

2. Desiree Henderson, "'What is the grass?': The Roots of Walt Whitman's Cemetery Meditation," *Walt Whitman Quarterly Review* 25 (Winter 2008): 89.

3. As Henderson notes, Whitman wrote at least seven articles referring to the prominent Greenwood Cemetery in Brooklyn while a journalist in the 1840s (97).

4. See, for instance, Justin Kaplan's description in *Walt Whitman: A Life* (New York: Simon & Schuster, 1980), 347.

5. This represents a poetic equivalent to the poet's wish to have his mother's body exhumed and relocated to his own enduring tomb in Camden upon his death.

6. Ulysses S. Grant, *Personal Memoirs of U.S. Grant*, 2 vols. (New York: C. L. Webster, 1885), 1:7. Hereafter cited parenthetically.

7. Gregory Eiselein, "Lincoln's Death," in *Walt Whitman: An Encyclopedia*, ed. J. R. LeMaster and Donald D. Kummings (New York: Garland, 1998), 395.

8. "A New Departure," *Baltimore American*, April 20, 1879. Reel 4, Harned Collection, LOC.

9. Eiselein, "Lincoln's Death," 395.

10. In a June 6, 1868, letter to his mother, Whitman writes, "We had the strangest procession here last Tuesday night, about 3000 darkeys, old & young, men & women. . .—it was quite comical, yet very disgusting & alarming in some respects—They were very insolent, & altogether it was a very strange sight—they looked like so many wild brutes let loose—thousands of slaves from the Southern plantations have crowded up here—many are supported by the Gov't" (*Corr*, 2:34–35). As with much of Whitman's prose following the war, his remarks here demonstrate the troubling attitudes about race that have been explored by Mancuso, Folsom, and other critics. His repetition of the word "strange" highlights how much the procession represented something new and unusual to the poet, a living symbol of the changing times.

Bibliography

Allen, Gay Wilson. *The New Walt Whitman Handbook*. New York: New York
 University Press, 1975.

Baldasty, Gerald J. *The Commercialization of News in the Nineteenth Century*.
 Madison: University of Wisconsin Press, 1992.

———. "The Nineteenth-Century Origins of Modern American Journalism."
 Proceedings of the American Antiquarian Society 100, no. 2 (October 1990):
 413–14.

Baldwin, David B. "Europe, the 72d and 73d Years of These States." In
 Walt Whitman: An Encyclopedia, edited by J. R. LeMaster and Donald D.
 Kummings, 212–13. New York: Garland, 1998.

———. "I Sit and Look Out." In *Walt Whitman: An Encyclopedia*, edited by J. R.
 LeMaster and Donald D. Kummings, 298–99. New York: Garland, 1998.

Belasco, Susan. "Walt Whitman's Poetry in Periodicals." In *The Walt Whitman
 Archive*, edited by Ed Folsom and Kenneth M. Price. ⟨http://www.whitman
 archive.org/published/periodical/general_introduction/index.html⟩.

Blight, David W. *Race and Reunion: The Civil War in American Memory*.
 Cambridge, MA: Belknap Press of Harvard University Press, 2001.

Bloch, Julius Marcus. *Miscegenation, Melaleukation, and Mrs. Lincoln's Dog*. New
 York: Schaum, 1958.

Bode, Carl. "Columbia's Carnal Bed." *American Quarterly* 15, no.1 (1963): 52–64.

Brown, Thomas J. *The Public Art of Civil War Commemoration*. Boston: Bedford/
 St. Martin's, 2004.

Buinicki, Martin. *Negotiating Copyright: Authorship and the Discourse of Literary
 Property Rights in Nineteenth-Century America*. New York: Routledge, 2006.

Childs, George William. "Important Announcement! (Wait and Get the Best.):
 Lossing's Pictorial History of the Great Rebellion." Publisher's Prospectus.
 Philadelphia: George W. Childs, 1862[?]. AAS stacks, Z780 C537 1862.

Clark, Leadie M. *Walt Whitman's Concept of the American Common Man*. New
 York: Philosophical Library, 1955.

Croly, David G., and George Wakeman. *Miscegenation*. 1864; Upper Saddle
 River, NJ: Literature House, 1970.

Cushman, Stephen. "Walt Whitman's Real War." In *Wars Within a War:
 Controversy and Conflict over the American Civil War*, edited by Joan Waugh

and Gary W. Gallagher, 137–56. Chapel Hill: University of North Carolina Press, 2009.

Dana, Malcolm McGregor. *The Norwich Memorial: The Annals of Norwich, New London County, Connecticut, in the Great Rebellion of 1861–1865*. Norwich, CT: J. J. Jewett, 1873. Making of America Database, University of Michigan, ⟨http://name.umdl.umich.edu/ac11756.0001.001⟩.

Davis, Robert Leigh. "Democratic Vistas." In *A Companion to Walt Whitman*, edited by Donald D. Kummings, 540–52. Malden, MA: Blackwell, 2006.

Duncan, Bingham. *Whitelaw Reid: Journalist, Politician, Diplomat*. Athens: University of Georgia Press, 1975.

Edwards, Rev. Tryon. "Mason and Dixon's Line." *Harper's New Monthly Magazine* (September 1876). Making of America Database, Cornell University Library, ⟨http://cdl.library.cornell.edu/cgi-bin/moa/moa-cgi?notisid=ABK4014-0053-75⟩.

Eiselein, Gregory. "*Drum-Taps*." In *Walt Whitman: An Encyclopedia*, edited by J. R. LeMaster and Donald D. Kummings, 193–94. New York: Garland, 1998.

———. "Lincoln's Death." In *Walt Whitman: An Encyclopedia*, edited by J. R. LeMaster and Donald D. Kummings, 395–96. New York: Garland, 1998.

Erkkila, Betsy. *Walt Whitman Among the French*. Princeton, NJ: Princeton University Press, 1980.

———. *Whitman the Political Poet*. New York: Oxford University Press, 1989.

Fahs, Alice. *The Imagined Civil War: Popular Literature of the North and South, 1861–1865*. Chapel Hill: University of North Carolina Press, 2001.

Faust, Drew Gilpin. *This Republic of Suffering: Death and the American Civil War*. New York: Knopf, 2008.

Feldman, Mark. "Remembering a Convulsive War: Whitman's *Memoranda During the War* and the Therapeutics of Display." *Walt Whitman Quarterly Review* 23 (Summer/Fall 2005): 1–25.

Fish, Stanley. "Interpreting *The Variorum*." In *Modern Criticism and Theory: A Reader*, edited by David Lodge and Nigel Wood, 382–400. 2nd ed. Harlow, UK: Pearson Education, 2000.

Folsom, Ed. "Lucifer and Ethiopia: Whitman, Race, and Politics before the Civil War and after." In *A Historical Guide to Walt Whitman*, edited by David S. Reynolds, 45–95. New York: Oxford University Press, 2000.

———. "When I Heard the Learn'd Astronomer." In *Walt Whitman: An Encyclopedia*, edited by J. R. LeMaster and Donald D. Kummings, 769. New York: Garland, 1998.

———. *Whitman Making Books / Books Making Whitman: A Catalog and Commentary*. Iowa City: Obermann Center for Advanced Studies, 2005.

Folsom, Ed, and Kenneth M. Price. *Re-Scripting Walt Whitman: An Introduction to His Life and Work*. Malden, MA: Blackwell, 2005. 〈http://www.whitman archive.org/criticism/current/anc.00152.html〉.

———. "Walt Whitman." 〈http://www.whitmanarchive.org/biography/walt_ whitman/index.html〉.

Foner, Eric, and Olivia Mahoney. *America's Reconstruction: People and Politics after the Civil War*. Baton Rouge: Louisiana State University Press, 1997.

Gailey, Amanda. "The Publishing History of *Leaves of Grass*." In *A Companion to Walt Whitman*, edited by Donald D. Kummings, 409–38. Malden, MA: Blackwell, 2006.

Gaskell, Philip. *New Introduction to Bibliography*. New York: Oxford University Press, 1972.

Genoways, Ted. "Civil War Poems in 'Drum-Taps' and 'Memories of President Lincoln.'" In *A Companion to Walt Whitman*, edited by Donald D. Kummings, 522–38. Malden, MA: Blackwell, 2006.

Gilette, William. *Retreat from Reconstruction, 1869–1879*. Baton Rouge: Louisiana State University Press, 1979.

Grant, Ulysses S. *Personal Memoirs of U. S. Grant*. 2 vols. New York: C. L. Webster, 1885.

Haddox, Thomas F. "Whitman's End of History: 'As I Sat Alone by Blue Ontario's Shore,' *Democratic Vistas*, and the Postbellum Politics of Nostalgia." *Walt Whitman Quarterly Review* 22 (Summer 2004): 1–22.

Harp, Gillis J. *Positivist Republic: Auguste Comte and the Reconstruction of American Liberalism, 1865–1920*. University Park: Pennsylvania State University Press, 1995.

Henderson, Desiree. "What Is the Grass?: The Roots of Walt Whitman's Cemetery Meditation." *Walt Whitman Quarterly Review* 25 (Winter 2008): 89–107.

Hesseltine, William B. *Ulysses S. Grant, Politician*. New York: Frederick Ungar, 1957.

Hirschhorn, Bernard. "To a President." In *Walt Whitman: An Encyclopedia*, edited by J. R. LeMaster and Donald D. Kummings, 726–27. New York: Garland, 1998.

Hubach, Robert R. "Three Uncollected St. Louis Interviews of Walt Whitman." *American Literature* 14 (May 1942): 141–47.

Hunter, Dard. *Papermaking: The History and Technique of an Ancient Craft*. New York: Dover, 1978.

Hutchinson, George. "The Civil War." In *Walt Whitman: An Encyclopedia*, edited by J. R. LeMaster and Donald D. Kummings, 124–27. New York: Garland, 1998.

———. "*Specimen Days*." In *Walt Whitman: An Encyclopedia*, edited by J. R. LeMaster and Donald D. Kummings, 678–80. New York: Garland, 1998.

———. "Stoicism." In *Walt Whitman: An Encyclopedia*, edited by J. R. LeMaster and Donald D. Kummings, 691–93. New York: Garland, 1998.

Ings, Katherine Nicholson. "Between Hoax and Hope: Miscegenation and Nineteenth-Century Interracial Romance." *Literature Compass* 3/4 (2006): 648–57.

Irving, Washington. "Rip Van Winkle." In *The Norton Anthology of American Literature*, edited by Nina Baym, 954–65. Vol. B. New York: W. W. Norton and Company, 2007.

Kaplan, Justin. *Walt Whitman: A Life*. New York: Simon & Schuster, 1980.

Kielbowicz, Richard B. *News in the Mail: The Press, Post Office, and Public Information, 1700–1860s*. New York: Greenwood, 1989.

Klammer, Martin. "A Boston Ballad (1854)." In *Walt Whitman: An Encyclopedia*, edited by J. R. LeMaster and Donald D. Kummings, 69–70. New York: Garland, 1998.

Levy, David W. "David Goodman Croly." In *American National Biography*, edited by John A. Garraty and Mark C. Carnes. Vol. 5. New York: Oxford University Press, 1999.

Lewis, R. W. B. *Trials of the Word*. New Haven, CT: Yale University Press, 1965.

Lindfors, Bernth. "Whitman's 'When I Heard the Learn'd Astronomer.'" *Walt Whitman Review* 10 (March 1964): 19–21.

Losey, Jay. "A Hand-Mirror." In *Walt Whitman: An Encyclopedia*, edited by J. R. LeMaster and Donald D. Kummings, 264–65. New York: Garland, 1998.

Loving, Jerome. *Walt Whitman: The Song of Himself*. Berkeley: University of California Press, 1999.

Mancuso, Luke. "Civil War." In *A Companion to Walt Whitman*, edited by Donald D. Kummings, 290–310. Malden, MA: Blackwell, 2006.

———. "*Leaves of Grass*, 1871–72 Edition." In *Walt Whitman: An Encyclopedia*, edited by J. R. LeMaster and Donald D. Kummings, 368–72. New York: Garland, 1998.

———. *The Strange Sad War Revolving: Walt Whitman, Reconstruction, and the*

Emergence of Black Citizenship, 1865–1876. Columbia, SC: Camden House, 1997.

McGill, Meredith. *American Literature and the Culture of Reprinting, 1834–1853.* Philadelphia: University of Pennsylvania Press, 2003.

McPherson, James M. *Battle Cry of Freedom: The Civil War Era.* New York: Ballantine, 1988.

Miller, James E., Jr. *A Critical Guide to Leaves of Grass.* Chicago: University of Chicago Press, 1957.

———. *Walt Whitman.* New York: Twayne, 1962.

Mott, Frank Luther. *A History of American Magazines.* 5 vols. Cambridge, MA: Harvard University Press, 1938.

Murray, Martin G. "Pete the Great: A Biography of Peter Doyle." *Walt Whitman Quarterly Review* 12 (Summer 1994): 1–51.

———. "*Specimen Days.*" In *A Companion to Walt Whitman*, edited by Donald D. Kummings, 553–65. Malden, MA: Blackwell, 2006.

Myerson, Joel. *Walt Whitman: A Descriptive Bibliography.* Pittsburgh: University of Pittsburgh Press, 1993.

Ness, William B. "Bathed in War's Perfume: Whitman and the Flag." *Prospects* 27 (2002): 247–70.

Nevins, Allan. *The Organized War to Victory.* Vol. 4. War for the Union. New York: Konecky and Konecky, 1971.

"A New Departure." *Baltimore American*, April 20, 1879. Reel 4, Thomas Biggs Harned Collection of the Papers of Walt Whitman, Manuscript Division, Library of Congress, Washington D.C.

New York Daily Graphic. December 7, 1874: 265. Newspaper Collection, American Antiquarian Society.

New York Daily Graphic. December 19, 1874: 357. Newspaper Collection, American Antiquarian Society.

Nora, Pierre. "Between Memory and History: Les Lieux de Mémoire." Translated by Marc Roudebush. In *History and Memory in African-American Culture*, edited by Geneviève Fabre and Robert O'Meally, 284–300. New York: Oxford University Press, 1994.

Perret, Geoffrey. *Ulysses S. Grant: Soldier and President.* New York: Random House, 1997.

Philadelphia Press. December 17, 1879: 8. ⟨http://www.whitmanarchive.org/ published/periodical/poems/per.00146⟩.

Rachman, Stephen. "By the Roadside." In *Walt Whitman: An Encyclopedia*, edited by J. R. LeMaster and Donald D. Kummings, 93–94. New York: Garland, 1998.

Ramsey, Julianne. "A British View to an American War: Whitman's 'Drum-Taps' Cluster and the Editorial Influence of William Michael Rossetti." *Walt Whitman Quarterly Review* 14 (Spring 1997): 166–75.

Reynolds, David S. *Walt Whitman's America: A Cultural Biography*. New York: Vintage, 1996.

Richardson, Heather Cox. *The Death of Reconstruction: Race, Labor, and Politics in the Post-Civil War North, 1865–1901*. Cambridge, MA: Harvard University Press, 2001.

Richardson, Todd. "Walt Whitman's 'Lively Corpse' in 1871: The American Press on the Rumor of Whitman's Death." *Walt Whitman Quarterly Review* 15 (Summer 1997): 1–22.

Rosenthal, Debra. *Race Mixture in Nineteenth-Century U.S. and Spanish American Fictions: Gender, Culture, and Nation-Building*. Chapel Hill: University of North Carolina Press, 2004.

Rotella, Guy. "Cummings' 'kind)' and Whitman's Astronomer." *Concerning Poetry* 18, nos. 1–2 (1985): 39–46.

Sanchez-Eppler, Karen. *Touching Liberty: Abolition, Feminism, and the Politics of the Body*. Berkeley: University of California Press, 1993.

Scharnhorst, Gary. "Rediscovered Nineteenth-Century Whitman Articles." *Walt Whitman Quarterly Review* 19 (Winter/Spring 2002): 183–86.

Scholnick, Robert. "Whitman and the Magazines: Some Documentary Evidence." *American Literature* 44, no. 2 (1972): 222–46.

"Shall the Hatchet Ever be Buried?" *New York Times*, June 14, 1869: 4.

Smeller, Carl. "To the States, to Identify the 16th, 17th, or 18th Presidentiad." In *Walt Whitman: An Encyclopedia*, edited by J. R. LeMaster and Donald D. Kummings, 731–32. New York: Garland, 1998.

Smith, David C. *History of Papermaking in the United States*. New York: Lockwood, 1970.

Smith, Jean Edward. *Grant*. New York: Simon & Schuster, 2001.

Sollors, Werner. *Interracialism: Black-White Intermarriage in American History, Literature, and Law*. New York: Oxford University Press, 2000.

Stark, Mary Virginia. "Clustered Meaning in Walt Whitman's *Leaves of Grass*: An Exploration of the New Clusters in the 1881 Edition." Ph.D. dissertation, University of Iowa, 1990.

Steffen, Charles G. "Newspapers for Free: The Economies of Newspaper

Circulation in the Early Republic." *Journal of the Early Republic* 23, no. 3 (Autumn, 2003): 381–419.

Sweet, Timothy. *Traces of War: Poetry, Photography, and the Crisis of the Union.* Baltimore: Johns Hopkins University Press, 1990.

Thomas, M. Wynn. *The Lunar Light of Whitman's Poetry.* Cambridge, MA: Harvard University Press, 1987.

———. "Whitman's Obligations of Memory." *Walt Whitman Review* 28 (1982): 43–54.

Traubel, Horace. *With Walt Whitman in Camden,* 9 vols. Vol. 1. Boston: Small, Maynard, 1906; Vol. 2. New York: D. Appleton, 1908; Vol 3. New York: Mitchell Kennerley, 1914; Vol. 4. Philadelphia: University of Pennsylvania Press, 1953; Vol. 5. Carbondale: Southern Illinois University Press, 1964; Vol. 6. Carbondale: Southern Illinois University Press, 1982; Vol. 7. Carbondale: Southern Illinois University Press, 1992; Vols. 8–9. Oregon House, CA: W. L. Bentley, 1996.

Turner, Hy B. *When Giants Ruled: The Story of Park Row, New York's Great Newspaper Street.* New York: Fordham University Press, 1999.

Wecter, Dixon. "Walt Whitman as Civil Servant." *PMLA* 58 (December 1943): 1094–1109.

Whitman, Walt. *The Correspondence.* 7 vols. Edited by Edwin Haviland Miller. New York: New York University Press, 1961–1964.

———. *Leaves of Grass.* Comprehensive Reader's Edition. Edited by Harold W. Blodgett and Sculley Bradley. New York: New York University Press, 1965.

———. *Leaves of Grass.* 1855 ed. In *The Walt Whitman Archive,* edited by Ed Folsom and Kenneth M. Price. ⟨http://www.whitmanarchive.org/published/LG/1855/whole.html⟩.

———. *Leaves of Grass,* 1860 ed. In *The Walt Whitman Archive,* edited by Ed Folsom and Kenneth M. Price. ⟨http://www.whitmanarchive.org/published/LG/1860/whole.html⟩.

———. *Leaves of Grass,* 1870–1871 ed. In *The Walt Whitman Archive,* edited by Ed Folsom and Kenneth M. Price. ⟨http://www.whitmanarchive.org/published/LG/1871/whole.html⟩.

———. *Memoranda During the War.* Edited by Peter Coviello. New York: Oxford University Press, 2004.

———. *Prose Works.* Edited by Floyd Stovall. 2 vols. New York: New York University Press, 1963–1964.

Wood, James Playsted. *Magazines in the United States*. 2nd ed. New York: Ronald Press, 1956.

Woolson, Constance Fenimore. "Rodman the Keeper." In *Constance Fenimore Woolson: Selected Stories and Travel Narratives*, edited by Victoria Brehm and Sharon Dean, 124–47. Knoxville: University of Tennessee Press, 2004.

Zboray, Ronald J. "Antebellum Reading and the Ironies of Technological Innovation." *American Quarterly* 40, no. 1 (March 1988): 65–82.

Zwinger, Ann, and Edwin Way Teale. *A Conscious Stillness: Two Naturalists on Thoreau's Rivers*. New York: Harper and Row, 1982.

Index

Abbot, Jacob, 20–21

African Americans: and election of 1872, 39–40; in Grand Review of the Union Army, 2, 3; "miscegenation," 32–35, 154n37, 155n41, 155n49; oppression of, 3; postwar protection of, 117; voting rights of, 3, 9–10, 38, 116, 117; in Washington, 149, 168n10

Alcott, Louisa May, 52, 55

Allen, Gay Wilson, 79, 80, 163n22

Andersonville prison, 19, 75–76, 160n27

Armory Square Hospital Gazette, 18

Army & Navy Official Gazette, 18

"As at Thy Portals Also Death" (Whitman), 13, 138–39

"As I Ponder'd in Silence" (Whitman), 149, 150

"As I Sat by Blue Ontario's Shore" (Whitman), 9

"As One by One Withdraw the Lofty Actors" (Whitman), 130

Associated Press, 46

"As the Time Draws Nigh" (Whitman), 13

Atlantic Monthly, 18, 24, 26

attorney general's office: dismissal of Whitman from, 123, 131; and Grant administration, 118, 123; and health issues of Whitman, 121–22; and Johnson administration, 109, 118

audience. *See* readership of Whitman

"A Backward Glance O'er Travel'd Roads" (Whitman), 8

Badeau, Adam, 143

Baldasty, Gerald J., 36

Baldwin, David B., 99, 162n13

"Bardic Symbols" (Whitman), 24

"Bathed in War's Perfume" cluster (Whitman), 78, 88, 91, 107

"Beautiful Women" (Whitman), 101

Belasco, Susan, 24, 29

Blight, David W., 33, 117

Blodgett, Harold W., 80, 162n10

bloodstains in notebooks, 7, 8, 20, 53, 54, 69–70

"A Boston Ballad" (Whitman), 84–86

Bradley, Sculley, 80, 162n10

Brady, Mathew, 49

Bryant, William Cullen, 40

Burns, Anthony, 85

Burroughs, John, 21, 83

Burroughs, William, 30

Butler, Benjamin, 113

"By Blue Ontario's Shore" (Whitman), 127–28

"By the Roadside" cluster (Whitman), 77–108; "Astronomer" in, 92–95; "by the roadside" phrase, 106–8; disparate observations in, 101; introspective observation in, 101–3, 104–5; order of works in, 92;

political context depicted in, 84–87; as prelude to "Drum-Taps" cluster, 11–12, 82–83, 84, 91–92, 103, 105, 161n5; and prewar passivity, 82, 95, 103–6; questions and answers in, 95–101; reassembly into *LG*, 79, 81–84; scholarly disagreement on, 80–81; speaker of, 87–89, 89–90, 103–4, 162n10

cemeteries and graves: of ancestors, 13, 136–40; of Confederate soldiers, 160n23; and "Decoration Day," 157n7; as embodiment of war, 66; and loss of memory, 141; as record of the war, 76; of Union soldiers, 139–40, 160n23; for unknown dead, 13, 59, 65; of Whitman's ancestors, 136–39, 140. *See also* deaths of soldiers

Century Magazine, 22, 142–43

chemistry of death, 65–66, 75–76, 135

Chicago Tribune, 40

Christian Commission. *See also* deaths of soldiers

Christ imagery, 67–68

Christmas Graphic, 30–32

Cincinnati Commercial, 40

Civil War: "awakening" generated by, 103, 105; casualties of, 112–13 (*see also* deaths of soldiers); centrality of, to Whitman's life, 80; commemoration of, 49, 50; Crusades analogy of, 7–8, 152n14; documentation of (*see* historicizing of the war); Grant's leadership in, 111–14; and health of Whitman, 7, 70; "interior history" of, 6–7, 58; and later work of Whitman, 11; and *Leaves of Grass*, 73, 77–79, 79–82; limitations of historical accounts of, 56–57; memorialization of, 49, 50, 59, 156n1, 157n7; and persona of Whitman, 12; as pivotal, redemptive event, 106; prisoner exchanges in, 113–14, 166nn5–7; public preoccupation with, 7, 8, 75; reminders of, 3; and Republican Party, 34; unrepresentable nature of, 6, 56–58, 64, 68–69, 71–72, 74, 140–41. *See also* memories of the war

Clark, Leadie M., 155n41

class issues, 39, 41, 42–43, 100, 116

Colfax, Schuyler, 120

Compromise of 1850, 103

A Conscious Stillness: Two Naturalists on Thoreau's Rivers (Zwinger and Teale), 152n9

Conway, Moncure, 109, 110, 116

corruption, 88, 103, 120, 121

Credit Mobilier scandal, 120, 121

critics, Whitman on, 131–32

Croly, David G., 29, 32–35, 36–37, 155n49

"Crossing Brooklyn Ferry" (Whitman), 89

Crusades, 7–8, 152n14

currency, paper, 40, 41

Cushman, Stephen, 57, 159n22

cylinder presses, 21–22

"The Dalliance of Eagles" (Whitman), 101

dandy-to-rough transformation, 16

Davis, Robert Leigh, 41

"Dear to the Muse" (Whitman), 148

"Death of Abraham Lincoln" (Whitman), 145–48

"Death of General Grant" (Whitman), 129

deaths of soldiers: chemistry of, 65–66, 75–76, 135; corpses in poetry, 84–85, 86; described in prose, 60–62, 64–65; as experienced by Whitman, 70–71; and memories of the war, 70; unknown dead, 13, 59, 65, 70–71, 72, 74, 134–35

"A Death-Sonnet for Custer" (Whitman), 43–44

Democratic Party: election of 1868, 115, 116; and labor issues, 39–42; postwar disarray of, 109; and race issues, 33–34

democratic vision of Whitman, 9

Democratic Vistas: on approach to poetry, 27; on labor issues, 40–42, 166n10; political topics of, 9–10; on racial issues, 38

documentary approach to history, 57, 61

Douglas, Stephen A., 102

Doyle, Peter, 28, 46, 115, 145, 167n21

Drum-Taps (Whitman), 19, 78, 79, 92

"Drum-Taps" cluster (Whitman): integration of, into *LG*, 78; poetic prelude to, 11–12, 82–83, 84, 91–92, 103, 105, 161n5; war poetry collected in, 80

Eiselein, Gregory, 92, 145, 148

Eldridge, Charles, 113

elections: election of 1868, 33, 40–41, 110, 115–18; election of 1872, 39–40, 42, 44, 122; election of 1876, 3, 124

electrotype printing and plates, 20–22, 51

Emerson, Ralph Waldo, 21, 30, 118–19

emotional experience, emphasis of Whitman on, 63

employment of Whitman: lecturer appearances, 4, 145–48, 157n8; with U.S. Department of Justice, 109, 118, 121–22, 123, 131; with U.S. Department of the Interior, 26, 118, 167n14. *See also* periodicals

Erkkila, Betsy: on election of 1868, 117; on Fugitive Slave Law, 85; on public/private self of Whitman, 88; on "To the States," 103, 106

"Ethiopia Saluting the Colors" (Whitman), 77, 107–8

"Europe, The 72d and 73d Years of These States" (Whitman), 86–87, 89, 98, 99, 162n13

Evarts, William, 118

execution scene, 60–62

Fahs, Alice, 17, 52

family genealogy, 13, 136–40, 144

"A Farm Picture" (Whitman), 101

Faust, Drew Gilpin. *See also* deaths of soldiers

Feldman, Mark, 56, 65, 158n10, 160nn24–25

Fern, Fannie, 24

Fields, James T., 18

Fish, Jim, 120

Fish, Stanley, 162n7

flashbacks, 56. *See also* memories of the war

Folsom, Ed: on "Astronomer," 93, 95; on "By the Roadside," 81; on *Drum-Taps*, 78, 83; on final edition of *LG*, 79; on *Memoranda*, 51; on "Prayer of Columbus," 153n23; on "The Sleepers," 37–38

Franklin Evans (Whitman), 34–35

Fugitive Slave Law (1850), 85, 162n12

future of the nation, 5, 6–7, 9–10

Gailey, Amanda, 6, 16, 24, 78

Galaxy, 23, 38

Gardner, Alexander, 49

Garrison, William Lloyd, 85

genealogy, 13, 136–40, 144

Genoways, Ted, 18–19

George III, King of England, 106

"A Glimpse of War's Hell-Scenes" (Whitman), 60–62

Godey's, 22

Godkin, Edwin L., 40

"Gods" (Whitman), 89–90

Gold Panic of 1869, 120–21

Gould, Jay, 120

Grand Review of the Union Army, 1, 2–3, 114

Grant, Nelly, 122–23

Grant, Ulysses S., 109–33; cabinet appointments, 118–20; as creative genius, 131–33; death of, 129–30; democratic nature of, 124–31; determination of, 111–12, 113; early impressions of, 110; as employer of Whitman, 118, 123–24; global tour of, 124–27, 129; as hero, 114, 124–26, 129–30; and Lincoln, 111–12, 167n19; memoir of, 143–45; military leadership of, 111–14; and political climate, 36; political leadership of, 118–24, 167n17; presidential campaigns and elections, 3, 110, 115–17, 122, 123, 124, 126; response of Whitman to, 10–11, 114; Whitman's pieces on, 121–23, 124–27, 129–30

graves. *See* cemeteries and graves

Greeley, Horace, 39–40, 44, 49

Haddox, Thomas F., 9–10

Halstead, Murat, 40

"A Hand-Mirror" (Whitman), 87–89, 91, 101, 104, 163n17

Harlan, James, 118

Harper brothers, 20–21

Harper's Monthly Magazine, 26, 28

Harper's Weekly: on events of the war, 18; on Grant's death, 129; on memory of the war, 50; and readership of Whitman, 24; on Reid, 44

Hartford Courant, 117

Hayes, Rutherford B., 3

health of Whitman: and employment, 121, 123–24; and political climate, 38–39; stroke and recovery, 29, 30, 70, 121, 123; trace of the war in, 7, 70

Henderson, Desiree, 138

Hirschhorn, Bernard, 98

historicizing of the war, 142–45; and

fading of memories, 50; Grant's
memoir, 143–45; and history-
literature boundary, 74–75; limitations of, 62–63; national interest
in, 142–45, 157n8; participation
of Whitman in, 51–52, 157n8; and
publishing industry, 49–50; reaction of Whitman to, 59. *See
also Memoranda During the War*
(Whitman)
Hoar, Ebenezer R., 118–19
Holmes, Oliver Wendell, 17–18
Hosmer, Horace, 19–20
hospitals and war casualties: and
health of Whitman, 70; and letter writing of Whitman, 134; and
memories of the war, 4; and publication in periodicals, 47–48; as
reminder of cost of war, 3; service
in, 6, 50; suffering in, documented
by Whitman, 7, 53, 141. *See also*
deaths of soldiers
Hospital Sketches (Alcott), 52
Howell, William Dean, 25
Hutchinson, George, 100, 135, 144,
168n1

infrastructure development, 5–6, 17,
23
Ings, Katherine Nicholson, 33,
154n37
instincts of Whitman, 55
intellectualism of Whitman, 30,
153n23
Irving, Washington, 12, 82, 105–6,
165n39

"I Sit and Look Out" (Whitman),
99–100, 101

Johnson, Andrew: and freed slaves,
117; and Grand Review of the
Union Army, 1; impeachment and
acquittal of, 3, 109; as reminder of
cost of war, 3
Johnson, Robert Underwood, 142–43
Jones, John Paul, 66
justification, 127–28

"A Kiss to the Bride" (Whitman), 122
Klammer, Martin, 85, 162n12
Ku Klux Klan, 3

labor unions and movements, 40–42,
116, 166n10
Leaves of Grass (Whitman): changes
to works in, 83–84; controversy
regarding, 26; critics on, 21; editions of, 47, 77, 79, 124; and health
of Whitman, 70, 124; identity
linked with, 68; mother's tombstone in, 139, 140; narrative progression in, 96; order of works in,
83; personalization of, 69; in postwar political context, 9; print runs
of, 23; and production advances,
23; promotion of, in periodicals,
16; scholarship on, 4; suffering
of war in, 20; unauthorized copies
of, 21; value place on, by Whitman, 84; war poetry in, 73, 77–83,-
96
"Leaves of Grass" clusters, 79, 81

lecturer appearances, 4, 145–48, 157n8

Lewis, R. W. B., 88

Lincoln, Abraham: assassination of, 1, 148; and election of 1860, 102; and Grant, 111–12, 167n19; lectures on, 7, 145–48, 157n8

Lindfors, Bernth, 164n27

literary movement, postwar, 9

"L. of G.'s Purport" (Whitman), 73

Lossing, Benson, 49–50

Loving, Jerome: on Credit Mobilier scandal, 121; on Croly, 32; on Grant's death, 129–30; on health of Whitman, 123, 124; on prisoner exchange, 114; on voting habits of Whitman, 166n8

Lowell, James Russell, 24

"Lucifer" section of "The Sleepers," 37–38

The Lunar Light of Whitman's Poetry (Thomas), 5

magazines. *See* periodicals

mainstream acceptance of Whitman, 23–29, 31, 32, 39

Mancuso, Luke: on integration of "Drum-Taps" into *LG*, 78; on liberation from domination, 79; on *lieux de mémoire*, 158n15; on political writings, 9–10, 116; on racial tensions, 165n40; scope of scholarship, 4–5; on Whitman scholarship, 150

"Marches Now the War Is Over" cluster (Whitman), 78

McGill, Meredith, 46

McPherson, James, 112–13

media infrastructure, 5

Memoranda During the War (Whitman): changes to material in, 7; discrepancies in shared material, 57–58; execution scene, 60–62; and fading of memories, 75–76; on Grand Review, 3; and health of Whitman, 124; influence of newspapers in, 19; and *lieux de mémoire* (sites of memory), 57; on limits of memory, 62–63; night battle scene, 62–64; pieces on Grant in, 123; on race issues, 35; on the "real war," 57–58, 134; relationship of text to events, 52; "Remembrance Page" in, 69; as reproduced in *Specimen Days*, 7, 12, 45, 56, 60, 135–36, 140; selections published from, 30; on unknown dead, 59, 135; on Upperville episode, 62

memories of the war, 49–76; and body of Whitman, 70–73; coming to terms with, 3–4; containment of, in writings, 73–76; discrepancies in shared material on, 57–58; embodiment of, 58–66; and feelings about the conflict, 8; flashbacks, 56; framing of, 8; integration of, 6; *lieux de mémoire* (sites of memory), 7, 58–64, 68, 73, 158n15, 160n24; loss of, 71–73, 75–76, 140–41; in notebooks, 50–55, 69–70; personal memory signifiers, 67; and publishing industry changes, 5; separation between history and, 55–58; topics worthy of remembrance, 68–69; unrepresentable nature of, 6–7, 71–72; and written accounts of the war, 71

Military History of U.S. Grant (Badeau), 143

Miller, Edwin Haviland, 32

Miller, James E., 80, 104, 166n7

"The Million Dead, Too, Summ'd Up" (Whitman), 59, 65

"miscegenation," 32–35, 154n37, 155n41, 155n49

Miscegenation (Croly and Wakeman), 32–35, 155n49

Modern Thinker, 36

money, paper, 40, 41

monuments, 49, 59, 156n1

Mosby's men, attack on, 60–61

"Mother and Babe" (Whitman), 101–2

Mott, Frank Luther, 21–22

Murray, Martin, 144, 145, 167n21

Myerson, Joel, 69

"My Legacy" (Whitman), 13

"My Picture-Gallery" (Whitman), 148–49

"My 71st Year" (Whitman), 73

Napoleon Bonaparte, 131–32

national themes, 28

"Nay, Tell Me Not to-Day the Publish'd Shame" (Whitman), 121

Ness, William, 165n40

newspapers: autonomy of, 36; delivery costs for, 23; demand for, 17–18; influence on Whitman, 18–19; and infrastructure development, 23; and news about Whitman, 45–47; and paper manufacturing, 19–20; and partisan politics, 36–44; reprinting among, 46–47; and visibility of Whitman, 29. *See also New York Daily Graphic*; periodicals

New York City, 23

New York Daily Graphic: association of Whitman with, 29–30, 35; *Christmas Graphic*, 30–32; content of, 37; and Croly, 32; on Grant, 121–22; on Lincoln, 147; and readership of Whitman, 23

New York Daily Tribune, 39, 43–44

New York Evening Mail, 121

New York Evening Post, 40, 45

New York Herald, 125

New York Ledger, 22

New York Times, 18–19, 52, 113

New York Tribune, 49

New York Weekly, 22

New York World, 36, 119

night battle scene, 62–64

Nora, Pierre: on creation of *lieux de mémoire*, 58, 59, 68; on definition of *lieux de mémoire*, 73–74, 160n24; on history compared to memory, 55–56, 66, 160n24; on history-literature boundary, 74–75; on maintaining memories, 62; on multiplying effect of *lieux de mémoire*, 73–74

North American Review, 22

notebooks from the war: attachment of Whitman to, 74; bloodstains in, 7, 8, 20, 53, 54, 69–70; essence of war captured in, 50–55; and *lieux de mémoire* (sites of memory), 60;

material nature of, 53, 54; reification of, 8; suffering documented in, 7, 20; as supplements of memory, 53, 58

obituary of Whitman, mistaken, 46
O'Connor, Ellen, 28
O'Connor, William, 34, 118
"Old Age Echoes" (Whitman), 123
"O Me! O Life!" (Whitman), 96, 98, 101, 104
oppression, 3, 99, 103
Osgood, James R., 83

paper currency, 40, 41
paper manufacturing, 19–20
Passage to India (Whitman), 78, 89
"Passage to India" (Whitman), 81
"Perfections" (Whitman), 96
periodicals, 15–48; archive of, 152n2; circulation figures, 22; culture of, 17; and dandy-to-rough transformation, 16; delivery costs for, 23; and infrastructure development, 5–6, 17, 23; *LG*'s promotion in, 16; and mainstream acceptance of Whitman, 23–29, 31, 32, 39; and memories of the war, 47–48; and paper manufacturing, 19–20; and partisan politics, 16, 36–44; and public persona of Whitman, 23–24, 30, 84; rate of publishing in, 6, 24; readerships of, 5–6, 16, 17–19, 24; rise of, 4, 49; scholarship on, 16; transformation of, 15–16; Whitman as topic of, 44–48. *See also* newspapers

Personal Memoirs of U.S. Grant (Grant), 143–45
photography, 49
Pictorial History of the Civil War in the United States of America (Lossing), 49–50
"Poem of Many in One" (Whitman), 9
political landscape: attentiveness of Whitman to, 109; complexity of, 40–41; and Compromise of 1850, 103; corruption of the 1870s, 88; disengagement of writings from, 37, 42; distrust in, 36; engagement of writings in, 9–10, 11–12, 162n13; malaise of, 105–6; and newspapers, 36–44; and prewar passivity, 12, 82, 95, 103–6; and race issues, 33–35; unity/reconciliation message in, 9–12
postal service, 17, 23
poverty, 43
"Prayer of Columbus" (Whitman), 26–28, 153n23
The Press, 126
Price, Abby, 118
Price, Kenneth M., 37–38, 78, 81, 153n23
"Proud Music of the Storm" (Whitman), 24–25
public figure of Whitman: and *Christmas Graphic*, 31; cultivation of national persona, 16–17; emergence of, 9; mellowing of, 31; and political engagement, 11; and publications in periodicals, 26, 30, 84
publishing industry, 17–23; expansion of, 4, 15, 49; and infrastructure de-

velopment, 5–6, 17, 23; production technologies, 19–22, 51, 153n10; readership of, 5, 6, 16, 17–18; reprinting practices, 46–47. *See also* periodicals

race issues: ambivalence regarding, 38, 168n10; concern of Whitman with, 34, 37–38; and labor issues, 39; "miscegenation," 32–35, 154n37, 155n41, 155n49; postwar racial tensions, 36, 165n40; statements on, 10; and stoicism, 100
Rachman, Stephen, 92, 161n6
railroad, 5, 23
Ramsey, Julianne, 92
readership of Whitman: and infrastructure development, 5, 6, 17, 23; and obituary of Whitman, 46; and publication in periodicals, 26; and publishing technology, 21, 22
Reconstruction Act, 117
Redpath, James, 51–52, 54
Reid, Whitelaw, 40, 43–44, 49
religion, 81
Republican Party: election of 1868, 115–18; and labor issues, 39–42; and *Miscegenation* pamphlet, 32–34; and *New York Daily Tribune*, 44; postwar split within, 109
revisions of poems, 37–38
Reynolds, David S., 34, 37, 45
Richardson, Heather Cox, 39, 42
Richardson, Todd, 46
"Rip Van Winkle" story, 12, 82, 105–6
"Roaming in Thought" (Whitman), 102

Rosenthal, Debra, 34
Rotella, Guy, 164n27
"rough" style of Whitman, 16, 45–46
"The Runner" (Whitman), 101, 161n5

Sanchez-Eppler, Karen, 155n41
Sanitary Commission, 135. *See also* deaths of soldiers
Schmidt, Rudolf, 28–29
scholarship on Whitman, 4–5, 150
scientific inquiry, 93, 95, 163n22, 164n27
Scribner's Monthly, 22
sexuality, 34, 163n16
Seymour and Blair: Their Lives and Services (Croly), 33
"Shooting Niagara: And After" (Whitman), 38
"The Silent General" (Whitman), 124
slavery: and Compromise of 1850, 103; conflicting views on, 9, 102; portrayed in poetry, 37–38, 107–8
sleep: as metaphor, 103; and political passivity, 12, 82, 95, 103–6; "Rip Van Winkle" story, 12, 82, 105–6
"The Sleepers" (Whitman), 37–38, 102
Smeller, Carl, 103
Smith, David C., 20, 153n10
soldiers: death scenes, 60–62, 64–65 (*see also* deaths of soldiers); in Grand Review of the Union Army, 2, 3, 114; as national body, 65, 66; night battle scene, 62–64; postwar lives of, 1; and publishing industry, 18; unknown soldiers, 64–65; wounded soldiers, 1, 3, 65

"Song of Myself" (Whitman): on chemistry of death, 66; graves described in, 138; retreat and renewal in, 94–95; speaker of, 88, 90, 101

"Song of the Redwood Tree" (Whitman), 26, 28

"The Song of the Universal" (Whitman), 37

"Songs of Insurrection" cluster (Whitman), 78–79, 80, 86

"Songs of Parting" (Whitman), 13

South, federal troops in, 1, 3

Specimen Days and Collect (Whitman): on blood-stained notebooks, 69–70; cautious assertions in, 159n18; chronology in, 140; discrepancies in shared material, 57–58; execution scene, 60–62; as fragmented work, 135, 141–42, 168n1; genealogy in, 12, 136–40, 144; on Grand Review, 3; material incorporated into, 142; *Memoranda* reproduced in, 7, 12, 45, 56, 60, 135–36, 140; on memory of the war, 56, 140–41; on newspaper publishing, 18; pieces on Grant in, 123; postwar period omitted from, 144; topics of, 12–13; on war and personal history, 135

spiritualist movement, 30

Springfield Republican, 45

Stafford, Harry, 81

Stanton, Edwin M., 113, 117, 143–44

Stanwood, Augustus, 19

Stark, Mary Virginia, 80, 102–3, 161n5

Steffen, Charles G., 17

"Still Though the One I Sing" (Whitman), 78–79

St. Louis Post-Dispatch, 153n23

stoicism, 100

Stovall, Floyd, 147

"The Strange Sad War Revolving": Walt Whitman, Reconstruction, and the Emergence of Black Citizenship, 1865–1876 (Mancuso), 4–5

stroke and recovery, 29, 30, 70, 121, 123. *See also* health of Whitman

"Sun-Down Poem" (Whitman), 89

Sweet, Timothy, 52, 58–59, 159nn19–21

Swinton, John, 113–14, 166n6, 166n7

tariff issues, 10, 41, 116, 120

Teale, Edwin Way, 152n9

Thayer and Eldridge, 15, 21

"This Compost" (Whitman), 13, 135, 163n17

Thomas, M. Wynn: on "interior history" of war, 6–7, 55; on obligations of memory, 62; on postwar struggles of Whitman, 5; on potency of memory, 71, 152n13

"Thought" (Whitman), 81, 102

"Thoughts" (Whitman), 91, 92

"To a President" (Whitman), 97–98, 103

"To Rich Givers" (Whitman), 100, 104

"To the States, To Identify the 16th, 17th, or 18th Presidentiad" (Whitman), 82–83, 103–6

"The Tramp and Strike Questions" (Whitman), 42

transportation infrastructure, 5

Traubel, Horace: on cabinet appointments, 119–20; on centrality of war, 80; on Grant, 121, 128; on Irving, 165n39; on poetic license of Whitman, 132–33; on publication pressures, 47; on voting habits of Whitman, 166n8

Troy Press, 46

The Truth about Love (Croly), 36

"Twenty-Second Presidentiad" (Whitman), 123

"A Twilight Song" (Whitman), 71–73

Two Rivulets (Whitman), 77, 124, 147

"The Unexpress'd" (Whitman), 74

unifying national figure, Whitman's desire for, 10–11

Union Army: cemeteries of, 139–40, 160n23; Grand Review of, 1, 2–3, 114; wounded soldiers, 1, 3

unity/reconciliation, message of, 9–12, 38–39

U.S. Constitution, 3, 85

U.S. Department of the Interior, 26, 118, 167n14

voting rights, 9–10, 38, 116, 117

Wakeman, George, 32–35

Walt Whitman Archive, 24

"Walt Whitman's Actual American Position" (Whitman), 44–48

Washburn, Elihu, 118–19

Washington Star, 24–25

Wecter, Dixon, 167n13

Westminster Review, 21

westward journey of Whitman, 124, 135

"What Best I See in Thee, [General Grant in Philadelphia, December–, 1879]" (Whitman), 126, 167nn19–20

"When I Heard the Learn'd Astronomer" (Whitman), 11, 92–95, 163n22, 164n27

White, Horace, 40

white supremacy, 33–34

Whitman, Edmund B., 139–40

Whitman, George: capture of, 113–14; and Grant, 111; and prisoner exchange, 166n7; return from war, 148–49; Whitman's search for, 69

Whitman, Jeff, 124

Whitman, Louisa Van Velsor: attachment of Whitman to, 139; death of, 4, 13, 29, 139; letters to, 2, 111, 121, 168n10; tribute to, 13

women's right to vote, 38

Woolson, Constance Fenimore, 50

Worthington, Richard, 21

written accounts of the war: limitations of, 51–52, 54, 55, 56–57, 64, 68; and memories of the war, 71; as "reminiscent memorial," 71. *See also Memoranda During the War* (Whitman); notebooks from the war

Youth's Companion, 22

Zboray, Ronald J., 23

Zwinger, Ann, 152n9